BUDDHISM GOES TO THE MOVIES

Buddhism Goes to the Movies: An Introduction to Buddhist Thought and Practice explains the basics of Buddhist philosophy and practice through a number of dramatic films from around the world. This book introduces readers in a dynamic way to the major traditions of Buddhism: the Theravāda, and various interrelated Mahāyāna divisions including Zen, Pure Land, and Tantric Buddhism. Students can use Ronald Green's book to gain insights into classic Buddhist themes, including Buddhist awakening, the importance of the theory of dependent origination, the notion of no-self, and Buddhist ideas about life, death, and why we are here. Contemporary developments are also explored, including the Socially Engaged Buddhism demonstrated by such figures as the Dalai Lama, Thich Nhat Hanh, Aung San Suu Kyi, and other Buddhist activists. Finally, comparisons between filmic expressions of Buddhism and more traditional artistic expressions of Buddhism—such as mandala drawings—are also drawn.

Ronald S. Green is Assistant Professor of Religious Studies at Coastal Carolina University.

BUDDHISM GOES TO THE MOVIES

An Introduction to Buddhist Thought and Practice

Ronald S. Green
Coastal Carolina University

 Routledge
Taylor & Francis Group

NEW YORK AND LONDON

First edition published 2014
by Routledge
711 Third Avenue, New York, NY 10017

and by Routledge
2 Park Square, Milton Park, Abingdon, Oxon OX14 4RN

Routledge is an imprint of the Taylor & Francis Group, an informa business

© 2014 Taylor & Francis

Library of Congress Cataloging-in-Publication Data
Green, Ronald S.
Buddhism goes to the movies : an introduction to Buddhist thought
    and practice / Ronald S. Green.
        pages cm
    Includes bibliographical references and index.
    1. Buddhism in motion pictures.   I. Title.
    PN1995.9.B795G74 2014
    791.43′682943—dc23
    2013022179

ISBN: 978-0-415-84146-7 (hbk)
ISBN: 978-0-415-84148-1 (pbk)
ISBN: 978-0-203-76569-2 (ebk)

Typeset in Bembo
by Apex CoVantage, LLC

Printed and bound in the United States of America by Publishers Graphics,
LLC on sustainably sourced paper.

This volume is dedicated to the many students, family members, and friends who have contributed and inspired ideas on these films. To mention a few, these include Jacob Beaver, Michael Dorman, Mary Green, Martha Kapek, Zack Moran, Emily Schrag, and Jake Sheehan. I wish to express my thanks to all of those at Coastal Carolina University who allowed and encouraged me to teach this subject.

CONTENTS

List of Figures   *ix*
Preface   *xi*
Introduction   *xiii*

1 Early Representations: *Broken Blossoms* and *Lost Horizon*   1

2 The Four Noble Truths: *Fight Club*   13

3 Buddhist Awakening: *Waking Life*   30

4 Dependent Origination: *I Heart Huckabees*   43

5 Korean Seon Buddhism: *Why Has Bodhi-Dharma
   Left for the East?*   56

6 Theravāda Buddhism, Socially Engaged Buddhism:
   The Burmese Harp   70

7 Tibetan Buddhism: *The Cup*   82

8 Japanese Shin Buddhism: *Departures*   94

9 The Buddhist Order of Nuns: *Windhorse*   106

10 Thai Buddhism in Horror Films: *Nang Nak* and *Uncle
   Boonmee Who Can Recall His Past Lives*   118

viii Contents

Glossary	*135*
Selected List of Films with Buddhist Content	*141*
Bibliography	*153*
Index	*157*

LIST OF FIGURES

1.1	Theda Bara in *The Soul of Buddha*, 1918	3
1.2	Lillian Gish (as Lucy) and Richard Barthelmess (as Yellow Man) in *Broken Blossoms*	5
1.3(a)	Screenshot of first glimpse of Shangri-la in *Lost Horizon*	8
1.3(b)	Potala Palace in Lhasa	8
2.1	*Trikāya* (three bodies) theory and *Fight Club*	28
3.1	Dream Yoga	39
3.2	The Wheel of Life	40
5.1	The *Ox Herding Drawings*	61
7.1	*Vajra*	86
7.2	Scene near the beginning of *The Cup*	89

PREFACE

This book describes the basics of Buddhist philosophy and practice within the contexts of a number of dramatic, not documentary, films. It introduces some of the main traditions of Buddhism, the **Theravāda** and various interrelated Mahāyāna divisions including Zen, **Pure Land Buddhism**, and **Tantric Buddhism**. Little or no knowledge of Buddhism is assumed of the reader. Instead, Buddhist concepts, practices, and histories are presented in progression so that this might serve as an introduction to Buddhism particularly accessible to those interested in film studies or who just enjoy a good movie. Likewise, this approach may appeal to individuals who primarily are visual learners. The book is divided into ten chapters, which can easily be considered units for a quarter or semester school term. Key terms in Buddhism appear in bold type and in the glossary. The text avoids using foreign words except in cases where such are conventional expressions in Buddhist Studies. Sometimes scholars leave these intentionally untranslated because they consider English equivalents inadequate. Such words are italicized and explanations are given. Those with more advanced knowledge of Buddhism may enjoy the discussions of how Buddhism reshapes cinema and is reshaped by it, how Buddhism is being used as a piece of a projection screen to criticize society, and how the cinema compares and contrasts with earlier Buddhists' visual mediums such as **mandala**.

Currently no text exists that treats Buddhism and film in a systematic fashion. Only a few articles have been published reviewing individual films tentatively related to Buddhism in some ways. However, there are an increasing number of films being made with Buddhist content. There is now a Buddhist Film Foundation that holds an annual film festival in San Francisco and a "Buddhism and Film" conference in Germany convened for the first time in 2011. The present study seeks to shed light on the Buddhist themes in certain films. It is hardly meaningful to call a film Buddhist with no qualifications. It is also misleading. In actuality, there are many Buddhist traditions and they sometimes hold seemingly contradictory ideas. This study introduces theories and practices of a variety of Buddhist traditions. It presents supporting information about Buddhism as portrayed in each film considered. The focus is on contemporary fictive films that are easily accessible. Most of these have been identified as "Buddhist" by the film-makers or critics. Each chapter begins with a short synopsis of a film and progresses to explanations of the Buddhist elements portrayed or associated with the film.

Notes on Conventions

1. The Pinyin system is used for Chinese terms; the Korean Government Romanization System revised in 2000, for Korean terms; and the Hepburn system, for Japanese words.
2. Diacritics are used on most Sanskrit and Pāli terms.
3. Foreign terms, those not included in the *Webster English Dictionary*, appear in italics.

INTRODUCTION

> This world is the movie of what everything is,
> it is one movie, made of the same stuff
> throughout, belonging to nobody, which is what
> everything is.
>
> *The Scripture of the Golden Eternity.* Jack Kerouac (1922–1969)

If ancient Buddhists had the medium of film, might they have used it instead of or in addition to mandala? Put another way, why use mandala when you have film? Can film serve the same purposes as mandala? Mandala drawings of Buddhas and **Bodhisattva** have been used for centuries for contemplating the attributes of those figures, attributes such as wisdom and compassion. A practitioner might sit in meditation in front of the mandala, using it as a tool of visualization in hopes of incorporating those ideal traits of wisdom and compassion into his or her own life. Do certain films fill this role today? Why or why not?

About his film *Why Has Bodhi-Dharma Left for the East?*, director Young-Kyun Bae said, "I would like the audience to see the film without preconceived knowledge or ideas."[1] Is this either possible or desirable? Doing so might require a Buddhist way of film viewing, a mindful method of suspending judgment and letting sounds and images flow over us. The implication is that if we can learn to do this while viewing films, we can learn to apply the skill to daily life. Bae also said he hoped to build a temple through his film.[2] Can sacred space be created cinematically?

In the documentary *Life as Cinema*, Khyentse Norbu, director of *The Cup* (1999), *Travellers and Magicians* (2003), and *Vara: A Blessing* (2012) speaks extensively of the Buddhist potential of film. Tibetan Buddhist masters have bestowed upon Norbu the title "**Rinpoche**," given to respected monks in their tradition. Even before hearing his explanations, we might wonder why a venerable Rinpoche would make movies. Theoretically, a Tibetan Buddhist's primary social task is to save all sentient beings from suffering the cycles of rebirth. A Bodhisattva, a Buddhist dedicated to awakening self and others, does this through **skill-in-means**, that is, by thinking of and putting in practice innovated ways to bring the **Dharma** (the teaching of the Buddha) to people according to their situations and abilities. Traditionally, one way of doing this is by using mandala to illustrate the Dharma. Certainly the technological situation in most of the world today is drastically different from when mandala were first drawn and the director understands this. Norbu Rinpoche says, "Illusion is what we see as something that is fake, something not permanent, something not solid, something that is not true. And reality is the opposite. But from the Buddhist point of view, everything is fake, everything is illusion, everything is dependent." He continues, "This idea I have, life as cinema, is that one's life is a movie, film, cinema. There're actors, there're producers, they're all there, the drama, all the romance, everything that's in cinema. And, the very idea, the very purpose of spiritual practice is so you can have control over how to direct our story [. . .] Most of the time we can't because we are always pulled apart by our passions, our aggressions, and these emotions, they write the story for us [. . .] All of this is directed by you, produced by you, and you are also the actor. And you are also the audience. You're just not clever enough to be a good critic. So you're always stuck with your own show thinking that what you have produced is good or real, you're convinced. That's how the power of life is, just like cinema. If you know that, then a certain kind of confidence and courage will come."[3] From this perspective, it seems that film may have the power to make the audience realize that life is as illusionary as scenes on the screen. If so, viewing film can be seen as a type of religious practice.

The idea that drama can serve as Buddhist skill-in-means to lure the viewers, unaware, toward awaking, is an old one. The famous Japanese Nō theater playwright and theorist **Zeami** (c. 1363–c. 1443 CE) wrote at length about it. According to Zeami, drama had been used in this way at the time of the Buddha. When the Buddha held up a flower and only the monk **Kāśyapa**, smiling, thereby received his mind-to-mind transmission of the Dharma, this exemplified the perfect skill actors must develop. Zeami taught that actors must conceal their minds even from themselves in order to display the flower to the audience. Later, Zeami said, Prince Shōtoku (574–622) imported Buddhist drama into Japan as a way of propagating the Dharma.[4] Throughout Asia over the centuries, plays, novels and poems have been extensively created to inspire in people Buddhist sentiments such as the realization of the transience of nature and life, and the eternal in the momentary. Buddhism and film continues this tradition. Can a director use symbolic expressions to evoke realization in the viewer like the Buddha with the flower? Is it possible for a film-maker to achieve a mind-to-screen-to-mind transmission of the Dharma? If so, the film-maker is a Bodhisattva and the viewer a practitioner, at least potentially.

The development of representations of Buddhism in film has not been free of controversies. Whereas in America and Europe Buddhism currently appears to be an alternative to conventional ways, in Asia it typically is a conservative tradition with all that goes with that, including censorship. Thai Buddhists called for a ban on the film *Angulimala* (2003) directed by Sutape Tunnirut, for distorting Buddhist teachings and glorifying violence. As a result, it was blocked from being released by government censors until some of the violent scenes were removed. Afterwards the monk Phra Phisan Dhammavadhi, deemed it acceptable and the banned was lifted.[5]

In 2006, the Thai Censorship Board objected to director Apichatpong Weerasethakul's depictions of a Buddhist monk playing guitar in movie *Syndromes and a Century*. They felt the portrayal was undignified. Apichatpong refused to make the cuts and withdrew his film from release in Thailand, although it had been shown in other countries. As a result, some artists petitioned the Board and the country subsequently revisited the rating system. Likewise, the release of the Thai film *In the Shadow of the Naga* (*Nak prok*, directed by Nasorn Panungkasiri) was delayed due to protests by Buddhists. The film depicts three criminals who become Buddhist monks in order to recover stolen goods buried beneath a temple. It was completed in 2008 and finally released in 2010.

Buddhist conservatism is not restricted to Asia. In America the release of the film *Hollywood Buddha* (completed in 2003), directed by Philippe Caland, was cancelled by the director because of protest by Buddhists in California. The film tells the story of Philippe, bankrupted film-maker on the verge of eviction. Philippe seeks the advice of a Buddhist master, who persuades him to purchase an expensive sculpture of a Buddha. The pre-release movie poster depicts Philippe, played by the director, sitting on the head of the large Buddha sculpture. Buddhist protesters found this out and the anticipated content of the film objectionable. It is interesting to note that such conservatism exists alongside Buddhist stories about masters who ripped up scriptures, chopped up the master's chair, and destroyed images of the Buddha so that practitioners would not become attached to them. Hence the Zen proverb: If you meet the Buddha on the road, kill him.

Such mixed messages in the history of Buddhism add to the complexity of analyzing Buddhist content in films and likely makes a single model impossible. It is equally difficult to develop a Buddhist analysis of film. Some might guess any Buddhist analysis of film would begin and end by saying desire and ignorance surrounds every aspect of the affair, film-making, representation, and spectatorship alike. This widespread understanding of Buddhism is, however, grossly mistaken. In its 2,500-year history, across vast borders and diverse political situations, Buddhism has developed deep analyses in areas we today call sociological, psychological, and phenomenological. On the one hand, through many historical changes, the basic formula of the Buddha's **Four Noble Truths** and the **Eightfold Path** remains intact, beginning with the assumption that life is filled with dissatisfaction. On the other hand, historical emphasis on one or another aspect of the Four Noble Truths and the Eightfold Path, and the degree of detail some traditions of Buddhism have developed to account for each of these has greatly complicated matters.

In today's world, is there relevance to the idea that life is pervasive dissatisfaction as the Buddha's first Noble Truth states? Dissatisfaction translates the Pāli language word *dukkha*, usually rendered into English as "suffering." In the modern world of plumbing and refrigerators, young people in countries where the majority has traditionally been Buddhist, now ask, "How is all life suffering? I have a new sports car." We are surprised to see in the film *The Cup* young Tibetan monks scheme to obtain a satellite dish in order to watch World Cup soccer. Many Asian monastics defrock upon immigration to America. Why be a monk in the land of plenty? But *dukkha* also expresses uneasiness in life we may not readily equate with suffering. This is the feeling we get from perpetually desiring things we don't have and wanting to rid ourselves of things we have but dislike. Maybe this is basic to humanity, compelling us to act, expand, reproduce, and innovate. But, it is also manipulated to drive a market economy capable of manufacturing "needs" for profit. No matter how much you have bought, you may not stop buying or the economy will collapse. Likewise, we are all given the parental advice from family and society, "Never settle." Doesn't this mean never be satisfied? In such a world *dukkha* is far from lost. We should not wonder when during the 2008 Olympics Ara Abrahamian of Sweden placed his bronze medal on the wrestling mat in protest of being judged only third best in the world. This and the things upsetting each of us take place at the same time wars rage, people are being raped and brutalized, and the basic conditions of sickness and death remain ever present.

Living in perpetual dissatisfaction is called ignorance in many Buddhist writings. Ignorance translates the Sanskrit word *avidyā*. It is the opposite of knowing, *vidyā*, which has the Sanskrit root *vid*. The Latin and Greek words *video* share this root, likely from a common Indo-European source. *Vidyā* may also be used to mean meditation (Sanskrit: *dhyāna*). It is interesting that this term, basic to Buddhist awakening, has entered our language in the word "video," relating to the topic of our study. More interesting is whether *vidyā* is possible through video. Professor Robert Sharf at UC-Berkeley taught a film series course called "Seeing Through the Screen, Buddhism and Film." The course outline says the course will, "as the double entendre of its title suggests, be looking at Buddhism through film, and film through Buddhism—using the medium of film to explore various themes and issues in the study."[6] We can imagine other senses to this title. One is seeing beyond the film to reality as it is or as Buddhists say it is, sometimes called "**thusness**" or "**suchness**" (Sanskrit: *tathātā*) in translations of Buddhist texts. For some Buddhists, this would be *vidyā*. But again, is it possible by viewing film to see through the screen in that sense, the screen of ignorance causing pervasive dissatisfaction or suffering? A similar possibility was forwarded by Francisca Cho, who suggests "a nonliterary approach to film by seeing it as a form of religious practice."[7]

As we watch these films and study their Buddhist content, we might ask who exactly is the subject seated before the screen, involved in an activity which has been described as everything from passive absorption to active production? How are we linked to screen, narrative, and character? A Zen teacher once told a student,

> If you really want to know your true nature you must orient yourself toward the source of delusive thoughts and get to the bottom of it. When you hear a voice, do not focus on the thing that you are hearing but, instead, return to the source of your own hearing. If you practice in this way with all things you will definitely clarify your true nature.[8]

Some time ago, ethno-methodologists engaged in activities such as viewing film, to study the social components of those behaviors. Perhaps a Buddhist viewing, if such is possible, would be somewhat similar. Whether we actually try this or not as progressing though this book, it is interesting to note the possibilities.

Notes

1 *Dharmaga tongjoguro kan kkadalgun*, South Korea, 1989. Quoted in the press release at the film distributor's website http://cdn.shopify.com/s/files/1/0150/7896/files/BodhiDharmaPK.pdf?1009, accessed 8/15/12.
2 http://cdn.shopify.com/s/files/1/0150/7896/files/BodhiDharmaPK.pdf?1009, accessed 8/15/12.
3 From *Life as Cinema*, included in the special features on the DVD release of *The Cup*.
4 Masakazu Yamazaki, *On the Art of the No Drama: The Major Treatises of Zeami*, p. 3.
5 See http://en.wikipedia.org/wiki/Angulimala_(film), accessed 3/22/11.
6 http://buddhiststudies.berkeley.edu/filmseries/, accessed 8/17/12.
7 Francisca Cho, "Buddhism, Film, and Religious Knowing: Challenging the Literary Approach to Film," in *Teaching Religion and Film*, p. 117.
8 "The Awakening of Mugai Nyodai (Died 1298)" in Addiss *et al.* (eds.), *Zen Sourcebook: Traditional Documents from China, Korea, and Japan*, p. 176.

1
EARLY REPRESENTATIONS
Broken Blossoms and *Lost Horizon*

Since the Middle Ages, some European writers have used "the East" or "the Orient" to revolt against rationalism. Their stories tell of adventurers in search of magical knowledge no longer found in Europe. Asian religions came to be used as philosophies of unity against what writers viewed as the fragmentation of existence produced by science and technology. Nineteenth-century Europe saw a renewed interest in this. William Butler Yeats and others used mystical images of Asia in reaction against positivism. In America, before the Civil War, the works of Henry David Thoreau and Ralph Waldo Emerson show Buddhist influence. Thoreau made the first translation of part of the *Lotus Sūtra* into English and was clearly interested in Buddhism. A few decades later, Asian religions were introduced to larger audiences in America under the sponsorship of various international-oriented groups interested in representing religions in certain ways. In 1875, the Theosophical Society was founded in New York City to promote their beliefs in spirituality largely pieced together from Asian traditions including Buddhism. It was founded by Helena Blavatsky and Henry Steel Olcott among others. Madame Blavatsky was a Russian psychic who had immigrated to America. Henry Steel Olcott was a US military colonel interested in mysticism. The two moved to India where Colonel Olcott became possibly the first American convert to Buddhism. He went on to become a hero in Sri Lanka's struggle for independence from Britain by defending Buddhism against strong attacks from Christian missionaries. Today there is a major street named after him in Colombo, Sri Lanka.

In 1893, the World's Parliament of Religions took place in Chicago. At the time, Swami Vivekananda impressed crowds by speaking about philosophical issues related to Hinduism. Japanese Buddhists and representatives of other Asian religions, funded in part by Colonel Olcott, also made impressions on those attending as reported in news media. These events of the 1870s–1880s led to curiosity and study, spurring what is seen today as a worldwide revival of Buddhism in the early twentieth century. At that time, the content of films began to change from simple projections of scenery, rightly called "motion pictures," to edited story narrations. An impact of the spread of limited information on Buddhism can be seen in a number of films shown over the next few decades. These films in turn likely influenced public opinion about Asian religions, spanning new writings and more films. Asian Buddhists in this period were typically portrayed in films by non-Asian actors and based on stereotypes. Likewise, Buddhist ideas and practices were typically molded to further the plot of the film in disregard for historical accuracy. Similar misrepresentations in novels and nonfiction have been described as examples of "orientalism," an expression analogous to racism.

A silent film called *Buddha* was made in America by an unknown director and cast in 1913. It was shown as half of a "split-reel," a silent film term meaning two short films on one real. It played together with *A Little Hero*, a comedy.[1] This may have been the first film made about Buddhism, although this is not certain. A few years later, *The Soul of Buddha* was made based not on Buddhism but sensationalized representations of a temple dancer popular in news stories. In 1917, a Dutch exotic dancer with the Indonesian stage name Mata Hari was put to death by a firing squad in Paris for allegedly selling secrets to Germany during World War I. She studied Indonesian dance and married a Dutch army officer. Affairs and scandals surrounding her life and death were popular themes in news and tabloids. *The Soul of Buddha* is a 1918 silent film that is currently considered lost. It was directed by J. Gordon Edwards (1867–1925), a Canadian-born director, producer, and a writer. The film starred Theda Bara, who allegedly wrote the story and starred in it as a dancing Buddhist priestess.[2] The story follows a Javanese girl Bava, whose name is obviously close to the actress's name Bara. Bava's mother, fearing for the chastity of her flirtatious daughter, sends her to a Buddhist temple so that she might dedicate herself to sacred dance.

However, Bava runs away with a British officer stationed in Java, and then moves with him to Scotland. The temple priest vows to kill her for her betrayal of Buddhism. The couple bears a child and the priest kills the baby. Later, Bava visits a cabaret and the desire to dance is renewed in her. Seeing her dance, a theatrical company offers her a contract. Now in her new life, Bava has an affair. When her husband learns of this he kills himself in her dressing room. In order to receive guests without interruptions, the cool-hearted Bava hides his body and then goes to dance. On stage, one of the Buddha statues seems to come to life and kills her with a knife. The statue turns out to be the Buddhist priest in disguise. About this film, a *New York Times* reviewer wrote, "None of this made much sense, but Bara melodramas were never strong on character motivation or logic. *The Soul of a Buddha* was filmed in the dead of winter at Fort Lee, New Jersey, a paper mache temple and the palisades standing in—uneasily—for tropical Java."[3] The association with Mata Hari must have seemed perfect for Theda Bara, who built a screen image of herself as a classic femme fatale, the seductive and dangerous female.

FIGURE 1.1   Theda Bara in *The Soul of Buddha*, 1918

In India, there is a tradition of offering dancing women to the deity of a Hindu temple. These women are known as *devadasi*, a Sanskrit term meaning "female servant of a deity." *Devadasi* are sometimes degraded to prostitution at temples. This is not a part of Buddhism and the tradition may have arisen as a sentence to former Buddhist nuns at the time of the fall of Buddhism in India during the sixth century CE.[4] There are also children temple dancers in Bali, Indonesia. Today, such a film would likely meet with protests by people offended by the misrepresentation of Buddhism as an evil, cult-like religion.

In 1919, the renowned film director D.W. Griffith (1875–1948) represented Buddhism in a more positive light. His protagonist in *Broken Blossoms* is a Buddhist who has come to England from China to spread the Dharma. The sentiment expressed in the film is that although English speakers at the time looked upon Asia as barbaric, in face of World War I this should be reassessed. A similar idea had been stated on the third day of the 1893 World's Parliament of Religions in Chicago when Japanese Buddhists spoke. Hirai Kinza (1859–1916), a lay delegate and Confucian scholar, took up the issue of how Asians were being treated in America, for example, they were not being allowed to attend school in San Francisco. He asked what should be thought of American Christianity "when there are men who go in procession hoisting lanterns marked 'Japs must go'? If such be Christian ethics, we are perfectly satisfied to be heathen." "Loud applause followed many of his declarations," reported the *Chicago Herald*, "which grew as the delegates were exposed to a thousand cries of 'Shame!' as he pointed out the wrongs which his countrymen had suffered through the practices of false Christianity."[5]

D.W. Griffith is considered among the pioneers of the film industry, perhaps the most influential directors of the early era. He is known to have developed such cinematic devices as the close-up shot to convey the psychological state of a character. Griffith's films often present certain archetypes, likely related to his own experiences and beliefs. Among these is the poor country boy struggling to survive in the harsh city. This reappears in his films as a retelling of his own story not tied to any time or country. His second archetype is the defenseless girl, a symbol of purity in the world plagued with evil. In the cold city, the wayward boy is only warmed by romantic love for the pure girl. His films also depict an ideal view of lone struggles against overwhelming injustice. These themes form the basis of *Broken Blossoms* (D.W. Griffith, USA, 1919).

Broken Blossoms begins with the male protagonist in a Buddhist temple in China. The intertitles, text displayed between scenes, only refer to him as "Yellow Man," although the part is played by American actor Richard Barthelmess. While the depictions of Buddhism in the Chinese temple are limited, there is a clear attempt at accuracy, in contrast to *The Soul of Buddha*. In the temple, a Buddhist is shown using prayer beads. Others bow before an altar. A master in the temple gives Yellow Man advice about taking "the lessons of the gentle Buddha" to "the barbarous Anglo-Saxons, sons of turmoil and strife." Once in England, however, he soon loses his naïve idealism about this task as he struggles with the realities of harsh city life. He becomes a shopkeeper in a depressed part of town and seems to find some consolation for his disappointment in opium dens. Meanwhile, a teenager named Lucy wanders through the streets after being abused by her father, a boisterous and often drunken boxer. Yellow Man sees her searching for tinfoil to sell for flowers and immediately recognizes a spark of human purity in her. When a man called Evil Eyes attempts to take advantage of the impoverished child, Yellow Man prevents it. Two Christians with religious pamphlets also come to the district. One tells Yellow Man, "My brother leaves for China tomorrow to convert heathens." The perception that Asians are heathens is clearly contrasted with Yellow Man's humanity and the boxer's brutality. However, there is a subtle message that the Christians' naïve arrogance is the same as that formerly displayed by Yellow Man in his idealism about Buddhist missionary work. That is, rather than nationality and wealth, it is something more basic to humanity that makes a person good. Likewise, religion does not make a person holy, love does.

Later, after Lucy is again brutalized by her drunken father, she limps out of the house and down the street, incidentally falling unconscious into the doorway of Yellow Man's store. He takes her upstairs so that she might recover, watching over her closely. At first we are unsure of his intent towards the helpless girl, especially knowing he has smoked opium. He draws slowly near her for a closer look

FIGURE 1.2   Lillian Gish (as Lucy) and Richard Barthelmess (as Yellow Man) in *Broken Blossoms*

(see Figure 1.2). We see extreme close-ups of his squinting eyes and her fearful ones. Then we are told through the intertitles, "his love remains a pure and holy thing." The titles also say the room is "prepared as for a princess" and he gives her "a magical robe treasured from an olden day." He sits in front of a Buddhist shrine in the room. A striking contrast is made between the room's delicate decorations and the dilapidated environment of the streets and Lucy's house, analogous to their purity compared to the corruption of the outside world. The simple kindness of each seems to transform the other into greater people. Yellow Man has found the principles he has lost in the city and Lucy has gained the flowers she sought. He fondly calls her White Blossom; clearly both have bloomed.

Tragically their happiness is short lived. Lucy's father is informed by a shop patron that his daughter is living with a foreigner. Enraged, the father goes to the shop while Yellow Man is out. He yells at his daughter, "You! With a dirty Chink?" He rips the robe and destroys a chair as she runs out into the river mist. Her father catches her outside and drags her home. Yellow Man returns to the shop to find the robe discarded. He falls to the floor in anguish and learns from the gloating Evil Eyes what has happened. Yellow Man grabs a gun and heads outside into the river mist. The foggy black and white scene partially concealing the man with the gun foreshadows what will later be classic images in film noir.

In a memorable scene in cinematic history, at home Lucy locks herself in a closet, which her father proceeds to break through with an axe. He pulls Lucy through the splintered door and beats her fatally. Viewers, upon first seeing this, reported becoming nauseated and physically ill.[6] She dies on her bed just as Yellow Man enters her room through a window. When her father sees him he raises the axe but Yellow Man shoots him repeatedly. We see a man informing the police of the development. The police officers have been reading the news of war, remarking, "Better than last week—Only forty thousand casualties." This again points to the barbarism of Europe. Yellow Man carries Lucy's body to his room, puts flowers on her and lights incense at the Buddhist shrine. He raises a Buddhist scripture to his head in an authentic fashion, and rings a bell. He then kills himself. The final scene shows the Buddhist temple in China. Buddhists ring the temple bell and more ships sail between Europe and Asia. Part of the message seems to be that relationships of purity and love among individuals are not allowed to develop because social prejudices based on religion and nationality.

In 1923, Indian director Dadasaheb Phalke made a documentary called *Buddha Dev* (*Lord Buddha*). In 1925, another silent film dramatizing the life of the Buddha was released, *The Light of Asia* (Hindi title: *Prem Sanyas*). This movie was made by the German film-maker Franz Osten. The script was based on the book *The Light of Asia* by the British poet Sir Edwin Arnold, distributed by the Theosophical Society in 1891. The film was a greater success in Europe than in India. It gives a somewhat romantic picture of the life of Buddha.

Broken Blossoms made the point to contrast individual good across political borders at the time of World War I. In 1940, the year before the United States entered World War II, *Broken Blossoms* was remade as the first film of director John Brahm (a.k.a. Has Brahm). John Brahm later went on to direct many television shows, such as *Twilight Zone* and *The Outer Limits*, which is interesting in that *Broken Blossoms* is also a fantasy of sorts. The following year, 1937, Frank Capra (1897–1991) directed *Lost Horizon*. Capra is another seminal director in film history, perhaps most popularly known for making *It's a Wonderful Life* with James Stewart. *Lost Horizon*, adapted from James Hilton's best-selling 1933 novel by that name, centers around Shangri-la, likely a literary adaptation of the mythical kingdom of Shambhala in Tibetan Buddhism. Madame Blavatsky of the Theosophical Society had earlier claimed that her undisclosed Tibetan Lama teacher had shown here the secret location of Shambhala. Similar to *It's a Wonderful Life*, *Lost Horizon* is about the search for what is really important in life, an issue Capra and others likely considered crucial just after the stock market crash and World War I. In both films, it does not matter that the entire story seems like an impossible fantasy. In fact, the aspect of escapism from the daily news played a part in the popularity of both films. But it is also important that the stories are consciously recognized as fantasies by the viewers. This underscores the value of the dreams and aspirations of humankind above lust and greed that the films present as driving society. An offshoot of this is that Buddhism is presented in *Lost Horizon* in a fantastic way that perpetuates Orientalism to this day.

The opening intertitles of *Lost Horizon*, shown as pages turned in a book, prepare us for the film's theme of universal human ideals.

> In these days of war and rumors of war haven't you ever dreamed of a place where there was peace and security, where living was not a struggle but a lasting delight? Of course you have. So has every man since time began. Always the same dreams. Sometimes he calls it Utopia, sometimes the Fountain of Youth, sometimes merely that little chicken farm.

In this way, a part of Tibetan Buddhism is removed from its historical context and presented as universal. "War and rumors of war" is a quote from Jesus found in Matthew 24:6–7. This Universalist message is repeated when later we learn the founder of the Tibetan monastery is a Catholic priest.

The story begins in 1935 and continues to around the time of the film's showing, 1937. Near China's border with Tibet there is a British diplomat named Robert Conway (Ronald Colman) helping to evacuate Europeans and Americans by airplanes during a frantic local revolt. Conway boards a plane along with his younger brother George (John Howard). Onboard are also an American swindler and fugitive named Henry Mitchell (Thomas Mitchell) who had cost investors a great deal during the stock market crash, a narrow-minded British paleontologist called "Lovey" (Edward Everett Horton), and Gloria Stone (Isabel Jewell), an American woman soured by doctors' prognoses that she only has a short time to live. In the air we get a feel for Conway's personality when he laments that 10,000 Chinese deaths do not count in terms of his government report. After some time, the passengers realize they have been kidnapped by a Mongolian pilot and are traveling towards Tibet rather than Shanghai. The plane runs out of fuel and crashes in the Himalayas, killing the pilot. Gloria laughs at the others for now being faced with imminent death, like her. The motif of ever-present mortality, at the heart of Buddhism, runs throughout the film.

Just as they are thinking there is no way out of the frozen wilderness, a group of Tibetans arrive, led by a soft-spoken Chinese man named Chang, played by English actor H.B. Warner.[7] The Tibetans provide heavy clothing and lead them to a portal where they behold Shangri-la, a warm and lush valley strangely protected from the surrounding cold by high mountains. From this mysterious vista a magnificent building can be seen, appearing somewhat like the **Potala Palace**, the traditional chief residence the **Dalai Lama** in Lhasa, Tibet (see Figures 1.3[a] and 1.3[b]). We are told it is a Lamasery, a Tibetan monastery, actually constructed by Columbia Pictures in a backlot of the studio in Los Angeles.

Inside the palace there are Buddha images and people dressed in robes. The visitors are treated to a delicious meal served to them by people who appear to represent the colonial ideal of benevolent natives. Throughout the film, the Europeans live in idle luxury as the natives work happily. "Lovey" complains that the place is too mysterious and Robert becomes anxious to leave. Conway, on the other hand;

FIGURE 1.3(a)   Screenshot of first glimpse of Shangri-la in *Lost Horizon*

FIGURE 1.3(b)   Potala Palace in Lhasa

comments, "I think I'm going to like it here." He asks Chang, "What religion do you practice here?" Chang replies,

> To put it simply, I should say that our general belief was in moderation. We preach the virtue of avoiding excesses of every kind, even including excess of virtue itself . . . We find in the valley it makes for greater happiness among the natives. We rule with moderate strictness and in return we are satisfied with moderate obedience. As a result, our people are moderately honest, moderately chaste, and somewhat more than moderately happy.

This reply may remind us of the Dalai Lama's well-known ecumenical quote, "**Loving Kindness** is my religion," which is often seen on buttons and bumper stickers today.

Buddhism is known as the **Middle Path** because it teaches the avoidance of excesses. However, Conway believes that a native Asian element cannot be responsible for the magnificence of Shangri-la. Instead, he suspects there is a "shrewd, guiding intelligence somewhere" who has somehow orchestrated the very "simple and naïve" life of the valley. Inquiring, he learns that indeed the community was formed in 1713 by a Belgian priest named Father Perrault. Father Perrault was "the first European to find this place and a very great man, indeed." He built Shangri-la, taught the natives, and began collecting treasures of civilization in order to preserve them from the apocalypses he saw for the world in the future. In this way, though the film appears to be about Tibetan paradise created by putting Buddhist principles into practice, the story turns instead to Christianity and the European culture for its guiding force, again Orientalism.

Soon Conway learns of many miraculous features of Shangri-la. In the paradise free from the struggles of the world, people live hundreds of years and remain healthy. Chang explains, "Age is a limit we impose upon ourselves." Conway also falls in love with Sondra (Jane Wyatt), another European there who plays an Eve-like character, swimming nude in a mountain pool and conversing with a squirrel. Conway is introduced to Father Perrault, the High Lama of Shangri-la who is miraculously still alive.[8] Father Perrault explains that Conway had been kidnapped because Sondra selected him, perhaps to be the next High Lama and her mate. "She has read your books and has a profound admiration for you," Perrault says. This sounds like a not so veiled personal fantasy of the writer, James Hilton.

The stay in Shangri-la has a profound effect on most of the visitors. Conway decides to give up his successful life as a statesman and pursue something that will truly benefit humankind: the preservation of Shangri-la. "Lovey" loses the stiffness of his personality and becomes a kind teacher to the local children. Henry repents of his evil ways as a Wall Street bear and returns to his youthful profession as a plumber for Shangri-la. Gloria seems to be recovering from her illness and has grown attached to Henry. In short, all the characters' previous woes have been overcome in paradise. However, George has met a Russian girl named Maria and the two refuse to stay in Shangri-la. The High Lama warns that Maria cannot leave because outside of Shangri-la she will become her natural old age and die. Although her part is minor in the film, Maria plays a role somewhat like **Mara** in Buddhism. She is the temptress who lies, saying the High Lama is deceitful, in order to lure George back to the mundane world. Using rational argument and Maria as a witness, George convinces Conway to honor national loyalty and family love above the irrational feelings for a higher good in his heart. This is also a dilemma faced by Buddhist monks, as featured in the film *Why Has Bodhi-Dharma Left for the East?*, and aspirants of many religions.

Conway, George, and Maria leave Shangri-la with a group of cruel traders from outside. After several days of grueling travel, Maria becomes exhausted and falls face down in the snow. When George calls to the traders to wait for them, the group instead fire guns at the three. As if illustrating Buddhist karmic retribution, the gunfire causes an avalanche, killing the traders. Afterwards, they discover Maria has become very old and died. Horrified, George loses his sanity and jumps to his death. Conway continues on and eventually meets a search party sent to find him. However, the ordeal has caused him to lose his memory of Shangri-la. On the voyage back to England, he remembers everything; he tells his story and then jumps ship. The searchers track him back to the Himalayas, but are unable to follow him any further and Conway returns to Shangri-la. In the end, a British statesman is telling the story and we see Conway rediscovering Shangri-la, seen through a wooden gate frame resembling a Buddhist *torana*, a gateway marking the entry to a sacred space. The title of the film, *Lost Horizon*, indicates the spiritual values and potentials modern people have misplaced in blind pursuit of worldly gain, illustrated by Conway metaphorically losing Shangri-la.

After World War II, Tibet appeared more prominently in the American news. In 1950, China invaded Tibet, proceeding afterwards to destroy centuries of Tibetan art, scriptures, temples, and monks. In 1959, the Fourteenth Dalai Lama, Tenzin Gyatso, left his country in secrecy and set up the Tibetan Government-in-Exile in Dharamsala, India.[9] Under his guidance, Tibetan teachers preserved their county's culture and religion in universities in America. In 1973, the Dalai Lama came to America for the first time. By 1987, at the request of the Dalai Lama, Tibet House was formed in New York by composer Philip Glass, actor Richard Gere, and Robert Thurman, father of actress Uma Thurman. In 1989, the Dalai Lama was awarded the Nobel Peace Prize and American interest in Tibetan Buddhism gained momentum. In 1997 its popularity reached a new peak in America. That year the Dalai Lama toured Washington, meeting separately with President Clinton and Vice-President Gore and the film *Seven Years in Tibet* was released starring Brad Pitt. Also in 1997, Director Martin Scorsese released *Kundun*, a dramatization of the early life of the Fourteenth Dalai Lama. Philip Glass created the musical score for the film. An October 1997 edition of *Time* magazine explored "America's Fascination with Buddhism."

On June 27, 1998 President Clinton and Chinese President Jiang held a joint press conference in Beijing. At that time Mr. Clinton mentioned the ongoing conflict between China and Tibet. In response, Mr. Jiang said,

> But still, I have a question. That is, during my visit to the United States last year, and also during my previous visit to other European countries, I found that although the education and the science and the technology have developed to a very high level and the people are now enjoying modern civilization, still quite a number of them have a belief in Lamaism. So this is a question that I'm still studying and still looking into. I want to find out the reason why.

In reply Clinton said, "I have spent time with the Dalai Lama, I believe him to be an honest man, and I believe if he had a conversation with President Jiang, they would like each other very much."[10]

Removed from America's and Europe's romantic, Orientalist cinematic and literary history of representing Tibet, the Chinese President appeared baffled at the fascination. Neither *Kundun* nor *Seven Years in Tibet* expose the historical realities according to a Chinese perspective, such as Tibet's feudal social and economic inequities, its reliance on shamanic magic for medicine in face of widespread disease, the internal violence among rival Tibetan Buddhist sects, etc. Instead, the films rely on the box office pulling power of Brad Pitt, Martin Scorsese, Yo Yo Ma, Philip Glass and other superstars to once again present a romanticized vision. One critic points out, "This selective oversight will be enough to put these movies in a continuum with *Lost Horizon*."[11]

According to the High Lama in *Lost Horizon*, when people of the world are finished crashing against one another in lust and greed, they will turn to Shangri-la that preserves the best in humanity with the one simple rule: "Be kind." This reminds us of the Buddhist *Metta Sutta, Discourse on Loving Kindness* that teaches we should open our hearts to the positions of others. Maybe film and other modern methods propagate at least a part of that message even if in an altered form. The film *The Cup* uses World Cup soccer for this purpose. Meanwhile, at social gatherings and over the internet, Tibetan monks in America sell incense, prayer beads, and bumper stickers that reiterate the Dalai Lama's words, "Loving Kindness is My Religion."

Perhaps along these same lines is Mr. Clinton's rather amazing statement assuming the dispositions of the two leading individuals hold the key to resolving world conflict in disregard for such issues as China's desire for Tibet's natural resources. Whether we chalk this up to naiveté, idealism, or correct insight, it seems to be the same approach preached by the High Lama in *Lost Horizon*, the very one sold to Americans in the image of magical Tibet. Will film imagery continue to influence the way America treats Tibet politically? If so, it could well determine the fate of that country.[12]

Further Reading and Viewing

Fields, Rick. *How the Swans Came to the Lake, A Narrative History of Buddhism in America*. Boston: Shambhala Publications, 1992.

Elison, William. "From the Himalayas to Hollywood: The Legacy of *Lost Horizon*." *Tricycle Magazine*, December 1997. See http://www.radioradicale.it/exagora/from-the-himalayas-to-hollywood-the-legacy-of-lost-horizon, accessed 8/15/12.

Broken Blossoms can be viewed in its entirety on Google Videos: http://video.google.com/videoplay?docid=5636171007327735796.[13]

Notes

1 The Selig Polyscope Company, Incorporated, production; distributed by The General Film Company, Incorporated. Released February 14, 1913.

2 According to a website dedicated to the actress Theda Bara which is no longer available.

3 Hans J. Wollstein, All Movie Guide. http://movies.nytimes.com/movie/111136/Soul-of-Buddha/overview, accessed 8/15/12.

4 See "Devadasis Were Degraded Buddhist Nuns" by K. Jamanadas, available at http://ambedkar.org/buddhism/Devadasis_Were_Degraded_Buddhist_Nuns.htm, accessed 8/15/12.

5 Rick Fields, *How the Swans Came to the Lake, A Narrative History of Buddhism in America*, p. 124–5.

6 Charles Affron, *Lillian Gish, Her Legend, Her Life*, p. 129.

7 H.B. Warner also played in a silent film version of *Paradise Lost*, which has a somewhat similar theme. In addition, he played the lead role in Cecil B. DeMille's silent classic *Jesus Christ*.

8 Father Perrault seems to be a strange caricature of the Dalai Lama, who would have been the 13th Dalai Lama Thubten Gyatso (1876–1933) at the time of the film and book. We are reminded of the masonic conspiracy theory that sees the leaders of all major religious as being secretly connected to the same secret European society that is controlling the world.

9 Officially called the Central Tibetan Administration of His Holiness the Dalai Lama.

10 For a full transcript by the Federal News Service and the Associated Press, see: http://www.zpub.com/un/china27.html, accessed 8/15/12.

11 William Elison, "From the Himalayas to Hollywood: The Legacy of *Lost Horizon*."

12 *Lost Horizon* was remade as a musical in 1973, directed by Charles Jarrott. The book was also made into a Broadway musical in 1956 and a drama for BBC radio that has been rebroadcasted a number of times, including March 2012.

13 Accessed 8/25/12.

2

THE FOUR NOBLE TRUTHS

Fight Club

1. Basic Plot Summary

Fight Club (David Fincher, USA, 1999) is a film depicting groups of men around the US who meet in basements and parking lots to fight. They are not angry when they fight and they do not keep score of who wins. Instead they find fighting exhilarating. Fighting also frees them from the stress of daily life. Even though they are often hurt badly, they view this too as a positive part of the activity. It makes them feel alive and unconcerned about the small things. There are three persons of focus: a main character and narrator who remains nameless (Edward Norton), his outgoing and thrill-seeking friend Tyler Durgen (Brad Pitt), and a love interest, or at least a sexual interest of both, who is also a strong female figure, Marla Singer (Helena Bonham Carter). Marla is a rather offbeat femme fatale, perhaps post-punk girl who might appeal to the tastes of those who like Mia Wallace (Uma Thurman) in *Pulp Fiction*. As the story continues, the men begin to find less excitement in fighting and so form Project Mayhem, a self-proclaimed terrorist group with few or no political goals. Again, the purpose in Project Mayhem's activities is personal satisfaction. The men are given homework assignments such as to start a fight with a stranger and lose the fight. They also buy guns but no bullets and burn a grinning demon face on the side of a city building. If they are caught, they are out of the group. The narrator and Tyler also urinate in soups at restaurants, splice pornography clips into children's movies at theaters, and steal human fat from a medical waste facility to make soap to sell in upscale department stores. All these and other overgrown-boyish activities apparently had wide appeal among film goers. Near the end of the film, the narrator becomes aware that he is Tyler Durgen and that he has been erroneously thinking they were separate people. Seeing this, he realizes that he has let Fight Club and Project Mayhem grow beyond control. He tries to stop the terrorist activities but learns there are Fight Clubs around the country and Project Mayhem members in the police department and elsewhere. He attempts to free himself from Tyler and the Project by suicide. Although Tyler disappears from his life, the narrator does not die. Instead he is united with Marla, who he now realizes he loves.

Fight Club gained popularity as an action-packed adventure. Young men have graphically bloody brawls, cars crash violently, buildings explode, there are allusions to wild sex, and there is much talk about how to make napalm and bombs. Although the adoring audience might not know this, none of it probably happened in the physical world. Instead, the narrator may be projecting all of this as manifestations of deep psychological disturbances. The audience might not want to consider that in the end he is successful in committing suicide. While the film makes it clear that the narrator's fights with Tyler have been struggles with himself, physical and/or psychological, are we as comfortable with the implication that the same applies to his ferocious erotic encounters with Marla?

One of the strengths of the film is that five different people watching it can potentially see five different plots, depending on their point of view. The first, perhaps most common, is outlined above. A second, psychological interpretation can come from the perspective of dissociative identity disorder (DID). A single person diagnosed with DID is said to have multiple personalities. Each personality displays its own individuality and alternately takes control of the individual's behavior. One takes control, the others lose memory. There are many references in the film and best-selling novel by Chuck Palahniuk that not only Tyler but Marla also may be an alternate personality of the narrator. This begins when Marla and the narrator both go to a testicular cancer support group meeting. Right away he recognizes that she is a reflection of him, a fake, a tourist at the meeting. The recognition of his own pretense ruins the effect he was looking for by going to the group. Likewise, the narrator never sees Tyler and Marla together. There are also numerous references to triads, perhaps indicating the narrator, Tyler and Marla are the same. For example, the place where the testicular cancer support group meets is the Trinity Episcopal Church. But perhaps all of those involved in all of the Fight Clubs are either distinct personalities of the same person, or illustrations of the struggles and interactions of the three main personalities. As the narrator says, he feels like a copy of a copy of a copy. If so, little of the overt plot may be taking place as the viewer assumes. Instead, the events are illustrations of what it might be like for a person experiencing DID.

From a third perspective, *Fight Club* is about the role of men in post-industrial capitalism. In short, men were once hunters and warriors. Women were household economists and primary caregivers in the family. The traditional male role is now obsolete. Violence is viewed in our society as heinous. The female role has become dominant. This is reflected in business, politics, and education, everywhere peace and civility are valued. For men to thrive in society, they must display traditionally female traits. This is illustrated in many ways in the film. Big Bob is a formally strong robust man who is now literally neutered and has breasts. He appears at a testicular cancer support group meeting. Marla speaks of animals that people love but neuter. A politician is threatened with castration as is the narrator. Help from the illness support groups comes in the form of talking and crying. Help in the Fight Clubs comes from violence. The narrator's change from reliance on support groups to the activities of Fight Clubs is illustrated by images of his face. Crying in a support group he sees the wet image of his face on Big Bob's shirt. In a Fight Club he sees the bloody image of his face on the floor. Also, the "power animal" in the support group visualization is a friendly penguin as opposed to the hard-hitting men visualized later. The narrator says we are a nation of men raised by women, abandoned by fathers. There are references to God as the father and abandonment by God. Several times the novel says father is our model for God. We've lost both in our society. In a sense, the film is about searching for God the father, so men can move on. This is similar to the quest by the replicant (Rutger Hauer) in *Blade Runner*, which also features a bizarre male-fantasy woman (Daryl Hannah). In *Fight Club*, the narrator says he is 6 years old again, delivering messages between his mother and father, referring to Marla and Tyler. Also like a son to his father, Tyler rails at his boss and society generally: "You don't care where I live or how I feel . . . yes I am stupid and bored and weak, but I am still your responsibility." Tyler as father and Marla as mother might also give the viewer an indication of what happened to the narrator to cause his DID. Tyler describes his father as never staying with one woman for more than six years, but setting up franchises of families around the country. This is exactly what Tyler and the narrator do with Fight Clubs. Both Tyler and Marla are pictures of terrible parents. Illustrating this, in the novel Marla tells Tyler she wanted to get pregnant and have his abortion.[1] The scar the father has left on both the mother and the child is illustrated in the film by the acid burns in the shape of a kiss on the hands of the narrator and Marla.

From a fourth perspective, *Fight Club* is about social disruption, culture jamming. Project Mayhem participants are like punk rockers in this respect or the anarchists of the 1886 Haymarket Incident who tried to destroy upscale businesses in Chicago. Chuck Palahniuk, the writer of *Fight Club*, was a member of the Cacophony Society, the alleged founders of Burning Man. Cacophony events often involve costumes and pranks such as those seen at SantaCon in San Fracisco, which encouraged people to dress as Santa Claus and perform spontaneously in the streets. The group would also take Barbies and GI Joes from department stores, switch their voice boxes and replant them in stores. Like the schoolboys in *Lord of the Flies*, the characters in *Fight Club* deal with the failure of industrial civilization in chaotic ways. They also look with favor at self-reliance as seen in the sustainable gardening at the Paper Street communal house. They speak with favor of a future when animals will roam the deserted streets and kudzu vines will grow up skyscrapers. They hope their pranks will hasten that advent.

And then there is the perspective of Buddhist themes in *Fight Club*, beginning with the **Four Sights**, the Four Noble Truths and the Eightfold Path.

2.   Buddhist Themes

Traditional accounts say the Buddha's parents were King Śuddhodana and Queen **Maya** of the Śakya kingdom in northeast India, present-day Nepal. Maya is said to have dreamed of a white elephant, a symbol of purity. This auspicious sign marked the conception of her son. While in the forest, standing up and holding onto a tree branch, Maya gave birth to the baby who would grow up and teach the path to awakening. Buddhist temples celebrate his birthday on or around the eighth day of the fourth month of the lunar calendar. Traditions vary but some say he was born in 563 BCE.[2] The baby was named **Siddhartha Gautama**. "Buddha" is an honorific title meaning "the perfectly awakened one." Celebrating the birth of the prince, soothsayers predicted his future, saying the child was destined to either be a great ruler who would extend the range of his father's kingdom or to become an awakened being, a Buddha. Hearing this, his father determined his son should broaden his ambitions as king. He decided to shelter his son from any-thing that might lead him to reflect on the harsh realities of life and cause him to seek awakening. Siddhartha was raised in comfort and luxury. When he was in his twenties, he ventured out from the palace grounds in his chariot on a pleasure trip to the forest. To keep him sheltered, his father ordered the roads to be cleared of any indications of suffering or discontentment. However, on the way to the forest, there happened to be an old man on the road. Seeing the man walking slowly and with difficulty, Siddhartha asked his chariot driver about the man's condition. He learned that old age, accompanied by physical pain and mental decline, is a natural development that most people will experience, including him. This was the first of Four Sights that would change him from a self-serving prince to a Buddha. On other occasions he saw on the road severe illness and death. Likewise, the chariot driver, a metaphor for his own thoughts, informed him of the inevitability of sick-ness and that all things that live must die. These were two more of the Four Sights. Later, seeing young women dancing, Siddhartha asks himself, don't these women realize that the things they hold most dear, their youth, health and life, will soon be gone.[3] He realizes that people get their minds off of this by acting unconsciously according to base desires and aversions.

Like Siddhartha's first life-changing experiences, early in *Fight Club*, the nar-rator sees old age, sickness, and death by visiting support groups for people with terminal illnesses. This profoundly affects him as we find in his comments such as "This is your life, and it's ending one minute at a time" and "Given a long enough timeline the survival rate is zero." Siddhartha too thought of the inevitability of old age, sickness, and death. Deeply troubled by these things, he sat in the forest with closed eyes. When he opened them he saw the fourth of the Four Sights. Standing before him was a Hindu ascetic holy man. Siddhartha learned from the ascetic that he had given up materialistic life in order to make his mind unlike ordinary worldly people.[4] In *Fight Club*, the narrator's fourth sight occurs on an airplane when he meets Tyler Durgen. Both the narrator and the Buddha eventually give up their reliance on these men. But, upon meeting them, both realize there is an alternative to the way they have been living. They feel that giving up materialism and intensely struggling with themselves may set them free from their overwhelming stress. Willing to try, both follow their leaders. Like Siddhartha's realization about diverting thoughts of death, the narrator in *Fight Club* speaks of Chloe in a cancer group. Chloe is close to death but all she thinks about is having sex. There is also a meditative practice in Buddhism to help overcome lust. Men should envision a woman as a "bag of bones" or a corpse, similar to how the narrator sees Chloe. We should also note Chloe wants sex, not love or even intimacy.

Siddhartha returns from the forest to his father's palace and announces his intention of becoming a hermit. His father forbids him to leave, but at night, when everyone is asleep, he gives up his life of luxury. In Buddhism this event is known as **going forth** or the **Great Departure**. As he is leaving he sees sleeping palace women with their clothes unfastened, but only sees them as corpses scattered about.[5] He goes to the forest and cuts off his hair that was tied in a royal topknot. Leaving home and cutting his hair (taking the tonsure) in the life story of the Buddha is seen as a model for Buddhists. In *Fight Club*, the narrator also makes a dramatic break from material life by destroying his apartment along with the furnishings he had cherished and worked to obtain. He later comments we are slaves to our possessions. He sees among the rubble a yin/yang table he had hoped would bring him happiness. He now rejects the mere symbol of balance in favor of action.

In the forest, Siddhartha experiments with Hindu meditation. He is taught techniques such as holding his breath in order to break the mind's attachments to materialism. In the group with Chloe, the narrator of *Fight Club* also learns a type of meditation practice, which helps at first but is ultimately unsatisfactory. This is a guided meditation involving closing one's eyes as a teacher leads your thoughts to another place. The novel mentions going up the hill to the palace of seven doors.[6] In Buddhism, the palace of seven doors is the head with its seven sense openings (two ears, two eyes, two nostrils, and the mouth).[7] Past that, the group is encouraged to imagine a white healing light floating around their feet and rising. This is a Tibetan Buddhist dream practice and visualization for healing and awakening. The narrator says it opens **chakras**, an idea found in Hinduism and Buddhism. Finally, the narrator is led to visualize his "power animal." His turns out to be a penguin, sliding on its belly down ice-covered floors in the cave of his mind. This is funny in the film because the penguin does not fit the description "power animal." The message seems to be, like the guided meditation practice, the penguin might relieve stress at first, but in the long run it does not have the power to address the large problems of life. This is the same conclusion Siddhartha reaches after trying Hindu meditation in the forest of ancient India. So, Siddhartha tries other methods the ascetics use and learns about self-mortification. In order to break their attachments to worldly pleasures, Hindu ascetics would keep themselves wet and uncomfortable or sit near fires on hot summer days. Meanwhile, mentally struggling with their self-identity, they would try to stop their thoughts. Undertaking these practices, Siddhartha's body becomes pitiful. His eyes are sunken and he becomes so skinny he can touch his backbone through his stomach. Along with the Hindu ascetics, he struggles with himself in such a way for six years in the forest. In the seventh year, he leaves the others to find his own way. He eats and regains his strength, then resolves to meditate alone until he finds release from his anguish. He sits beneath a tree known as the **Bodhi Tree**, the tree of awakening. There, having rejected both harsh asceticism and the overly lavish life of the palace, he discovered the Middle Path between these extremes. Buddhism is the Middle Path. But, on his own, the discovery did not come easily. It involved meditational practices and new insights that his mind tried to hinder by playing tricks. This is one of our realities when we try to meditate. Sitting calmly, our minds naturally begin to wander. We have thoughts about the past or future, keeping us from being serene. In the life story of the Buddha, these thoughts keeping us from attainment are personified as a demon named Mara. In *Fight Club*, there is a mental distraction in the form of Marla. At least, this is how she appears to the narrator at first. Not only the similarity of names, but the characteristics of the two figures are close enough to suggest the author is making this connection. The Sanskrit word *māra* is etymologically related to the English word "murder." It is also close to the name of Siddhartha's mother, Maya. *Maya* literally means "illusion." It may seem strange that the mother of the Buddha, metaphorically that which gives rise to all awakening, is illusion. But this is natural in Buddhism. The same metaphor can be found in the Buddhist symbol of the lotus flower. A lotus grows from the swampy muck of the world, emerging as a clean and beautiful flower. This is seen as the same as awakening. In this way, the profane and the sacred are connected. In *Fight Club*, as well, from violence comes release from attachments to materialistic society that is the root of suffering.

In Buddhism, Mara is, in part, the personification of death. Mara is also the Buddhist equivalent of Hindu *kama*, lust. As with Chloe, there is a connection between sex and death. Lust leads us mindlessly to death. Early in *Fight Club* Marla is connected with death. The narrator first sees her in a cancer support group meeting. Afterwards, the support groups no longer help him with his anguish. Marla as death is in the mind of the narrator, just as Mara is in the mind of Siddhartha and all of us. It is, in fact, the central factor in Siddhartha's pursuit of Buddhahood. Likewise, the narrator of *Fight Club* states at the beginning of the film that all of this has something to do with a girl named Marla Singer. As with Mara for Siddhartha, the appearance of Marla may represent the narrator facing his fear of death, which disrupts the practices that were previously comforting. Marla's connection to death is further established when she walks through traffic from the Laundromat to the vintage clothing store. While the narrator has to stop and avoid oncoming cars, Marla strolls fearlessly and unfeasibly through traffic. The impossibility of this act should be a hint to the audience that this is only happening in the mind of the narrator. The name "Paper Street" also indicates this. A paper street is a road that is planned but doesn't really exist, appearing on a map showing projected construction. There are many examples of impossible events in the film that serve the same function, such as walking away from a major car crash and surviving a suicide attempt with a gun in the mouth. Marla also smokes heavily, breathing smoke like a demon, like Tyler and like the narrator when he shoots himself in the mouth near the end of the film. When the narrator says he wants to destroy something beautiful, which is what illness and death do to the body, he adds he wants to breathe smoke. Marla and Tyler do this repeatedly. The narrator is the only one who doesn't smoke. Marla also says she receives phone calls from dead people, who do not speak when she answers. After Marla ruins the effect of support groups for the narrator and miraculously walks through traffic, she tempts him with sex. Marla's constant smoking is like hell that is a part of his life. In a support group after Chloe has just died, the narrator holds Marla. He says, "I open my arms to receive my inner child, and the child is Marla smoking her cigarette."[8] In the novel the narrator has a hole in his cheek that will not heal. Death, which is part of him, as much as Marla is, manifests itself in the half of his face that looks like a grinning skull. But Marla changes in the film as the narrator's perception changes. Marla calls him to her house to check her for a lump in her breast. We come to see Marla as fearing death, a condition that may have led her to the support groups. The narrator tries to come to grips with Marla throughout the film. In fact, this is the main plot to the film and the book: the narrator tries to deal with Marla and death through that part of him that is personified as Tyler.

When Siddhartha is about to awaken, Mara first threatens to shoot him with an arrow, representing the fear of death. Mara says, "Rise up, O Warrior, afraid of death . . . I won't shoot men servile to their lovers and delighting in sexual pleasures."[9] When Siddhartha ignores Mara and continues to meditate, the demon sends an army to fight him. Again Siddhartha is unperturbed. So, Mara sends his three beautiful daughters to seduce him. They are the personifications of Desire, Lust, and Aversion.

After Siddhartha overcomes all of the tricks his mind plays in the personification of Mara, he begins to achieve meditative attainments. Each attainment is marked by the time of night it occurs, not in hours but following the watches of the night in ancient India. During the first watch of the night he remembers all of his past lives. As an analogy, late in the movie, the narrator realizes his alternate life as Tyler. In the second watch of the night Siddhartha realizes the interconnectedness of all things. This is known in Buddhism as **dependent origination**. It means nothing exists independently, including what we call the "self."[10] The cinematic correspondence comes when the narrator sees the undeniable connection with himself, Tyler and Marla. In the third watch of the night Siddhartha awakens and becomes the Buddha. This state is **nirvana**, extinction of passions, along with notions of self and other. In *Fight Club*, this may be illustrated by the narrator finally realizing how to take control of his mind, willing the gun away from Tyler's hand into his own, shooting himself and thereby destroying the illusion of self and other.

After awaking, the Buddha stays at the Bodhi Tree for seven weeks formulating his teaching method. Afterwards, he searches out the five Hindu ascetics he had known in the forest and teaches them the path to awakening. He begins his instructions by saying he had realized Four Noble Truths. The First Noble Truth is that life is filled with perpetual dissatisfaction, suffering, or disease. This is what the narrator in *Fight Club* comes to realize at the beginning of the film. The Second Noble Truth is that dissatisfaction in life is cause by desire. This means, not only do we have desires for things and conditions that we don't have, but we desire to rid ourselves of things we have and don't want. In other words, when Mara tempted Siddhartha with his three daughters, Desire, Lust, and Aversion, it was personification of the mental state we all live in, the state described by the Second Noble Truth. The narrator in the film realizes that his desire for material possessions is causing his suffering. The Third Noble Truth is: to end suffering we must end desires. The narrator realizes this and responds by blowing up his apartment. The Fourth Noble Truth is: to end desires we should follow the Eightfold Path.

The Eightfold Path is the step-by-step method discovered by the Buddha for overcoming suffering and becoming awaken. To follow the Eightfold Path is to enter the way of Buddhism and become a Buddhist. The writer of *Fight Club* was influenced by the traditional way people start practicing Buddhism at Zen temples in Japan. He bases the layout of the Paper Street house on a Zen temple as well as the way men come to live in the house and the activities they do there. It is easy to see this if we refer to the documentary film *Principles and Practices of Zen*.[11] In the documentary we see a young man come to a Zen temple in Japan and ask to enter for study. He is told to go away, that there is no room in the temple for him. But he does not leave. Instead, he waits in the entryway for three days, knowing this is the traditional test of his resolve. This is also seen in *Way of the Tiger, Sign of the Dragon*, the film that spawned the television series *Kung Fu*. In it, boys wait outside the Shaolin Temple in China hoping to be admitted. Some are told to leave and do so. Others wait in the rain. In Japan, the waiting place and period are known as *tangaryō*, literally "hut where days are passed." This tradition of testing a student's worthiness appears in Indian and Chinese classic tales, including *The Katha Upanishad* of Hinduism and the story of the aspiring student Huike waiting in the snow for Bodhidharma's Chan (Zen) teachings in China.

In *Fight Club*, those who hope to live in the Paper Street house are told to go away. However, they remain waiting in the porch. When Big Bob is told to leave he starts to do so, only to be stopped by the narrator, who tells him it is a test. In the novel this is explained: "This is how Buddhist temples have tested applicants going back for bah-zillion years, Tyler says. You tell the applicant to go away, and if his resolve is so strong that he waits at the entrance without food or shelter or encouragement for three days, then and only then can he enter and begin the training."[12] *Principles and Practices of Zen* reveals the meaning behind several other features of the Paper Street house. Inside a Zen temple, one seemingly odd way a master gives encouragement when needed is to strike a student with a staff know as the "compassion stick." Viewers will remember in *Fight Club* that, as men stand on the porch hoping to be admitted, the narrator comes outside and hits them with a broomstick. This method of training is famous in Zen lore and is found in writings of Zen including the Chinese classic *The Blue Cliff Record* and the Japanese *The True Dharma Eye* by Zen master **Dōgen**.[13] Some Zen masters use shouting, others prefer blows of a stick to knock out the tendency toward book learning in favor of direct experience. As an illustration, the monk Lin-chi went to his master to ask what was the basic meaning of Buddhism. Before he could get the question out, the master hit him.[14] It also follows Master Te Shan's principle[15] "If you can speak it's thirty blows, and if you can't speak it's thirty blows."[16] We also read about "Zen Master Pao-shou [who] was suddenly enlightened to his true nature by the sight of a street fight."[17] If the men on the porch of the Paper Street house prove their worthiness, they are allowed to enter. Inside, they become a part of the community by shaving their heads, just as Buddhists do when becoming monks or nuns in a temple. The writer may be using the three days in Zen also as another indicator of the triad of the narrator, Tyler, and Marla. When Tyler is burning the narrator's hand the latter must promise three times to improve his life. These promises may be for the narrator, Tyler and Marla. In Buddhist scriptures, sometimes a request must be made three times before it is granted. For example, the Buddha only agrees to teach the truths contained in the *Lotus Sūtra* after being asked three times.[18]

Both novice Buddhist monastics and the new Paper Street admittees must cook, rake, and garden. Some Zen monasteries in China, Japan, and Korea have been known for farming, sustainability, and rugged self-sufficiency. For example, Silsang-sa Temple in the Jeolla Province of South Korea is the center for ecological Buddhism in that country today. Continuing its long history of environmentalism, it regularly teaches classes to reeducate people about organic farming practices. Zen temples sometimes feature Zen rock gardens with raked gravel around larger stones. Used as places of quiet contemplation, the raked lines in the rocks suggest ripples in a stream around a boulder. In *Fight Club* we find all of these elements appear in the rented home on Paper Street, with its raised beds and rock gardens behind the house. Those who live in the house are called space monkeys, because monkeys who were shot into space were sacrificed to help humankind. In Buddhism, a person who sacrifices him or herself to help others gain attainment is a Bodhisattva. Tyler speaks at length about ancient places where human sacrifices were carried out, connecting the fat of those beings with soap, an emblem of purification. The occupants of the Paper Street house are Bodhisattvas, as are monastics in temples. They are willing to sacrifice themselves to purify humankind from the stain of desire and materialism.

The film and novel's repetition of the word "rented," in regards to the Paper Street house, reminds us of impermanence. We have already learned that the narrator was a constant traveler, homeless like a Buddhist monk. He speaks about the prison of a home and makes an explosive break. Like the male-oriented monastic-like tough living on Paper Street, is Buddhism male-oriented? There may be something of stereotypical "male thinking" in vowing to sit under the Bodhi Tree without arising until attaining awakening. Likewise, monasteries appear at times to be exclusive to men. In most countries of Southeast Asia where Theravāda Buddhism is strongly supported, there is no order of Buddhist nuns. The *Pure Land Sūtras* say only males can be saved; women must first hate their female aspect and be reborn as a man. While Buddhism is generally egalitarian, there are numerous historical indications like these of gender discrimination.

The first two steps of the Eightfold Path have to do with wisdom. The first is Right Understanding. This means understanding that life is filled with perpetual dissatisfaction caused by desires. The second is Right Resolve. This means making a firm resolution to do something about dissatisfaction, that is, to end desires by following the Buddha's method. By coming to the Paper Street house the men have accomplished these steps, realizing their dissatisfaction with life and resolving to change it. The next three steps of the Eightfold Path are about ethical conduct, which helps others and oneself in his or her own practice. The third is Right Speech, the fourth is Right Action, and the fifth is Right Livelihood. These involve rules including the basic **Five Precepts**, which are basic guiding principles for being a Buddhist. They are:

1. To refrain from destroying living beings
2. To refrain from stealing
3. To refrain from sexual misconduct (adultery, rape, etc.)
4. To refrain from false speech (lying)
5. To refrain from intoxicants which lead to heedlessness.

As the Paper Street house grows as a community of men who renounce materialism, new rules similar to the Five Precepts are applied. Even so, although they are not supposed to drink alcohol, the narrator does. This reminds us of accounts of drunken Japanese Zen masters and the Chinese immortals portrayed by Jackie Chan in *The Forbidden Kingdom*.[19] Throughout the film we hear the now famous rules of *Fight Club*. The first rule of Fight Club is you don't talk about Fight Club. The second rule of Fight Club is you don't talk about Fight Club. This repetition, according to the basic interpretation of the film, serves to add emphasis. However, if we interpret these as rules the narrator is making for his own internal struggles with aspects of himself personified as Tyler and Marla, the first two rules may mean don't talk to Tyler about Fight Club, don't talk to Marla about Fight Club. Tyler tells the narrator to never speak to Marla about him or he would never be seen again. The third rule of Fight Club is when someone says stop, or goes limp, even if he's just faking it, the fight is over. According to our interpretation, this implies don't take the self-struggle too far, seek the Middle Path between extremes. However, later in the film after the narrator hurts a man badly, the third rule is dropped and the internal rule, to not talk to Marla or Tyler about Fight Club, no longer applies either. The fourth rule of Fight Club is only two guys to a fight, the fifth rule is only one fight at a time. This implies when the narrator is struggling with things Tyler represents, he cannot be fighting with those things Marla represents. The sixth rule is to fight without shirts or shoes. This may indicate the male nature of Fight Club in contrast with the support groups. The seventh and eighth rules of Fight Club are fights go on as long as you have to and, if this is your first night at Fight Club, you have to fight. These rules are introduced later in the film and indicate an evolving understanding of the narrator's struggle with himself. Project Mayhem also has rules: (1) You don't ask questions, (2) You don't ask questions, (3) No excuses, (4) No lies (which is also one of the Five Precepts), and (5) You have to trust Tyler, indicating the growing cult-like nature of the gatherings. Buddhism also developed more rules and vows beyond the basic five as time went on.

The "you" in these rules is not accidental. The narrator is addressing us, the audience. Throughout the film he and Tyler break character to address us as an audience and their situation as characters in a film is made clear. When the narrator has revelations, the film we are watching appears to slip on it reels. When Tyler is editing a pornographic clip into a children's film he is projecting, the narrator faces the camera and explains there is a cigarette burn circle that tells a projectionist when to change reels. As he speaks, Tyler points to the white circle that flashes on our screen: Tyler functions as a projectionist. He is also a projection of the narrator's mental progress, a projection of us as viewers and he is one who projects for us the ideas we are discussing. He also refers to "flashback humor," recognizing that the film in which he is a character is out of sequence. All of these serve at least three functions. They tell us that the events we are witnessing are not real but a story that has been created in someone's mind. They tell us that reality in general is unreal, like a film. They tell us that, not only are Tyler and the narrator actors in this mental drama, but so are we. We find very similar self-references and identification of us as the viewing audience as well as a part of the film in *Waking Life*.[20] Interestingly, in *Waking Life* the unnamed narrator wants to wake up; in *Fight Club* he wants to go to sleep. Both want this for the same reason, because they cannot distinguish the dream state from "reality." In *Fight Club* the narrator says, "With insomnia, nothing is real." As in Buddhism, in these films life is depicted as a dream the characters want to awaken from.

We are in the same predicament the narrator struggles with: life is suffering caused by desire, and there is a path to overcome this. To tell us this is our situation, not only his, the narrator of *Fight Club* speaks not of himself but of "you." He says, "You wake up at Seatac, SFO, LAX. You wake up at O'Hare, Dallas-Fort Worth, BWI. Pacific, mountain, central. Lose an hour, gain an hour. This is your life, and it's ending one minute at a time." Sometimes in films and novels, leaving a character nameless underscores that he or she is just like everyone. This may be a function of the namelessness of the narrator as well as the main character in the film *Waking Life*. It may also point to the idea that the narrator is not an independent entity: he is Tyler Durgen, the name he begins to use by the end of the film. He may be the other characters as well and, in that sense, the audience.

The last three of the Buddha's Eightfold Path are about mental discipline. The sixth is Right Effort. This means working diligently to realize and maintain the Buddhist path, including rooting out ill towards others and replacing that with good wishes. The seventh and eighth are Right Mindfulness and Right Concentration, both dealing with meditation. After the Buddha explained the Four Noble Truths and the Eightfold Path to the five ascetics in **Deer Park**, they became his followers on the path to awakening. Soon others joined him and he gave more instructions about how to meditate. This is recorded, for example, in the *Discourse on The Four Foundations of Mindfulness*.[21] These instructions are the bases of **Insight Meditation (*Vipassana*)** practiced in Southeast Asia and growing in popularity elsewhere. This method teaches the practitioner to meditate by paying "bare attention" to four things, (1) body; (2) feelings; (3) mind; and (4) mental qualities. The scripture explains that the method of meditation the Buddha used for awakening was to control his mind's cravings and aversions, its fear of death and desire for everlasting life. This was achieved by first thinking only of basic bodily activities in this way: "I am breathing in. I am breathing out."[22] Naturally, when trying this, other thoughts arise. But the practitioner should only acknowledge those thoughts briefly and continue to consider, "I am breathing in. I am breathing out." If we can do this, over time we will develop mindfulness of our thoughts and gain control over the discursive process that is leading us around beyond our control. This can also be seen as related to the fourth and fifth rules of Fight Club, only two guys to a fight, one fight at a time. Today we tend to multitask. Technologies such as cell phone texting and internet chatting may lead to mental developments that aid in multitasking. This may be good for filling certain jobs in society, such as working on Wall Street. But, it may also come at the expense of the opposite way of thinking, concentrating. Paying bare attention to one basic thing helps us to become mindful. To multitask is to be unmindful. Fight Clubs seem to reject the multitasking of society in favor of paying attention to immediate experience.

Another element of Zen Buddhism in *Fight Club* can be seen in the narrator's haiku poems. When he copies one of his poems he says in the novel, "I get totally ZEN right in everyone's hostile little FACE."[23] His poem is, "Worker bees can leave—Even drones can fly away—The queen is their slave."[24] This poem addresses the problem of attachment. His next poem says, "Without just one nest—A bird can call the world home—Life is your career."[25] This poem is about embracing homelessness as the means to truly living. His next haiku says, "A tiger can smile—A snake will say it loves you—Lies make us evil."[26] This poem is about false appearances and their personal consequences to our lives and practice. Haikus have been used by Zen Buddhists for centuries. Not only can haiku express Buddhist ideas, but they are thought to indicate the "Zen moment." That is, a haiku might make us stop and experience our immediacy in this moment here and now, the "Ah-ha" instant.

If the characters in *Fight Club* are to be taken at face value and not as metaphors for mental states, from a Buddhist perspective, can we like any of them? The narrator is a suicidal sociopath who wants to hurt others as he goes toward his own death. He asks his doctor how he can obtain the hepatitis virus because he wants to spread it. Tyler puts pornography in children's films and makes them cry. He urinates in food. He says we shouldn't recycle and that he wants to destroy pandas. Marla steals pants from laundries, takes food from meals for elders, and sleeps with lots of bizarre men. The film is filled with bomb-making instructions and for this reason it was outlawed in China. In America, it is doubtful it would have been released if it had been made a year or so later, due to similar terrorist bombings in New York on 9/11. In a sense, however, attacking these basic values of society takes us beyond them. There is this idea in Zen Buddhism as well. Zen masters are depicted as tearing up the Buddhist scriptures. Even the Buddha himself is disparaged so the practitioner does not become so attached to the method that the goal is lost. For this reason, when asked "What is the Buddha," a Zen master once replied, "A dung stick."[27]

To come to grips with an enemy we must first battle ourselves. In the case of Buddhism where the perceived enemy is death, a mild internal struggle is inadequate. Instead we must ultimately hit bottom, as Tyler says, doing away with everything we wrongly consider ourselves. As the narrator says, only in death are we no longer part of Project Mayhem. Project Mayhem here is our lives of suffering while being led by the desires of the ego-self. If we can struggle and hit bottom with our ego-selves, we will realize that death is not an external enemy but inherently us. In Zen Buddhism there is a saying: "If you meet the Buddha on the road, kill him."[28] This sounds like a shocking statement. Perhaps it is understandable in the following way: as you progress in meditative practice you will use the method of the Buddha, the Eightfold Path; but when you reach a certain point, you must abandon the method or it will become an obstacle to final release from suffering. After all, neither the method nor anything else can be the ultimate realization. Killing it is like killing Tyler in order to go further.

Coming to grips with Marla and death through Tyler works. But, eventually the method itself must be abandoned if the narrator is to completely embrace his life and death. In Buddhism, the way to do this is to destroy the ego-self. In the film, this is Tyler, the part of the self that has a name. Only in death does a person have a name, the film tells us, and you are not your name or your possessions. In the Paper Street house, everyone is nameless like the narrator. In Buddhism, practitioners can realize destruction of the ego-self and extinction of desires that control our lives. This is nirvana. We are only completely free of these at death, called ***parinirvana***, final nirvana. Does the narrator die at the end of the film? He shoots himself through the mouth and Tyler falls to the ground with the top of his head blown off. The narrator appears to miraculously live, talk and watch out the window as buildings explode, holding hands with Marla. There is little doubt that ridding himself of Tyler was the only way to completely come to terms with Marla. Marla and death are no longer as he had conceptualized them but are a part of him. The novel has a radically different ending. The narrator has a gun in his mouth atop of the tallest building in the world and the members of all of the support groups come to talk him out of suicide. When Marla approaches, Tyler disappears for the last time. From the point of view of DID, Marla wins over Tyler as the gatekeeper or dominating personality. However, when the building they are in fails to explode, the narrator shoots himself. The final chapter of the novel appears to take place in heaven. There, all the rooms and furnishings are white and attendants in white clothes bring him medications. Heaven sounds a lot like a sanatorium. The narrator says it is like *Valley of the Dolls*,[29] a film depicting three successful women, rather than three personalities, whose lives are ruined or affected by drug usage. Earlier, there are many references to Marla taking pills. She also sings the theme song to *Valley of the Dolls* as she leaves the Paper Street house. Now that the narrator is the one relying on pills, the reader suspects Marla has become the dominant personality or has merged with him as she does at the end of the film. In the sanatorium, he receives letters from Marla that say she hopes he returns soon. Men working there tell him "We miss you Mr. Durden" and "Everything's going according to the plan."[30] The letter implies Tyler knew this would happen and told people in advance or the narrator imagines he did.

The triad of the narrator, Marla and Tyler can be analyzed in many ways. Likely, any way that considers only one theoretical perspective will be inadequate in terms of the big picture. Certainly Buddhism is only one part of the film, but an important part. The novel refers also to *Sybil*,[31] a book and film about multiple personality disorder and it mentions *Psycho*.[32] In the documentary, *The Perverts Guide to the Cinema*,[33] the philosopher Slavoj Žižek evaluates *Psycho* in a way particularly relevant to *Fight Club*. Although his analysis is derived from Freudian psychology, it may be useful to us. Žižek says Norman Bates' (Anthony Perkins) house has three levels, as if reproducing the three aspects of personality.

> Ground floor is ego. Norman behaves there as a normal son, whatever remains there of his normal ego taking over. Up there is the superego, the maternal superego, because the dead mother is basically a figure of superego. And down in the cellar it is the id, the reservoir of these illicit drives.[34]

When Norman carries his mother's corpse from the upstairs to the cellar it is as if he is transposing her in his own mind as a psychic agency from superego to id. According to Freud, superego and id are deeply connected. The mother complains first as a figure of authority. Superego is an obscene agency bombarding us with impossible orders and laughing at us when we cannot fulfill its demands. The more we obey its insanity, the more guilt we feel. The superego criticizes and prohibits behaviors. In contrast, the id acts according to basic drives and the pleasure principle. It is immoral and egocentric. When Norman moves his personality from the restrictions of the superego to the immorality of the id, there is trouble. This same scenario might be applied to *Fight Club*. Marla often appears upstairs as in the Paper Street house and her apartment. Tyler appears downstairs, making noise in the house and organizing Fight Clubs in basements of bars. In this way, the narrator is the ego, struggling to bring himself back from imbalance. Tyler is the out-of-control id from which the narrator hopes to escape, returning to balance with the moral superego, Marla.

In **Mahāyāna** Buddhism, there is a somewhat related theory called *trikāya*, the three bodies.[35] The theory says reality can be thought of as consisting of three interrelated bodies or *kāya*. *Nirmāṇakāya* is the physical body of the Buddha and all of us. *Sambhogakāya* is thought of as clear light of the mind that manifests through meditation. It is not a physical body like those in *Nirmāṇakāya*. *Dharmakāya* is the body of the Dharma, the teachings of the Buddha. According to the *Parinirvāṇa Sūtra*, when the Buddha was dying his followers asked him what they were to do without him. He replied that, although his body would be gone, the body of his teaching, the Dharma, would remain. Accordingly, the Dharma can be seen everywhere. The *Dharmakāya* is the universe itself and ultimate reality. How do we realize the truth of *Dharmakāya*? The physical body (*Nirmāṇakāya*) can only realize the ultimate truth of the universe (*Dharmakāya*) through meditative insight (*Sambhogakāya*). Discriminative thoughts, those about objects in the physical world, are part of *Nirmāṇakāya*. *Sambhogakāya* and *Dharmakāya* do not exist as physical realms. In fact, *Nirmāṇakāya* does not exist as we think it does because the discriminative mind is subject to illusion. The physical realm, *Nirmāṇakāya*, only exists provisionally. The Buddhist philosopher **Nāgārjuna** (*c.* 150–250 CE) describes **two truths** or two kinds of truths: provisional truth and ultimate truth. Provisionally we can say there is a real world with practitioners and there are three bodies in Buddhism. However, ultimately all things are empty of inherent, individual existence, including the three bodies. In Buddhist art, some famous statues of the Buddha, such as the large Buddha in Nara Japan, do not represent the historical Buddha, Siddhartha Gautama. Instead, they represent a non-physical, meditative realm, personified as a cosmic Buddha, who is the universe and emptiness. This is known as a *Dharmakāya* Buddha, as mentioned in the *Lotus Sūtra* and other Mahāyāna scriptures. However, since the terms "universe" and "emptiness" are also conceptual, we must add that the *Dharmakāya* Buddha is not the universe nor emptiness.

Figure 2.1 is a conceptualization of *Trikāya*, the three bodies of Buddhism. But again, as a conceptualization it is necessarily incorrect. Still, it may be provisionally true if it can help us understand or go beyond understanding. Here *Nirmāṇakāya* is the physical realm within the greater realm of what is, *Dharmakāya*. Between *Nirmāṇakāya* and *Dharmakāya* is *Sambhogakāya*. Only through the light of meditative insight are we able to perceive *Dharmakāya* from our physical positions as *Nirmāṇakāya*.[36] *Nirmāṇakāya* is us as bodies, the historical Buddha, and the

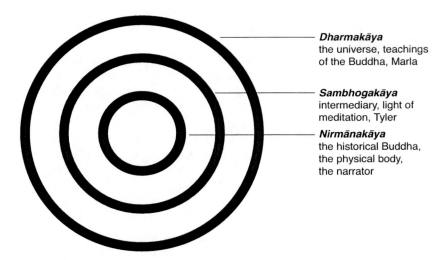

FIGURE 2.1   *Trikāya* (three bodies) theory and *Fight Club*

narrator in *Fight Club*. *Sambhogakāya* is the intermediary realm of practice meant to take us beyond ordinary consciousness. It is Tyler. *Dharmakāya* is the universe, the universal, the teachings of the Buddha that takes us beyond life and the fear of death. It is merging with Marla. Žižek says Norman Bates moves from the super-ego, past the level of the ego and into the realm of the id, so there is trouble. In *Fight Club*, to the contrary, the narrator in the physical realm goes from the basement through Tyler, representing attainment through practice, and moves to unity with the *Dharmakāya*, Marla upstairs, where they are finally at peace together on the top floor at the end of the film.

Further Reading

Cleary, Thomas (trans.). *The Blue Cliff Record*. Boston: Shambhala, 2005.
Loori, John Daido and Kazuaki Tanahashi (trans.). *The True Dharma Eye: Zen Master Dogen's Three Hundred Koans*. Boston: Shambhala, 2009.
Basho, Matsuo and Sam Hamill (trans.). *Narrow Road to the Interior: and Other Writings*. Boston: Shambhala, 2000.
Palahniuk, Chuck. *Fight Club, A Novel*. NY: W.W. Norton, 2005.

Notes

1 Palahniuk, Chuck, *Fight Club*, p. 59.
2 Most scholars date his birth between 563 BCE and 483 BCE.
3 Aśvagosha, 4.55; Patrick Olivelle (trans.), *Upanishads*, p. 105.
4 Aśavagosha 5.17; Olivelle, p. 131.
5 Aśavagosha 5.60; Olivelle, p. 147.
6 Palahniuk, p. 20.

7 This is illustrated as a palace with seven empty doors and windows in Buddhist Wheel of Life paintings.

8 Palahniuk, p. 37.

9 Olivelle, pp. 375–6.

10 Dependent Origination is treated in more detail in Chapter 4 in this volume.

11 *Films in the Humanities*, 1988.

12 Palahniuk, p. 129.

13 John Daido Loori and Kazuaki Tanahashi (trans.), *The True Dharma Eye: Zen Master Dōgen's Three Hundred Koans*, p. 44.

14 Lin-chi, died 866. *Lin-chi Record* in Addiss *et al.*, p. 45.

15 Lived 782–865 CE.

16 Case 34 in *The Zen Teachings of Master Lin-Chi*, translated by Burton Watson, p. 92.

17 So Sahn, *The Mirror of Zen*, in Addiss *et al.*, p. 231.

18 The "Expedient Means Chapter" of the *Lotus Sūtra*.

19 A 2008 Chinese-American collaboration directed by Rob Minkoff.

20 See Chapter 3 in this book.

21 *Satipaṭṭhāna Sutta*, number 10 in the *Majjhima Nikaya* and number 22 in the *Digha Nikaya*.

22 *Majjhima Nikaya* 10.

23 Palahniuk, p. 63.

24 *Ibid.*

25 Palahniuk, p. 64.

26 Palahniuk, p. 71.

27 *The Gateless Gate* (*Mumonkan*), Case 21.

28 See *Lin-chi Record* in Addiss *et al.*, pp. 49–50.

29 *Valley of the Dolls* is an American film directed by Mark Robson and released in 1967.

30 Palahniuk, p. 208.

31 Palahniuk, p. 196. *Sybil* is a 1976 film directed by Daniel Petrie.

32 Directed by Alfred Hitchcock, 1960.

33 A 2006 documentary directed by Sophie Fiennes.

34 Slavoj Žižek in *The Pervert's Guide to the Cinema*.

35 Charley Reed has suggested that the three main characters in *Fight Club* each represent one of the three bodies of the Buddha. What follows agrees but restructures Professor Reed's analyses; "Fight Club: An Exploration of Buddhism."

36 In a sense, we might very roughly equate *Sambhogakāya* to the Holy Ghost, the intermediary between physical beings (*Nirmānakāya*) and God (*Dharmakāya*). But this is also misleading, because the scheme is provisional and only a conceptual model.

3
BUDDHIST AWAKENING
Waking Life

1. Basic Plot Summary

Waking Life (directed by Richard Linklater, USA, 2001) is a film that makes us wonder if the main character is asleep and dreaming it all. It has a dreamlike look created by animators who drew on digitally shot live film footage.[1] The story begins with a young man (Wiley Wiggins) asleep on a train. He dreams of a boy who is probably him. The boy is playing with a girl who has a cootie-catcher paper puzzle. She opens a panel of it and we see "Dream is destiny" written there. The boy sees a shooting star and floats off the ground. Grabbing a car door handle he keeps from floating away. The young man on the train seems to wake up from this apparent dream. But the film continues to look dreamlike so we are not sure if he is awake. His train arrives at a station, where he disembarks and makes a phone call to someone who does not answer. He makes several phone calls throughout the film but no one ever answers. Going outside the station, a car that looks like a boat pulls up. The driver, who is wearing a sea captain's hat, offers him a ride and he accepts. But the young man is unable to say where he is going, a likely indication that this is a dream. Another passenger in the backseat (the director, Mr. Linklater) suggests he gets out at a random location, which he does. After getting out he is hit by another car, only to wake up in an apartment. However, it appears the dream continues.

The man then visits a number of people who tell him about various philosophical outlooks on life. A professor (Robert Solomon of the University of Texas, who Linklater knew as a student) speaks of Jean-Paul Sartre and tells him, "Your life is yours to create." An excited man who seems to be a scientist says evolution is moving faster and faster, leading to a "neo-human" unrestricted by time and space. The young man again appears to wake up in bed, noticing that where there should be numbers on a clock there is only flickering. He floats off the bed. The scene changes and he begins walking down a street with someone (J.C. Shakespeare), saying humans have become passive observers, drawn to chaos and destruction. The young man himself seems to be a passive observer of the others in this dream. Then, the other man sets himself on fire with gasoline. People walk by, appearing unconcerned.

In a number of scenes the young man does not appear to be present. Yet, there is a sense that these images too are a part of his dream. One of these includes characters from *After Sunrise*, another film by Mr. Linklater. In it, a woman and man (Julie Delpy and Ethan Hawke) lie in bed discussing dreams, the collective unconscious, and reincarnation. In another scene an angry prisoner (Charles Gunning, who also appears in Mr. Linklater's *Slacker* and *The Newton Boys*) speaks aloud to himself about the revenge he will take on those who put him behind bars. Later a conspiracy theorist (Alex Jones) drives through the streets ranting about dehumanization. His words blast through a speaker mounted on the roof of his car.

The protagonist returns and continues listening to people speak about philosophy, dreams, and free will. Eventually he comes to believe he is asleep and unable to awaken. He also considers that he might be dead. He now takes a more active role, not only listening but talking with people about lucid dreaming, the ability to realize a dream is a dream and thereby taking control of it. One man says people should become lucid dreamers because it's fun. He says a test to find out if you're dreaming is to try to turn off the lights. The young man tries this and discovers he cannot. Another test is to check the time on a clock. If you cannot see the numbers, you are dreaming.

In addition to repetitive talk of nihilist philosophy and dreaming, there are many references to film and film-making. For example, in one scene the young man flies into a movie theater and watches a film interview with film-maker Caveh Zahedi. During this layering of films, actors, and audiences the interviewer speaking with Mr. Zahedi declares, "everything is layers." Coming back to this theme, Mr. Linklater reappears near the end of the film and describes one of his own dreams, giving the young man advice about how to wake up. Eventually he returns to the house where we saw him as a boy. He begins to float and again reaches for the car door handle. But this time he lets go of the handle and floats away into the sky.

2.   Buddhist Themes

In a scripture called the *Dona Sutta* a man of the Indian Brahman caste named Dona says to the Buddha:

> When asked, "Are you a deva?" you answer, "No, Brahman, I am not a deva." When asked, "Are you a gandharva?" you answer, "No, Brahman, I am not a gandharva." When asked, "Are you a yaksha?" you answer, "No, Brahman, I am not a yaksha." When asked, "Are you a human being?" you answer, "No, Brahman, I am not a human being." Then what sort of being are you?

The Buddha responds, "I am awake."[2]

The title *Waking Life* contrasts to what we might think the film should be called: "Dreaming Life." This draws attention to the idea that what we consider ordinary waking consciousness is like a dream according to Buddhism. In many Buddhist scriptures our lives are compared to bubbles or mist. The Buddha says in the fourth verse of ***The Dhammapada***, a widely read collection of his teachings, "Consider this body to be as foam, awakening fully to its nature as a shimmering mirage."[3] It is possible to interpret "waking" in the title in this way, not as an adjective describing "life" but as a present participle: life that is in the process of awakening fully to its nature. This is what the nameless main character does in the film. Because of the quick moving dialogues and depth of changing ideas, we are likely to miss this. Buddhists might say this is also the case in our own lives.

The expression "waking life" is used twice in the film. Both times the speakers are questioning the assumed reality of what we call "waking life." In Buddhism, awakening is a goal attainable by each person. Various Pāli languages, Sanskrit, Chinese, and Tibetan words in Buddhist sūtras have been translated as "enlightenment" in English, including the word *bodhi*. However, if we think of the Buddha's awakening in terms of the European enlightenment period, we are misunderstanding. The word *bodhi*, the root of *buddha* and bodhisattva, means "awakening." The awakening person undergoes a cognitive reorientation, in part about epistemological assumptions: the origin, nature, methods, and limits of knowledge. Awakening is the process of realizing that we are mistaken in our ordinary assumptions about reality. Buddhist scriptures say this occurs in stages, similar to those experienced by the main character's progress in *Waking Life*.

According to Theravāda tradition, the type of Buddhism predominant in Southeast Asia, there are four stages of awakening. At each stage, the awakening person achieves a particular attainment. The first stage is called "**stream entry**" (Pāli: *sotapatti*) because the practitioner enters the stream that leads to nirvana.[4] The Buddha defines the stream as the Eightfold Path: "This noble eightfold path— right view, right resolve, right speech, right action, right livelihood, right effort, right mindfulness, right concentration—is the stream."[5] *The Dhammapada* says, "Better than sole sovereignty over the earth, going to a higher world, or dominion over the cosmos is the fruit of entering the stream."[6] In order to reach this stage of awakening a person must break free from three **fetters** of mind. The fetters are (1) Belief in an eternal or non-eternal "self" that is different from the body and mind, (2) Doubts about the Buddha's teachings, and (3) Clinging to practices of self-mortification or any rituals in hopes of salvation.[7] These fetters are considered a natural part of ordinary thinking. As long as we have these notions tying us down, we will continue to go through life with anxieties and stress. However, a person who has overcome these obstacles to awakening has entered the stream that inevitably leads to full awakening within seven lifetimes.[8] Such a person has opened the "**Dhamma-eye**" (Pāli: *dhammacakkhu*, also called **Dharma-eye**), an eye that looks towards the Dharma or sees by the wisdom of Dharma rather than viewing objects with desires and aversions as we usually do, as if asleep.[9] Would it be possible to watch a film with the Dhamma-eye opened?

Some texts say there are four conditions one must meet in order to overcome the three fetters to awakening. "Association with people of integrity is a factor for stream-entry. Listening to the true Dhamma is a factor for stream-entry. Appropriate attention is a factor for stream-entry. Practice in accordance with the Dhamma is a factor for stream-entry."[10] All of these are life choices and may be difficult ones. For example, *The Dhammapada* tells us to not associate with evil companions but to seek out encouraging friends.[11] Although we all know this is a good idea, it is easier said than done. Often when we try to improve our lives, our old "friends" do not want to see the change and try to hold us back. This is also happening in *Waking Life*, as some of the main character's friends advise him to enjoy the dream.

Beyond stream entry there is the stage of awakening called **once-returning**. This is gained by diligence of practice. The once-returner is free of the first three fetters and has weakened two more: sensuous desire and ill-will. This stage gets its name from the idea that upon reaching it the person is partially awakened and only has one more lifetime until full awakening. The next stage is **non-returning**. A person of this stage has finally overcome the five fetters and will not be reborn again. In Buddhism, not being reborn again is good. It also means you will not have to suffer and die again.

The fourth stage of awakening is that of the ***arahant*** (Sanskrit: *arhat*), an awakened being according to the Theravāda tradition. The term *arahant* means "worthy one" and is sometimes used as a name for the Buddha. An *arahant* has gained control over thoughts and the sensations thoughts produce. Because of this, *arahants* do not feel the stress of ordinary life. They see impermanence in all things, not a philosophical acknowledgment of this idea. *Arahants* destroy desires, which are the cause of suffering. *The Dhammapada* says the following about such a person:

> The person for whom there is not ensnaring, entangling craving to lead him anywhere at all, that one is awakened, of limitless sphere, trackless [. . .]. Difficult is the attainment of a human birth. Difficult is the life of mortals. Difficult is the hearing of the good way. Difficult is the appearance of those who have awakened.[12]

Some have even suggested *arahants* never dream because they do not need the mental relief dreams provide.[13]

The main character in *Waking Life* also goes through stages in his awakening process. Once he realizes he is dreaming, he experiences a sensation of waking up, but only from one situation and not fully. This occurs many times. Before he realizes he is dreaming, the audience comes to this conclusion and sees him wake up time after time. This situation is one of several instances of layering throughout the film. According to Buddhists, most of us are not awake and the world is like a dream. Add to this that we, the audience, are viewing an unreality, which is the fictional story of the film. In the film, the main character watches films. He also dreams layer upon layer of dreams. He meets the writer/director Richard Linklater, who had dreamed up his character in this film. At the same time and in the same stages, the character realizes his notion of reality is false, as the audience potentially realizes this about our own situation. Neither the character, the film, nor our own reality can be called ultimately real. If Mr. Linklater successfully helps the audience realize this, he leads us to stream entry. In Buddhism, a person who does this is called a Bodhisattva, an awakening being.[14] Are Richard Linklater and his character Bodhisattvas, ones who are becoming awake and awakening others along the way?

From the perspective of Buddhist ideas, the young man in the film goes through the following stages of awakening.

1. He is a child. While watching him play, we have no indication he is dreaming. The child floats and grasps a car handle. Grasping is the second of the Buddha's Four Noble Truths. The Buddha says life is suffering (Pāli: *dukkha*, stress or anguish) and this is caused by our desires in the form of grasping and pushing away.[15] We also cling to our cherished notions of self-identity or ego-self.

2. He awakens from his dream of childhood and arrives by train. He is now interested in learning about various philosophies describing reality. He searches for a vehicle. The various paths of Buddhism are also called vehicles, for example, the Mahāyāna (Great Vehicle) and **Vajrayana** (the esoteric or *Vajra* Vehicle). He enters a vehicle but not due to a considered choice. It is a car that looks like a boat. In Buddhism there is the "Parable of the Raft" about using the vehicles of Buddhism only as long as they are useful, abandoning them before becoming attached to any method.[16] We might also draw a parallel between the boat and stream entry. The driver or captain of the boat (Bill Wise) says it is "*see* worthy" and it is a vehicle that will help him on his path toward seeing the truth. Neither the main character, the others in the boat, or the viewers know its direction or destination. At this stage of awakening he has tentatively entered a vehicle but he is drifting. Although he is guided by Richard Linklater, who is a fellow passenger along with the audience, the guidance is arbitrary.

3. He speaks with lots of people about Western philosophy, science, and pseudoscience. None of these people realize they are a part of a dream. Instead, they interpret the dream as reality in complex detail. By doing so, they perpetuate the dream. In Buddhism, this is known as **prapancha**, the tendency of the mind to elaborate on the bare perception of the senses. This inclination toward worldly knowledge keeps us away from awakening. Buddhists see a need to go beyond this type of thinking about the world because it is inevitably inaccurate. That is to say, Buddhists feel the world cannot be rightly understood by any system claiming it can.

4. He slowly begins to see people he feels he recognizes but he is not sure he has really seen them before. This sensation occurs in dreams and sometimes in ordinary consciousness as *déjà vu*. *Déjà vu* is from French meaning "already seen." Some Buddhists believe we have karmic connections with others, connections with people we have already seen in the past. The Buddha and

his mother, for example, were connected by their karma in previous lives. Likewise, some say we cannot hear the words of the Buddha unless we have karmic connections with him.[17] The first stage of the Buddha's awakening under the Bodhi tree was remembering his past lives. The second was seeing the connections of all things (dependent origination).[18]

5. He realizes he is stuck in a dream. He meets lucid dreamers who want to control their dreams. But the lucid dreamers do not hope to awaken. To the contrary, they enjoy dreaming and seek to optimize their dreaming pleasure. By concentrating on things like sex and attaining 360-degree vision they perpetuate the unreality of life. This is similar to Buddhist notions of seeking worldly gain or even delving into religious practices. Buddhists sometimes say Buddhism is not a religion but a system for overcoming suffering. According to this outlook, religion involves beliefs in such things as an afterlife and practices like sacrifice and prayer. The Buddha considered these outside the purpose of the Dharma, awakening.

6. He comes to hate dreaming. He rejects lucid dreaming and puts his hands to his face in anguish at still being asleep. Around this time, he is told of two related possibilities: he might be a character in someone else's dream or he might be dead. According to Buddhism we should come to dislike the illusion of ordinary existence. This leads to resolve to overcome the illusion. Likewise, realizing he might be a character in someone else's dream indicates a weakening of the belief in the ego-self. It also indicates a new openness to the idea of dependent origination, that none of us are independent beings. Zen Buddhists sometimes consider themselves dead to the world as they awaken. In Tibetan Buddhism there is a scripture called *The Bardo Thodol*, commonly titled in English the *Tibetan Book of the Dead*. The book describes **bardo**, states in between life and death. This is also the theme of the film *Jacob's Ladder*.[19] In *Jacob's Ladder*, a traumatized Vietnam veteran begins to feel he is not what he had believed he is, but that perhaps he is in a *bardo* state. Traditionally, the Tibetan text would be read aloud by priests to a dying person. The purpose is to guide that person from the moment of death to liberation from the cycles of rebirth. It teaches that awareness creates its own reality like a dream. The dream is projected and proceeds in certain ways, some frightening, others beautiful. Awareness of this dream can be guided. The person is instructed to not become attached during the *bardo* states. If there is attachment, there will be suffering and rebirth. If one can be unattached, nirvana can be achieved. *Bardo* states are not only between life and death, this life and the next life, but also in our current, ordinary lives. In life we have various stages we might go through. The same advice about non-attachment is applicable to transitions to better states in our lives.

Considering the idea of being a character in someone else's dream, the main character in the film asks someone what that is like, accusing her of being just that. Being a dream, these characters and their advice are part of him. His phenomenal reality proceeds from his own mind, it is "led by mind, formed by mind."[20] Although he now knows this is true, he questions how it can be. It seems that other characters' creations are separate from him, but they are not. Since he realizes this is his dream and asks what it is like to be a character in someone else's dream, he is asking himself this question. Again there are various layers to being in another person's dream. The film and all of its characters are from the director's vision and it is a vision for the audience. In our reality outside the theater, the ego-self is a character of our imaginations, not independently existent but subject to dependent origination, inner-connectivity. Realizing that we have a fabricated self-image is portrayed in *Waking Life* as meeting yourself in a dream. While the character has previously been confronted with this idea, eventually an artist in a park (Edith Mannix) sketches a portrait of him and holds it up to his face.

After the character realizes his world is a dream, he takes an active role for the first time in the movie. Before this we saw him exit the boat at a destination randomly chosen by another and listening to various philosophies without responding. Now he begins to ask questions and make statements. Although he is beginning to take control of his direction, this does not indicate that he is asserting an ego consciousness of self. Instead, he feels it might be liberating to realize he is a character in someone else's dream. These developments are similar to the first two steps along the Eightfold Path: Right Understanding and Right Resolve. Right Understanding in Buddhism is realization that life is filled with persistent dissatisfaction due to our desires for something different. Right Resolve is making a commitment to do something about it. Specifically it is resolving to follow the Buddha's method for overcoming suffering, which is the same as awakening. This means you are taking an active role in your situation, not just remaining negligent by letting thoughts and suffering arise beyond your control. In *The Dhammapada* the Buddha says, "Those who are negligent are as the dead."

7. He stops grasping and gives up his self-notion. This occurs when he returns to the place he started, the home of his childhood. There he goes back to the car he clung to earlier in life. In a sense, in this revisiting, he is reexamining his previous material grasping. This time, when he begins to float, meekly he starts to grab the door handle, perhaps out of habit, but then he lets go. When he does this, he also gives up his self-notion. We see him float away into the sky and the void. He disappears as an independent ego and has attained nirvana, the extinguishing of passions and suffering.

Tibetan Dream Yoga and Lucid Dreaming

In 1989, the *New York Times* reported the Dalai Lama wished to promote exploration of connections between Buddhism and science.[21] The Dalai Lama is known to have a long-time interest in science and technology, as portrayed in the film *Kundun* when he is called upon to repair the generator in a temple no one else knows how to fix.[22] Some psychologists quickly pointed out that not only could science potentially improve Buddhist practice, but centuries of writings and experiences of Tibetan **Dream Yoga** might inform psychologists' studies of dreams. Since that time, psychologists have advanced studies in dreaming, including those on lucid dreaming, a dream during which one realizes he or she is dreaming. Also, a number of writings have been translated from Tibetan about Dream Yoga. Dream Yoga is practiced to become lucid while dreaming in order to understand illnesses, to face and overcome fears, to transcend mental boundaries, and ultimately achieve Buddhist awakening. Based on psychological studies of Lucid Dreaming and writings on Dream Yoga, non-academic individuals and groups around the world have also experimented with taking control of dreams for various reasons. Many videos about this can be found on the internet. Motives for learning to lucid-dream include the possibility of enhancing creativity in fiction writing, to better experience the sensation of dreaming, and to invoke nights filled with erotic dreams, as a lucid dreamer (John Christensen) says in *Waking Life*. Some of these areas have been explored in popular media, such as the bestseller nonfiction books by Dr. Patricia Garfield *Pathway to Ecstasy: The Way of the Dream Mandala*, *Your Child's Dreams*, and *Creative Dreaming*.

In 1981, the Dalai Lama came to Madison, Wisconsin, for a ceremony to initiate monks and nuns into the Buddhist order. During the week-long ceremony, he instructed initiates about how to dream, telling them to put *kusha* grass under their mattresses and pillows so they might have clear dreams and cleanliness of mind. *Kusha* grass, also known as *dharba* grass and *kusa* grass, is considered a special or sacred substance for meditation. It appears in the Hindu writings as the seat of the Gods and in various Buddhists texts. *Kusha* grass under a pillow at night before initiation is used to produce clear dreams. It is also used in Buddhism to enhance the clarity of visualization and meditation. The Dalai Lama also said to sleep in the lion's position and pay attention to dreams occurring near dawn. The dreams were believed to predict the effect of the initiation on the individual. The lion's position is achieved by using the right hand as a pillow under your cheek while lying on the right side of your body. This is considered the correct sleeping position for humans by many Buddhists. This is also the position the Buddha rested in at *parinirvana*, his final nirvana or death. Dreams that occur around dawn are considered particularly significant spiritually. At different times of the day, our bodies are said to be more strongly influenced by one or another internal factor. At dawn it is wind.[23] Not only is a connection assumed among the body, consciousness, and dreams, but also that what happens in dreams can influence the waking body.

The Dalai Lama's instructions show how dreams remain important to Tibetan Buddhism. Since the sixth century, there have been Dream Yoga writings about the various uses of dreams. While the character in *Waking Life* found the dream state annoying, in these Tibetan writings dreams are considered useful for awakening. In *Waking Life*, the main character begins to consider the possibility of being a character in someone else's dream. In terms of Buddhist interconnectedness (dependent origination), our thoughts and dreams are connected with those of others. Likewise, the self that appears in dreams is understood as a part of shared experiences. Individual dreamers and universal symbols meet and mix. In our culture, many people have reported experiencing shared dreams with another person. In Dream Yoga, the assumed boundaries between dreams and ordinary reality, ignorance and awakening, the self and others, are not distinct. Awake or asleep, the cognitive universe is not enclosed in individual skulls.

In the Tibetan texts we find the expression "seeing a dream" where we might expect "having a dream." This may point to the idea that dreams are experienced as given to us from outside sources rather than created by us internally. This also suggests dreams are objective rather than subjective. Since it is assumed that we are connected to others, it is believed that a physician may discover another person's illness and a treatment in a dream. Dream healing can also be found in the Roman Empire, early Christianity, and among Native Americans. In Buddhism there is the *Sūtra of the Medicine Buddha* and other texts concerned with spiritual healing. Likewise, Buddha has been called "Great Physician" and Dharma is the "King of Medicine." Many medicinal practices were discovered in monasteries and drinking tea was considered a healthy practice that also contributes to meditation.

In addition to being beneficial for healing, in Tibetan Buddhism dreams have been considered useful for Buddhist attainment and for awakening. Tibetans modified the Indian idea that dreams are caused by gods. Instead, the appearance of a Tantric deity is considered a sign of spiritual accomplishment. Tantric deities are the Buddhas and Bodhisattvas that are often depicted in mandala painting used for concentration and visualization. If a Buddhist dreams of such a being, it is considered a sign of the achievement of **siddhi**, attainment or perfection. This is similar to shamanism, where the first signs of shamanic power often follow dreams. The achievement of *siddhi* in a dream can be transformative. The dreamer can wake up with greater meditative abilities than before. In Tibetan biographies dreams mark stages of Buddhist development. Texts also tell of procedures to obtain two kinds of dreams, those that generate the thought of awakening and those that bestow attainment. However, *Waking Life* portrays dreaming as a state we should hope to escape. By promoting this understanding in the viewers it generates the thought of awakening. For this reason, from the dream that seemed bad comes the thought of awakening. This is like the Buddhist metaphor that from the mud of the earth comes the pure and clean lotus flower.

A famous Buddhist named Nāropa (1016–1100 CE) systematized certain Tibetan Buddhist practices in a document known as the "Six Yogas of Nāropa." Dream Yoga is one of the six. Accordingly, just as one can transform consciousness during the day through meditation, one can also transform dream consciousness. Ultimately this means that an individual will be able to transform consciousness during the *bardo* state at the time of death. Although dreaming can be provisionally useful

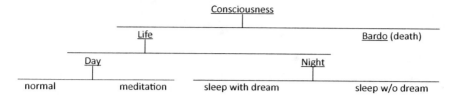

FIGURE 3.1 Dream Yoga

according to Tibetan Buddhism, ultimately waking consciousness, dreaming, and death are all equally illusory and need to be transcended. Dream Yoga uses all three states. In order to do so, we are instructed to remind ourselves during the day that everything is a dream, unreal, and empty. At night, practice Dream Yoga first by gaining awareness that we are dreaming. Then transform the dream into a scenario for advancing, such as ascending to a celestial plane and receiving teachings from a Buddha.

Meditative states are considered close to dream and *bardo* states, as well as keys to realizing the continuum of consciousness. Buddhists want to change consciousness, and dreaming is a form of consciousness. Figure 3.1 shows one possible conception of the various states in the continuum of consciousness.[24] In short, consciousness can be divided into two broad categories: life consciousness, including various states; and *bardo* consciousness of how the universe appears as we die. Life consciousness can be divided into the kinds of awareness we usually have in the day when we say we are awake and that we have at night. Daytime consciousness can be what we call normal or it can be the special awareness gained through meditation. Nighttime consciousness can come in sleep through dreams or in sleep without dreams.

Other Aspects of *Waking Life* Related to Buddhism

In the film, in addition to seeing the main character's stages of awakening, we see activities of others as if the main character were not there. Each of these other characters can be seen as representing a different mode of existence. There are musicians blissfully unconcerned with the outside world and there is a loving couple talking in bed. There is Alex Jones who turns red and purple. There is a group of four situationalists talking about social disruption, a theme also found in *Fight Club*. There is a man in prison (Charles Gunning), red and enraged by his growing desire for vengeance. *The Dhammapada* says, "In this world hostilities are never appeased by hostility. But by the absence of hostility are they appeased." This is the message in this scene as well.

These modes of existences are similar to the states depicted in the famous Buddhist drawings of the **Wheel of Life** (Figure 3.2). The Wheel of Life shows four circles, one inside another. Each of the circles depict circumstances in life

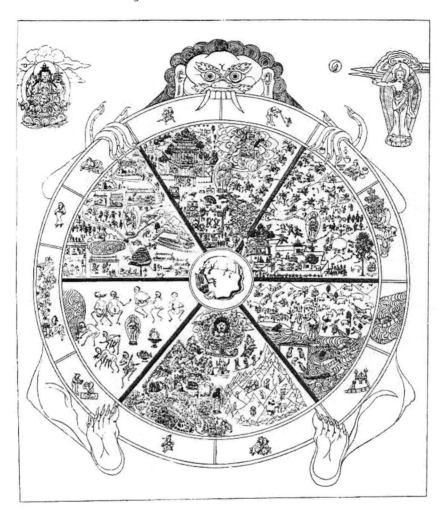

FIGURE 3.2 The Wheel of Life

and our reactions to them that keep us from awakening and living in a vicious circle of craving, lust, and aversion. These are the Three Poisons feeding upon one another in the central circle, shown as a bird, a pig, and a snake. Our reactions determine what state we will be in, as depicted in the next circle. Life can be a living hell, a chase after animal desires, an endless hunger never satisfied, or something more fitting to humanity. The red man in prison is in a hell of his own construction.

Likewise, as previously mentioned, another man in the film lights himself on fire. Again, these scenes are happening inside a dream and so are also states of mind. Like the Wheel of Life, there are many layers of dreams and imaged scenes. These layers in the film are also like circles: reawakening over and over, scenes from Mr. Linklater's other films reappearing, flipping TV channels and returning to previous channels. As in the film *Groundhog Day*, when Phil (Bill Murray) keeps waking up to the same day, all of this reminds us of reincarnation, doing it over until we get it right. This is also the theme of the outer circle of the Wheel of Life, known as the twelve-stage cycle of rebirth (*niddana*). As long as we continue our typical patterns in life, we will remain subject to suffering again and again. This is how Mara, the personification of illusion and death, keeps a grasp on us and on the Wheel of Life. Outside the wheel is awakening from this dream, with the Buddha pointing the way.

There are many other motifs in the film we could relate to Buddhism. After a lucid dreamer tells him he can have any kind of sex in a dream, the main character pulls away from a woman (Marta Banda) who is kissing him. Like many Buddhists, he appears to reject becoming lost in sensuality. That would only be embracing the dream instead of working to awaken, for us and him.

Several characters in *Waking Life* discuss theories about the unreality of time and space, which is an idea attributed to Chinese Tiantai Buddhist Zhiyi (538–597 CE). Zhiyi said there are "three thousand worlds in one instant of thought." When Richard Linklater is in the boat with the main character, he remarks, "There's only one instant, and it's right now, and it's eternity." Caveh Zahedi also speaks in the film within the film of the "holy moment" in a way that sounds a lot like the "Zen moment" found in haiku poetry, also used in *Fight Club*.[25] There are a few instances in *Waking Life* when an image of the Buddha appears. His shadow seems to be behind Mr. Linklater at the pinball machine and on John Christensen's jacket as he talks about lucid dreaming.

Perhaps one of the most important indications of the director's Bodhisattva activity is his decision to leave the main character anonymous. Like Clint Eastwood's *High Plains Drifter*, he rides into town a stranger and remains nameless. This calls into question the self and has the effect of universalizing the character. There is also the circular return to the telephone to make a call that we are still waiting to be answered. He leaves messages but only identifies himself by saying, "It's me." But who is he calling? Is he calling to his sleeping self to remind him of a dream he had? Is he calling to the director out of whose mind he comes? I think he is calling to us, the audience, and it's a wakeup call. He has left a message for us to respond.

Further Reading

Fremantle, Francesca and Chogyam Trungpa (trans.), *The Tibetan Book of the Dead: The Great Liberation through Hearing in the Bardo*. Boston: Shambhala, 2003.

Tenzin Wangyal Rinpoche. *The Tibetan Yogas of Dream and Sleep*. Ithaca, NY: Snow Lion, 1998.

Laberge, Stephen. *Exploring the World of Lucid Dreaming*. New York: Ballantine, 1991.

Further Viewing

Dreams (Akira Kurosawa, Japan, 1990). Also called *Akira Kurosawa's Dreams*.

Dream (Korean title *Bi-mong*, directed by Ki-duk Kim, South Korea, 2008). After a car crash, a man discovers his dreams are linked to the life of a woman he has never met.

Jacob's Ladder (Adrian Lyne, USA, 1990). A man wounded in the Vietnam War continues to live a nightmare in New York. His path of intrigue and horror seemingly leads to hell or heaven. Allegedly partly based on the *Tibetan Book of the Dead* (*Bardo Thodol*).

A Scanner Darkly (Richard Linklater, USA, 2006). Based on a short story by Philip K. Dick, this film examines memory and its connection with what we consider reality. By the director of *Waking Life*, it uses the same technique of coloring film.

Notes

1 A process known as Rotoscoping.
2 *Anguttarra Nikaya* 4:36. For a translation, see http://www.accesstoinsight.org/tipitaka/an/an04/an04.036.than.html. Deva, gandharva and yaksha are deities and earth spirits.
3 Wallis, *Dhammapada, Verses on the Way*, p. 12.
4 Another interpretation is the person begins to cross the stream to nirvana, which is metaphorically on the other side.
5 *Samyutta Nikaya* 55.5. Further discussion of the Buddha's Four Noble Truths and Eightfold Path can be found in Chapter 2 in this volume.
6 Wallis, p. 39. *Dhammapada gatha* 178.
7 *Sabbasava Sutta* in the *Majjhima Nikaya* 2. For a discussion of the belief in the self, see Chapter 4 in this volume.
8 Seven lifetimes can also be thought of as seven periods of one's life.
9 Reference to the Dhamma-eye can be seen in the *Mahavagga* collection of Buddhist writings, 1.23.1–10, and in the *Majjhima Nikaya* 56.
10 *Samyutta Nikaya* 55.5.
11 Wallis, p. 18. *Dhammapada gatha* 78.
12 Wallis, p. 40. *Dhammapada, gathas* 180 and 182.
13 Anuruddha *et al.*, *Compendium of Philosophy*, p. 50.
14 Using film to elicit a higher state of consciousness might also be called shamanistic.
15 The Buddha explains this in his First Sermon called "The Sutra Setting the Wheel of the Dharma into Motion" (*Dhammacakkapavattana Sutta*). See http://ww2.coastal.edu/rgreen/First Sermon.htm.
16 *Majjhima Nikaya* I. 134. Also see Chapter 4, note 16 in this book.
17 Khenpo Karthar Rinpoche, *Dharma Paths*, p. 38.
18 Aśvaghoṣa, *Life of the Buddha*, p. 417.
19 *Jacob's Ladder* is a 1990 film written by Bruce Joel Rubin and directed by Adrian Lyne.
20 This is the opening line of *The Dhammapada*. Wallis, p. 3.
21 Daniel Goleman, "The Dalai Lama Has Ideas for Neuroscience." *New York Times*, October 8, 1989.
22 *Kundun* is a 1997 film written by Melissa Matheson and directed by Martin Scorsese.
23 Serenity Young, "Dream Practices in Medieval Tibet," p. 25.
24 *Ibid.*, p. 32.
25 See Chapter 2 in this volume.

4

DEPENDENT ORIGINATION

I Heart Huckabees

1. Basic Plot Summary

In *I Heart Huckabees* (David O. Russell, USA, 2004) Albert (Jason Schwartzman) is a dedicated environmental activist and poet. He leads a citizens' coalition in an effort to save a wooded area from development by a large department store chain called Huckabees. Albert is also concerned about a series of experiences in his life that seem random but he believes may be connected in some strange way. In part, these involve crossing paths three times with an unknown individual he calls the "African man" (Ger Duany). After finding a business card in the pocket of a suit jacket provided to him by a restaurant, Albert decides to visit that address on the card, which is that of Vivian Jaffe, Existential Detective. At the detectives' office, he agrees to hire Bernard and Vivian Jaffe (Dustin Hoffman and Lily Tomlin) to spy on him. Although he does not understand the detectives' business or their methods, he hopes they will find something in his life to help explain his experiences. Bernard begins the investigation by zipping Albert inside a bag, where he experiences apparent hallucinations. Bernard explains this, saying Albert is beginning to see the interconnectedness of all things, the truth behind all experiences.

Brad (Jude Law) is an executive at Huckabees and Albert's nemesis in the film. He tries to persuade Albert and members of the coalition that he too wants to protect the environment by minimizing Huckabees' construction impact and by building parks near the projected store location. Able to convince other members of the group, Brad manages to remove Albert as their leader. When Albert continues to protest, Brad attempts to undermine him further by visiting the detectives on the pretence of wanting them to run his own Self investigation. To Albert's dismay, the Jaffes agree to take Brad as a client. The detectives also introduce Albert to his "other," another one of their clients named Tommy (Mark Wahlberg). Albert and Tommy believe they have been paired because both have deep concerns for the environment. Their bond is further solidified when Tommy pushes Brad at a party in order to help Albert steal his own file from the detectives. Albert and Tommy run from the party and begin to explore explanations of their life experiences that are contrary to the Jaffes' theory of interconnectivity.

An alternative is ultimately provided by Caterine (Isabelle Huppert), a European philosopher. Caterine teaches Albert and Tommy that not only are experiences unconnected, but life consists of random and utterly meaningless events. This being the case, she concludes, there is no justification for moral behavior. Instead, one may as well engage in hedonistic abandon and let the environment die. As a result, Albert burns down Brad's expensive house. Surprised at the sympathy he feels for Brad, Albert realizes the truth of the Jaffes' theory of interconnectedness. Likewise, Tommy has engaged in abandonment of humanity, yet in the process falls in love with Brad's fiancée, Dawn (Naomi Watts). Because both Albert and Tommy return to the Jaffes' position by using Caterine's method, they suspect she and the Jaffes, as well as their seemingly opposite philosophies, have secretly worked together for a long time.

2.   Buddhist Themes

In the special features included in the DVD, director David O. Russell explains many of the film's concepts that are related to Buddhism as he understands it. His excellent commentary could stand on its own in this respect. Likewise, there is a promotional video of Dustin Hoffman and Lily Tomlin in costume interviewing Dr. Robert Thurman, Chair of the Department of Religion at Columbia University and Dr. Joseph Rudnick, Chair of the Department of Physics and Astronomy at UCLA. While these tell the viewers about ideas from Buddhism that appear in the film, they do not explain them. In addition, there are a number of elements related to Buddhism in the film that are not mentioned in the commentaries.

The film begins and ends with blurry shots Mr. Russell says is how "everything is when we are not separate." This points to the major themes of the film in terms of Buddhism: the ideas of **"No-self"** and that all things are fundamentally empty of inherent existence. That is to say, everything is interconnected and nothing exists in isolation. The blurriness is also interesting because the film-makers are using cinematic effects to bring Buddhist ideas to the viewers, not just storyline. Another example of this is that the story moves so quickly the audience is likely to be confused from time to time. According to Mr. Russell, this creates a feeling that we are not getting it all. This corresponds to the Buddhist notion that believing the conventional truth is all there is means misunderstanding the nature of existence. A third and more obvious example of cinematic effect to convey an idea from Buddhism is the floating squares used to illustrate the meditative process and interconnectivity. There is also a scene near the end of the film where the viewer sees Brad from Albert's changed point of view. Lying on his back, Albert sees Brad upside down. Albert has come to see Brad as himself, flipping his earlier impression.

The concept of "no-self" is one of the most famous and pervasive ideas among the many varieties of Buddhist traditions around the world. Yet, not only is it puzzling to those hearing it for the first time, but it can continue to perplex long-time practitioners and even be denied by them. The first questions that are likely to arise include: To what conception of "self" do the Buddha's teachings refer? Did he mean there is (1) no "soul" or eternally abiding spirit, (2) no ego-self, (3) no physical, bodily self? How well does the English word "self" correspond to the sixth-century-BCE Indian notion of "*ātman*" (Pāli: *atta*) and, in fact, the other terms referred to by the Buddha for which we simultaneously use "self" as a translation? Is the Buddhist concept of "no-self" a statement about the nature of ultimate reality or about an ideal goal believed to be attainable by a few or all through meditation and other practices such as acts of charity and compassion? Where did the doctrine of no-self originate and how has it developed over time in Buddhism? Perhaps most striking: how can Buddhists believe in both no-self and reincarnation? After all, if there is no self to survive death, no soul, what is there left to be reincarnated?

Characters struggle with their conceptions of self throughout the film. Tommy is so concerned with finding answers that he is willing to leave his family. This mirrors the Buddha's "Great Departure" from his family, which is the model for monastic "leaving home," as entering a monastery is called in East Asia. Albert curses aloud to himself at several points when he is having an identity crisis. When he visits the detectives' office, this search to understand who he is begins. He has trouble locating the office and, walking down a maze of hallways, he begins to run. At one point in this running in search of his identity, he gets a glimpse of himself rounding a turn in the hallway ahead. Finally, meeting detective Vivian Jaffe, he describes first seeing the African man at a store that sells celebrity photographs and autographs. Like some celebrities, part of Albert's crisis is he feels his public image is not really who he is. The detectives later discover Albert was planting pictures of himself in with those of celebrities. Part of his dissatisfaction with his public image is due to the fact that he is an unknown poet. As the store is being shown on screen, we see the African man holding a picture of Jim Carrey in costume for the film *The Mask*.[1] *The Mask* also deals with self-identity and images. We learn the African man is also a doorman, which may be a reference to *Alice in Wonderland*, as he also metaphorically opens the door to another way of seeing the world.

Albert explains his questions about the possible interconnectedness of events, such as seeing the African man three times, and asks for the detectives' help. Yet he fails to mention his own identity crisis that is bound up with this. Albert is concerned by the question of who he is and how this relates to the material world, a basic question in Buddhism as well. Instead of accepting the case immediately, however, Vivian tells him to go home. She explains that most people stay on the surface of things without asking such questions. But this apparent rejection is a test of the subjects' worthiness of the teachings, similar to *tangaryō*, making potential students wait outside the temple in Zen Buddhist settings. This also occurs in the film *Fight Club* for the same reason.[2]

Albert does not give up and is instead shown into another room, where detective Bernard Jaffe is examining dirt. The dirt or dust of the world is a frequent expression in Buddhist sūtras, a metaphor for material life. Bernard shows Albert a blanket, holding his hands underneath it. He explains that existence is like this, all interconnected and of the same material. Mr. Russell says he learned this from Dr. Robert Thurman, professor of Buddhist Studies at Columbia University. Mr. Russell studied under Dr. Thurman when he was at Amherst. He also modeled the physical appearance of Bernard after Dr. Thurman and asked cast members to listen to recorded lectures by the professor. Albert and the audience learn through the metaphor of the blanket that not only is everything connected but our apparent reality is not total reality.

Afterwards, Bernard zips Albert inside a large black bag, although Vivian says it is too early for him to experience the bag. Russell explains the bag represents meditation, beginning by closing the eyes and quieting the mind. It appears to be a body bag, which corresponds to a notion in Zen and some other traditions of Buddhism that, upon embarking upon the path of the Buddha, the practitioner should die in terms of his or her former life. Inside the bag, Albert begins to "dismantle" the material conditions of his life and disassociate himself from these. As he begins to lose his self-image, Albert panics. Bernard unzips the bag and comforts him. How does this correspond with what Buddhism says about the nature of existence and self?

Existence, Non-Existence, and "No Soul" in Buddhism

Buddhist scriptures (Sanskrit: *sūtra*; Pāli: *sutta*) surviving in the Pāli language are typically considered the earliest accounts of the Buddha's words. In these, scholars have searched in vain for a phrase equivalent to "the doctrine of no-self" often used to describe the Buddha's view. Although there may be no early mention of a specific "doctrine," a number of interrelated ideas are expounded by the Buddha in these texts. Early scriptures record the Buddha critically reevaluating two contrary religious or philosophical tendencies prevalent in India around the time he lived.[3] Buddhists believe these tendencies are common to people throughout history and across geographical borders but that their underlying assumptions are incorrect. The beliefs are in existence (*sassatavada*) and non-existence (*ucchedavada*). In the *Kaccayana Gotta Sutta*, the Buddha says the following to his learned disciple Kaccayana:[4] "This world, O Kaccayana, generally proceeds on a duality of the belief in existence and the belief in non-existence. . . . All exists, Kaccayana, that is one extreme. Naught exists, Kaccayana, that is the other extreme. Not approaching either extreme the **Tathāgata**[5] teaches you a doctrine by the middle way."[6] This corresponds to the tension between the two sides in the film: existence represented by the Jaffes and non-existence represented by Caterine. Ultimately Albert discovers the **Middle Way** between the two extremes.

Buddhism is called the Middle Path for a variety of reasons. It rejects extreme asceticism as well as extreme hedonism. It also refutes beliefs in existence and beliefs in non-existence. Many Buddhist writings address these issues, some explicitly elaborating on the positions, others proceeding on the assumption readers accept the Middle Path. But what exactly the Buddha meant by existence and non-existence is a matter of contention. Nor is it entirely resolved in Albert's life. Many Buddhists feel that by "existence" the Buddha was referring to the Indian equivalent of the Western philosophical idea of substantialism, the doctrine that real matter constitutes phenomena. In this case, non-existence is interpreted as the equivalent of nihilism. Interestingly, Buddhism has often been variously charged with being either a substantialist or nihilist philosophy by critics, allegations Buddhists soundly deny.

Others find support in early Buddhist writings for saying the Buddha was referring to various Indian doctrines that attempt to explain humanity by positing the existence of a permanent soul that is distinct from the body.[7] An example of this we are likely most familiar with is found in the *Upanishads* of Hinduism. There and elsewhere, the true essence of an individual is said to be a permanent metaphysical self, independent of the physical body. This metaphysical self (*ātman*) is often called soul in English translation, or Self with a capital "s" to distinguish it from a physical self. It is envisioned as eternal and unchanging. Most, if not all, of the Indian religions at the time of the Buddha seem to have incorporated this view, either as a development of Vedic thought or reaction against it. For this reason, it might be assumed that by "existence" the Buddha was referring generically to all the beliefs in an immortal soul. It is quite likely that the Buddha's rejection of the belief in existence precludes both substance and soul. In the first sermon, *The Sūtra Setting the Wheel of Dharma in Motion*,[8] he explains that the individual is nothing beyond a composite of "**five aggregates**" or "five heaps": form, feelings, perceptions, mental fabrications, and consciousness. So that none of the five aggregates would be seen as eternally substantial, the Buddha said, "Form is *anatta* (not soul/Self), feelings are *anatta*, so too are perceptions, mental fabrications, and consciousness."[9] A famous phrase the Buddha uses in a number of scriptures to refute notions of existence is "*na me so atta*," "this is not my Self/soul."[10]

In a similar way, the Jaffes teach Albert and others to dismantle what they wrongly believe constitute their selves. Can the refutation of the doctrine of Self be called a doctrine? Some would argue the Buddha did not create a doctrine of no-self but simply refuted what he saw as incorrect views of his time. In part, Caterine does this also by attacking the Jaffes' position. Among those who used this technique is perhaps the most famous of all Buddhist theorists, the Indian philosopher Nāgārjuna (150–250 CE). Claiming he was not an innovator but only a spokesperson for the Buddha's original messages, Nāgārjuna set about refuting all notions of reality, including those that had subsequently developed within Buddhism. In the end, Nāgārjuna claimed neither he nor Buddhism had a doctrine of any kind.

If this was all of Caterine's role, she would be like a Zen master, attacking even Buddhism so that it does not become another doctrine to impede awakening. But she goes further by also advocating nihilism and, in a sense, "non-existence." Whereas Vivian's business card reads "Crisis Intervention & Resolution," Caterine's says "Cruelty, Manipulation, Meaninglessness." In the *Kaccayana Gotta Sutta* and in other scriptures, the Buddha also opposes non-existence. But again, what does this mean? It may be, as some suggest, the Buddha is referring to another widespread belief of his time, the belief that the physical body itself is a type of soul.[11] According to this non-Buddhist view, the body is an individual's real essence and is annihilated at death. From the viewpoint of many modern Buddhists, any form of "materialism," past or present, which advocates a theory of the ultimate reality of a physical self that ends with death, is subject to the Buddha's rejection of theories of non-existence. Such a reading of the Buddha's message sees beliefs in non-existence and existence as instances of theories of the soul or Self (Pāli: *attavada*; Sanskrit: *atmavada*). One sees the soul as permanent and transcending. The other sees it as material, temporary, and passing to nothingness. Concerning the latter the Buddha says, "Both formerly and now, I have never been a *vinayika* (believer in nothingness), never been one who teaches the annihilation of a being, rather I taught only the source of suffering, and its ending."[12]

For many Buddhists, the refutation of the view that there is an unchanging soul is a denial of any transcendental reality that would serve as ultimate grounds for existence. Others see it as less a specific denial of the possibility of such a reality than a part of the Buddha's broader ban on speculative philosophy. The Buddha discouraged talk about things we can never possibly know, whether about the existence of God or gods, the soul, or as imagined by Billy (Jack Nicolson) in *Easy Rider*,[13] a universe just like ours underneath a fingernail. Spending time musing about unanswerable questions only distracts practitioners from the goal of overcoming suffering. This is one reason Buddhists often see Buddhism not as a religion but a way of practice, as focused on humanity rather than divinity. The Buddha says the following in *The Shorter Instructions to Malunkya*.

So, Malunkyaputta, remember what is undeclared by me as undeclared, and what is declared by me as declared. And what is undeclared by me? "The cosmos is eternal," is undeclared by me. "The cosmos is not eternal," is undeclared by me. "The cosmos is finite" is undeclared by me. "The cosmos is infinite," is undeclared by me. "The soul and the body are the same," is undeclared by me. "The soul is one thing and the body another," is undeclared by me. "After death a Tathāgata exists," is undeclared by me. "After death a Tathāgata does not exist," is undeclared by me. "After death a Tathāgata both exists and does not exist," is undeclared by me. "After death a Tathāgata neither exists nor does not exist," is undeclared by me. And why are they undeclared by me? Because they are not connected with the goal[14]

In this way, the Buddha's idea of ***anātman*** is not a doctrine stating definitively that there is no soul but a tool to critique ideologies. Accordingly, the Buddha addressed these issues out of concern for the "psychological" wellbeing of meditative practitioners on the path to liberation from suffering. In order to overcome suffering, the Buddha taught we must eliminate our desires and attachments. Among the most deep-seated of these may be the desire to live forever. Hoping for this so strongly, various individuals have posited the existence of an immortal soul. However, cherishing this vision becomes a hindrance to liberation from suffering because it is a strong attachment. On the other hand, the belief in non-existence or non-being, if interpreted to mean nothing survives death, may have arisen from the human desire to be free from responsibility for living an immoral life or doing anything that weighs heavily on the conscience. The belief that nothing survives death or that nothing exists at all, frees an individual from the fear of moral retribution whether that is culturally envisioned as a day of reckoning, in terms of karma or otherwise.

In short, the Buddha does not say there is no soul. He says those who believe there is a soul are mistaken and those who believe there is nothing after death are equally wrong. The first major problem with both views is that reality cannot be conceptualized through such categories. You are justified in asking now: since the Buddha rejected views of existence *and* views of non-existence, on what do Buddhists rely for dealing with life and the world? This lies at the heart of Albert and Tommy's struggles with the conflicting theories. The Buddhist idea of understanding phenomenal reality (or realities) is in fact different from the conceptions of most theorists. Buddhism rejects the very notion that it is possible to understand the phenomenal world by means of a theory. In the *Brahmajāla Sutta*, for example, the Buddha criticizes the promotion of any theoretical viewpoint and concludes that the world cannot be understood from the limitations set by any theory. Accordingly, theoretical understanding of the phenomenal world originates from our expectations and preferences rather than what actually happens.[15] If this seems like a theory, the Buddha said, then it too should eventually be abandoned as a boat that helped you in the difficult crossing of barriers in the journey toward overcoming suffering.[16]

What happens to a person who begins to feel that reality cannot be understood in the way we have believed it can? In the film, there is panic. This is experienced by both Albert and Brad, showing they are alike in essential ways. Buddhist texts refer to "fearlessness" as one of the qualities a practitioner needs. Afraid of what would happen if fully accepting that self-identity is a falsehood, Albert and Brad attempt to regain the illusion of control, control of their own lives as imagined individuals and control of the process leading to the destruction of this falsehood. They do so by trying to sabotage their respective investigations. Albert does this by telling the Jaffes his workplace is off limits to them. It is one thing to examine our lives for 15 minutes a day in the solitude of home and quite another to keep this up at work and in public. But once the process begins in earnest, it is inevitable. Brad tries to regain control by firing the detectives, only to find it is impossible. In contrast, Mr. Russell describes the scene showing Albert and Tommy running out of the Jaffes' office, as taking the investigation out of the hands of the so-called experts. The Buddha also suggested to followers that they not believe something just because an expert said it is truth. Instead, one of the qualities of the Dharma is that it is open to individual investigation. One of the Buddha's famous sayings is "*Ehipassiko*," "Come and see."[17] The "seeing" he is about to experience is not simply "viewing" (Pāli: *diṭṭhi*) but insightful "vision" (Pāli: *dassana*), a distinction made by the Buddha.[18]

Dependent Origination and "No-Self" in Buddhism

You have probably been asked or asked yourself the following question at some time in your life. "If you could be anyone else in the world, who would you be?" This is also a popular question online, where the most common answers are movie stars and musicians. But what if we add a twist? You can be anyone else in the world but you will no longer be you. Would you still want to do it? In some conceptions of reincarnation (or even heaven) the situation imagined is some-what analogous: you will be reborn but you will not remember this life.[19] While Buddhist traditions vary in their interpretations of what reincarnates, since it is not *ātman*, typically the answer is karma. That is, only the results of your actions continue and nothing you might call "you."[20] For those suffering from the fear of death who consciously or subconsciously hope to find consolation in a doctrine of eternal life, the idea that you will not be you is unlikely to be completely satisfying. Nor is it likely to match our view of soul connected with personality. Maybe even less satisfying are the Buddhist suggestions that you are not who you think you are now and ultimately there is no independent you at all. This is the frightening prospect facing Albert, Tommy, Brad, and Dawn.

We have seen above that the Buddha rejected ideas of permanence and anni-hilation as valid ways of understanding reality, and we questioned whether this applies to non-Indian conceptions of the soul. In a similar manner, we should ask to what extent the sixth-century-BCE Indian conception of self corresponds to the twenty-first-century European, perhaps Judeo-Christian or even Freudian-influenced idea of the self, both in Albert's mind and in our current conception of the self. Even though the Buddha did not live in our time, we can venture that, regardless of the differences, he rejected any possible conception that posits the existence of a real entity such as the independent self. This can be found specifi-cally in his teachings about dependent origination.

Buddhism does more than simply reject the seemingly relentless conflict between existence and non-existence. It answers those concerned with such issues with the principle of dependent origination or dependent co-arising (*paticcasa-muppada*).[21] Most Buddhist traditions hold that this idea is the foundation of all other Buddhist ideas, that it is the Middle Path itself. The Buddha said, "Whoever sees dependent co-arising sees the Dhamma; whoever sees the Dhamma sees dependent co-arising."[22] This means, it is generally held in Buddhism, that the attainment of awakening is based on comprehension of the principle of dependent origination.

The principle of dependent origination proposes that individual existences are composed of interdependent physical and psychological elements that mutually condition one another. One element of this principle is the important Buddhist idea of non-substantiality. Since all "things" exist only as dependent on other "things," nothing is independently substantial. Likewise, everything is changing and exists only in process, including what Albert and the audience have been calling "self." References to "oneself," "I," "me," etc. are for Buddhists made merely for the sake of convention. Through meditative practice and acts of charity we are to realize the hollowness of these concepts. In this connection, Albert tries theatrical versions of a number of Buddhist meditative practices aimed at dismantling his false notion of self. He visualizes images from his past sitting in a tree. Later, in hope of overcoming his animosities, he pictures Brad having been in every human role in his life or possible past lives, including a nursing mother feeding him. Mr. Russell says he takes these from actual Tibet meditations. When Albert and Tommy hit themselves and each other in the heads with a large red ball, this is an illustration of Zen meditation to clear the mind of discursive thoughts and experience the suchness of the moment. Although Zen Buddhists do not have this practice, Mr. Russell compares it to the stick of compassion famously used by Zen masters to strike a sleepy meditator on the back. The director saw this in a Manhattan Zen training center (Zendō) he frequented. Albert also seems to be applying a meditative technique during an argument in the house of the Christian family that has provisionally shared their home with the African man out of charity.

It might seem troubling that there is nothing we can point to as being an independent and unchanging entity that is the self. If we look at it another way, the principle of dependent origination destroys our ego-centered worldview. When the Buddha advises us to observe all events from an interrelated perspective, this sets the guidelines for a symbiotic outlook on life. It rejects hostility toward an "other," antagonisms with neighbors, conflicts with "other" countries, attacks on animals and nature. In short, Buddhists believe if otherness is rejected, ego-centeredness is destroyed. As Albert hopes, modern Buddhists often say that as a result peace and environmental responsibility can be realized.[23] Albert's continual work for the environment also indicates that he has compassion, which, along with wisdom, is a necessary feature of one seeking awakening. According to scriptures, practitioners of meditation who are able to overcome their fear and finally renounce the belief in the ultimate reality of the five aggregates and the self, realize a release from suffering caused by clinging to those ideas. They experience an unattached bliss and abide in *prajñā*, insightful wisdom.

Because dependent origination advocates viewing with equal value what we conventionally call "ourselves" and "others," it encourages equal treatment of all. Not only should we live without being attached to self, we should not even give priority to what we call our self. When we hear on the news that a certain number of soldiers from the alleged "other side" were killed in battle, we should feel the same sympathy for them and their families that we feel for those killed from our country. In addition, the Buddhist notion of non-substantiality paves the road for another of its central themes: non-violence. By extension, according to the ideas of dependent origination and non-substantiality, to hurt others means to hurt ourselves. These ideas reject both the extreme egoist view focusing on maximizing one's own benefits and the extreme altruist view that only concentrates on the benefits of others. Neither oneself nor others should be prioritized. Seeing other human beings as the same removes potential bases of discrimination such as age, gender, race, nationality, and class. According to this outlook, we should consider all sentient beings, including the smallest of animals, equal in value.

Again the Buddhist philosopher Nāgārjuna illustrates dependent origination by offering a series of examples and metaphors that bring into question common perceptions of reality and the self. Nāgārjuna asks about a burning log, where does the wood end and the flame begin?[24] If we consider the changes taking place on the surface of the log, beneath and above the surface, the exact range of the fire becomes uncertain at best and in a constant state of change. Likewise, all "things" including the "self" are impermanent and in a constant state of flux. Any entity that exists only does so in dependence on other entities that condition its arising and are non-eternal. Therefore, whatever concept one might have of an abiding self is regarded as a delusion. Conceptualization of the self is just that, and not ontological truth.

This appears to contrast with Judeo-Christian positions in several respects. First, in distinction from this Buddhist egalitarian outlook, Judeo-Christianity typically views the world as a creation with God the creator at the top of a hierarchy, followed by humans, and animals.[25] In addition, if the principle of dependent origination is accepted, we should not presuppose external forces or any *prima causa* to explain the origin of beings. Even God would have come from **dependent co-arising**. To conceive "I" as being in a process and not within fixed borders, removes boundaries between creator and created, subject and object, you and me, and other pairs often conceived of as polar opposites. Nor should we look for accidental forces to explain the origin of beings or events in history. According to Buddhists, when something happens we should seek to understand it objectively and neutrally without looking for explanations in heavenly powers or accidental forces.

One reason Albert and all of us hold on firmly to our love of a supposedly independent self is that we fear losing control of our lives. The Buddhist notion of "letting go of" or "giving up" our egocentric selves likely seems like a loss of self-control to many. If that is your fear or objection, you should ask yourself how much control you have over your life now. Buddhists feel we are ordinarily led around by desires and hardly ever stop to think about it. What will we have for lunch, how can I meet a love interest, what car should I buy? We live with a constant barrage of such desire-driven questions or, more often, unacknowledged impulses. Maybe the desires are our own as human beings. But advertisers are betting high stakes that they can decide the direction of them. Did you really need the SUV you were persuaded to buy two years ago? Now you are being told to trade it in. Likewise, Tommy has come to the conclusion that we do not need to be addicted to fossil fuels. Buddhists believe that it is not your life that you are giving up by letting go of your tendencies to grasp for things. Instead, those who are unconsciously led around by such desires are as if dead.[26] Only when we give up desires and false beliefs are we capable of living.

Later Buddhist writers illustrated the holistic worldview of dependent origination with a famous metaphor known as "the Jewel Net of Indra," Indra being a deity of ancient India. This metaphor is also central throughout the film as portrayed with dismantling squares that float before Albert's eyes. Buddhist scriptures have us imagine a large net spreading on and on across the heavenly abode of Indra. In each knot of the net there is a glittering jewel so that in all directions there appears to be an infinite number of them. When you look at one jewel, all of the many other jewels are reflected in its polished surface. Such is the case for each and every jewel. This symbolizes the universe as a potentially infinite number of connected relations among all beings with inter-identity and interdependence.[27] Buddhists see this as analogous to our situation. If we come to understand dependent origination, we awaken to the fact that each person, element of nature, planet and existent is not a separate "self" but an interactive and continually changing reflection of all those we erroneously supposed to be "others." Not only do such squares hang before Albert and Tommy, they appear as the logo for Huckabees, the poster and box cover for the film, and on the blackboard in the Jaffes' office. Mr. Russell says the blackboard was an afterthought by a set designer who based it on the blackboard paintings of artist Cy Twombly. Accidental or not, when Bernard leans against the board and the squares are imaged on his back, he becomes yet another set of infinite connections.

The film ends where it begins: on a rock highly suggestive of a Zen rock garden where practitioners come to contemplate. Albert's opening poem at the rock is also reminiscent of Zen haiku, as is used in *Fight Club*. What has changed by the end is Albert and Tommy's understanding. They are now able to take what is helpful from the Jaffes and from Caterine, without adhering to a doctrine of any kind. A famous saying in Zen is: "Before Zen mountains are mountains, during Zen mountains appear different, after Zen mountains are mountains." The address on Vivian Jaffe's business card is Circle Dr. and Albert has gone full circle. Only now, when mountains are mountains, he can live with that. The screen fades in a blur of interconnectivity.

Further Reading

Bhikkhu Bodhi (trans.). *The Connected Discourses of the Buddha* (a complete translation of the *Samyutta Nikaya*). Somerville, MA: Wisdom Publications, 2000. Alternative translations appear online at http://www.vipassana.com/canon/samyutta/index.php and elsewhere.

Fronsdal, Gil (trans.). *The Dhammapada: Teachings of the Buddha*. Boston: Shambhala, 2008. Alternative translations appear online at http://www.suttas.net/english/suttas/khuddaka-nikaya/dhammapada/index.php and elsewhere.

Further Viewing

Zen Noir (Marc Rosenbush, USA, 2004). In this comedy/drama, a detective investigates himself as a part of what seems to be a murder at a California Zen temple.

Enlightenment Guaranteed (Doris Dörrie, Germany, 2000). Doris Dörrie creates a comic work about two brothers who travel to Japan for a retreat in a Zen monastery in hopes of getting their lives back together.

Notes

1 Released in 1994, directed by Chuck Russell.
2 See Chapter 2 in this volume for more details.
3 The dating of the life of the Buddha is currently controversial among scholars. Conventionally his birth is dated around the mid-sixth century BCE.
4 Kaccayana is traditionally considered one of the Ten Great Disciples of the Buddha.
5 The Tathāgata is a name for the Buddha, literally meaning "thus-come." He is the one who has come from "thus-ness," reality exactly like it is, or "thus."
6 *Samyutta Nikaya* XII.15; II.17. Available online at https://mywebspace.wisc.edu/jrblack/web/BU/PDF/samyuttanikaya2.pdf, accessed 8/4/2013.
7 Evidence of this position may be found in *Digha Nikaya* I.157, 188; *Samyutta Nikaya* IV.392; *Majjhima Nikaya* I.157; and elsewhere.
8 *Dhammacakkappavattana Sutta*, *Samyutta Nikaya* LVI.11. See T.W. Rhys Davids and Herman Oldenberg (trans.), *Vinyaya Texts*, in F. Max Mueller (ed.), *The Sacred Books of the East*, vol. 13, pp. 94-7, 100–102.
9 *Samyutta Nikaya* III.196.
10 For example, *Samyutta Nikaya* III.46.
11 *Digha Nikaya* I.34, 35; *Digha Nikaya* I.157, 188; II.333, 336; *Samyutta Nikaya* IV.392.
12 *Samyutta Nikaya* IV.400.
13 Directed by Dennis Hopper, 1969.
14 *Cula-Malunkya Sutta, Majjhima Nikaya* 63.
15 See the first of the long discourses of the Buddha: *Digha Nikaya*, Maurice Walshe (trans.), *The Long Discourses of the Buddha*.
16 "Parable of the Raft," *Majjhima Nikaya* I.134.
17 *Dhajagga Sutta* (*The Crest of Banners Scripture*), *Samyutta Nikāya* XI.3.
18 *Samyutta Nikāya* III.152.
19 It should be noted that in Indian religions—Hinduism, Buddhism, and Jaina—being reborn is not a good thing. Religious practices in these traditions are typically aimed at releasing from the cycles of rebirth.

20 Some Buddhists suggest what we call "reincarnation" actually takes place in this life. For example, if your actions produce negative results you come to live in a kind of hell on earth. See Takashi Tsuji's article "On Reincarnation" at http://www.buddhanet. net/e-learning/reincarnation.htm, accessed 8/17/12.

21 For an account and critical analysis of this idea, see David J. Kalupahana, *Causality: The Central Philosophy of Buddhism*.

22 "Dhamma" is the Pāli language equivalent of "Dharma" in Sanskrit. *Majjhima Nikaya* 28; http://www.accesstoinsight.org/tipitaka/mn/mn.028.than.html#t-4, accessed 8/17/12.

23 As with adherents of most religious traditions, Buddhists have not always lived up to these ideas. See, for example, *Zen at War* by Brian Daizen Victoria.

24 *Nāgārjuna, A Translation of his Mūlamadhyamakakārikā*, by Kenneth Inada, chapter 10.

25 Other entities such as angels are seen as interspersed.

26 See verse two of *The Dhammapada: Teachings of the Buddha*.

27 See *The Flower Ornament Scripture, A Translation of the Avatamsaka Sutra*.

5

KOREAN SEON BUDDHISM
Why Has Bodhi-Dharma Left for the East?

1. Basic Plot Summary

Why Has Bodhi-Dharma Left for the East (*Dharmaga tongjoguro kan kkadalgun*, Young-Kyun Bae, South Korea, 1989) contrasts secular family life with Buddhist renunciation in the mountains of Korea. It focuses on three monks of different ages: Haejin (Hae-Jin Huang), who is a young orphan monk; Kibong (Sin Won-Sop), a middle-aged monk; and Hyegok (Yi Pan-Yong), the old master of a remote monastery on Mount Chonan where the three live alone except for the animals and plants. The story follows Kibong, who struggles with his shaky resolve to remain on the mountain and attain awakening in face of his deep guilt over leaving his blind mother to fend for herself in the city below. The film opens with a lengthy scene of Kibong standing at a railroad crossing, having just left his mother. He stares ahead sadly as if at his life on the other side of the tracks. A train passes, and through the spaces between cars we see glimpses of his face, emblematic of his broken life and indecisive self. Out of focus in the foreground, the train signal flashes stop, ringing a warning. In the life story of the Buddha, the prince leaving home to discover the truth is known as the Great Departure. Crossing the train tracks will be Kibong's great departure from secular life.

In contrast, Haejin was orphaned at such a young age that he does not remember his parents. It is implied that this may make him a better candidate for Buddhist monastic life than Kibong. The older man, Hyegok, is famous for his longstanding and unshakable dedication to Buddhist practice. He attempts to help Kibong overcome his attachment to his family by teaching him meditative techniques aimed at dissolving his notion of self. We also learn Hyegok had found the abandoned boy Haejin on the streets and taken him to the mountain temple to raise him. So, even the old renunciant does not turn his back on someone who cannot take care of himself. Also, a previous master sent Kibong to the mountain temple for the dual purpose of learning Seon (the Korean version of Zen) from Hyegok and to take care of the elderly monk. Hyegok developed a long-term illness due to the severity of his ascetic practice. Again, even in the monastery, invalid care is needed, adding to Kibong's guilt about abandoning his blind mother. There is irony in the fact that Kibong takes care of Hyegok, who doesn't really need him, but left his mother, who does. Kibong later visits the city and sees her feeling around on the floor for her medication while calling out his secular name, Yongnan, and asking, "Are you back so soon?" Also while in the city, he notices a man about his age who has become homebound in order to care for a developmentally disabled man, who is likely the man's son. This motif of separation and guilt is highlighted as the film continually returns to a bird that seems to be haunting the young Haejin. In one scene Haejin shows his empathy for living creatures by saving a drowning bug that has fallen into a stream. However, after this he thoughtlessly throws a rock that kills the bird's mate. Haejin is disturbed by the immediate immorality of his act, but also by the longer-term, perhaps karmic, repercussions of it. This is represented in metaphor by a tooth pulled from Haejin's mouth.

In Korea and Japan there is a folk tradition of children throwing a lower tooth up on the roof of their house to symbolically encourage the new tooth to grow upward. An upper tooth should be thrown under the house to encourage the new tooth to grow downward. When throwing the tooth on the roof, Korean children sing a song to a magpie bird, a symbol of good luck. The bird is supposed to pick up the old tooth and bring a new one. However, Haejin has killed the bird that should take his tooth and the bird's mate seems to be haunting him. Later, Haejin finds his tooth on the ground. The bird was not there to take it. Seeing his obsession with the tooth, the master says Haejin is attached to an item that is no different from a rock. This statement is especially aimed at Kibong, his attachment to his family, and the problems his abandonment has caused.

In this way, a correlation is drawn between the bird losing its mate, Kibong leaving his family, and Haejin having no mother. Haejin's guilt over the bird is like Kibong's guilt over leaving his mother. Near the end of the film, master Hyegok dies, in a sense leaving Kibong without care. There is a camera shot of the single bird as if it represents Kibong. Following Hyegok's last instructions, Kibong cremates his master's body. The viewer wonders if his attachments to the world have not been broken. As he sifts through the cooled ashes for remaining traces of his master's bones, there is a camera shot from above, a classical cinematic expression of doom as if from the eye of heaven. In contrast, from a hillside, young Haejin watched the cremation with a detached attitude and walked away. As Kibong thoughtfully scatters the ashes as if they were important, Haejin is nowhere to be found. Having finished the task, Kibong returns to the temple and gives Haejin the master's robes. Kibong announces he has decided to return to secular life and will send someone to look after the boy. After Kibong has gone, Haejin burns the master's robes, further illustrating his detachment and his Buddhist attainment. The bird squawks in a way that previously frightened him, but now Haejin is unmoved. Having achieved this, the bird flies away as Kibong and Hyegok have done.

2. More Buddhist Themes

Like its relative, Japanese Zen, Korean Seon is a tradition with roots in Chinese Chan Buddhism. All three of these traditions trace their origins to an event in the life of the Buddha. According to a scripture known as the *Flower Sermon*, the Buddha once gathered his followers for a lecture. To the congregation's bewilderment, instead of speaking, he only held up a flower. In the crowd was a monk named Kāśyapa, also known as Mahākāśyapa (that is, the "Great Kāśyapa"). Only Kāśyapa understood the direct message of the teacher and smiled. Knowing that he had given Kāśyapa an extraordinary mind-to-mind transmission, the Buddha remarked, "I possess the true Dharma eye, the marvelous mind of Nirvana, the true form of the formless, the subtle dharma gate that does not rest on words or letters but is a special transmission outside of the scriptures. This I entrust to Mahākāśyapa."[1] This event is acknowledged in the poem at the beginning of *Why Has Bodhi-Dharma Left for the East?*: "To the disciple who asked about truth without a word, he showed a flower." In this line, "without a word" might refer to the silence of both Kāśyapa and the Buddha.

Seon, Chan, and Zen get their names from the Sanskrit word *dhyāna*, which means "meditation."[2] While we might think all Buddhist traditions are schools of meditation, this is not true. In Korea, the two dominant modern traditions focus on doctrinal and meditative wisdom respectively. Earlier in China some felt Buddhism had strayed from its meditative roots and degenerated into political factions or rival schools of doctrinal thought that were not practical. Around the year 520 CE, the Indian Buddhist meditation master **Bodhidharma** traveled to China. Bodhidharma is said to be the twenty-eighth master in the meditative Dharma lineage transmitted mind-to-mind, beginning with the Buddha and first passed along to Kāśyapa. In China, Bodhidharma became the first patriarch of Chan Buddhism and, therefore, is also considered a patriarch of Korean Seon and Japanese Zen. Legends say, after coming to China, Bodhidharma simply entered a cave and began to meditate. However, hearing that a great Indian Buddhist master had arrived, Emperor Wu of Liang sent retainers to bring him to court. The political and doctrinal Buddhists had given the Emperor the impression that he could gain merit for better future rebirth and prosperity in this life by financially contributing to Buddhist temples and priests. At court, the Emperor asked Bodhidharma what he could do for him to gain merit. Following the ideas of his Chan tradition of Buddhism, Bodhidharma replied in short, "No merit." Puzzled by this response, the Emperor asked, what then is the supreme truth. Bodhidharma answered, "Expanse of emptiness—nothing sacred." Hearing that Bodhidharma did not have words to teach like other Buddhists, the Emperor demanded to know then who it was standing before him. Bodhidharma replied, "I do not know," and walked out.[3]

Bodhidharma went to the Shaolin Temple in northern China, which is known for martial arts training and prominently featured in the American television series *Kung Fu* as well as in numerous martial arts movies. Bodhidharma is said to have entered a cave behind the temple and meditated facing a wall for nine years.[4] He is famous for his meditative endurance. In Japan, egg-shaped folk images of Bodhidharma (Japanese: *Daruma*) are sold with rounded, weighted bottoms. When knocked down, the egg-shaped figure rocks back but pops back upright, symbolizing Bodhidharma's endurance. Supposedly, to stay awake Bodhidharma cut off his eyelids. Likewise, master Hyegok in the film had stayed alert in long meditation by sitting beside ice. As a side effect, he developed an adverse medical condition: chilblains. This diligence contrasts with Kibong's weak resolve. Students came to Bodhidharma for instructions, but followers of his lineage believe the truth of Buddhism cannot be expressed in words or doctrine. As illustrated in the story of Kāśyapa and the flower, it must be experienced directly. The tradition developed a number of techniques to help students realize this. One is the **koan**, a strange saying, story, or riddle given to a student by a master. In American pop culture, we know the *koan* "What is the sound of one hand clapping?" The student is asked to concentrate on the *koan* and tell the master what is behind it. Since there is no regular answer, it is an exercise in surpassing ordinary logical thinking in order to realize extraordinary truth. A famous *koan* asks, "Why has Bodhidharma left for the East?" giving the film its title. Since Bodhidharma went east from India only to sit in a cave, no one knows why he did not just stay in India. If we interpret Kibong's return to secular life as a rejection of Seon celibate monasticism, the film's title is more than an unanswerable *koan*. It can be seen as a rhetorical question, asking what good there is in Bodhidharma's brand of Buddhism. Kibong's question to his master, "Why do you stay in these mountains?," appears directly related to the *koan* and the title. Reproaching Kibong for going to his mother's house and thinking of giving up before awakening, the master replies, "Idiot! I have to be here for fools who are looking for me!"

Notice the title is active, why *has* Bodhidharma left, not past tense: "Why did Bodhidharma leave?" Likewise, there is no sense that Bodhidharma has arrived yet. This can be related to the process in the film, the ongoing struggle of the characters to bring Bodhidharma's teachings to the East. The idea of leaving is related to Kibong's decision to leave his family and not knowing if this was a good move. It is related to the overall feeling of "Why is any of this happening?" Is there a reason? What is the meaning of this kind of life and the purpose of meditation? Buddhist scriptures view these as ill-formed questions we typically ask, seeking meaning even where there is neither meaning nor no meaning. For example, is there life after death or is there nothing after death? The Buddha said those who answer either way are necessarily wrong.[5] We cannot know such answers, in part because the conceptual limitations inherent in forming this kind of questions. In other words, we are used to forming questions about death based on our life experiences that are biased and mistaken as well as extremely limited. Zen attempts to lead the practitioner beyond the desire for meaning and, thereby, to another kind of realization beyond words and other types of conceptualization. It uses strange puzzles to break attachments to logical concepts and to the notion of self that has been falsely constructed with such concepts. In the film, the master says to Kibong,

> Here is a log of wood with a crane's head, a dragon's back and a lizard's breast engraved upon it. It has no name. It's your face before you were born. It's your body before the birth of your parents. With that you must solve the mystery of birth and death.

With these confusing words, Hyegok then gives Kibong his *koan*:

> When the moon takes over in your heart, where does the master of my being go? Kibong! I give you this *koan*. You must be ardent and persevering to understand it and show it to me. If you think about this *koan* day and night, if you concentrate on meditating, you will come to enlightenment. The *koan* is a tool to cross the sea of passion and illusion so as to discover the roots of the true self.

When Kibong is in his mother's house and when he flashes back to secular life, he sees his father's picture hanging. It is clear his feelings of guilt at abandoning his mother are related to not doing the right thing in the eyes of his father. This highlights the tensions between Confucianism and Buddhism in East Asia that have existed for centuries. The director, Young-Kyun Bae, spent over a year during high school living as a hermit in the mountains. He is credited with having later said, "Hermann Hesse saved me."[6] These two facts seem to explain much about the perspective on mountain monasticism presented in the film. Hesse's novel *Siddhartha* was made into a film by the same title. Like the three main characters in *Why Has Bodhi-Dharma Left for the East?*, Hesse's story follows Siddhartha in three phases of life: his idealistic youth, his years of searching, and his revelations. Siddhartha in the novel is not the Buddha but a Brahman who meets the Buddha and declines to become his disciple. It appears that the sequence and method proposed by Buddhism is a point of contention for Hesse and Young-Kyun Bae. Yet neither entirely rejects Buddhism. Instead, they propose the path to enlightenment cannot be conferred to another person, nor by simply listening to or obeying an enlightened one. Words and teachings may describe the truth but are not the truth itself. When Siddhartha decides not to become a disciple of the Buddha, but to seek the truth by himself, he rejects the community of monks and nuns (the *sangha*), but embraces the spirit of the Buddha. After all, among the Buddha's last pieces of advice to his followers was, "Be lamps to yourselves" and "Seek your own salvation with diligence."[7] Likewise, Kibong's return to the secular world appears to be a rejection of Seon awakening but may actually embrace it. A further key to

FIGURE 5.1 The *Ox Herding Drawings*

the director's point of view on this can be found in the film's many references to the *Ox Herding Drawings* from Chinese Chan Buddhism (Figure 5.1). Bae uses the basic ideas expressed in the *Ox Herding Drawings* but interprets the images. Again, this is what Hesse does with Buddhism in *Siddhartha* to express the same ends as Bae's film: rejection of the monastic life in favor of a naturalistic and non-institutional realization of the same truth. The twelfth-century Chinese Chan master Kuoan Shiyuan drew a set of ten pictures using images of a monk and an ox to depict stages of awakening. A modern version by Japanese woodblock artist Tomikichiro Tokuriki became known to English readers through the wide-selling book compiled in the 1930s by Paul Reps, *Zen Flesh, Zen Bones*. In Tokuriki's version, the monk is a boy who looks quite similar to Haejin in his robes. This is likely no coincidence since Bae films sequences closely based on *Ox Herding Drawings*.[8] In fact, both the ox and the boy Haejin in the film represent Kibong's attainment, at least in part.

Paul Reps suggests the ox signifies "the eternal principle of life, truth in action."[9] In Mahāyāna Buddhism, this principle in known as **Buddha Nature**. Buddha Nature is the innate awakened state within all of us, yet to be discovered by most of us. Buddhism is the way to find it. The first of the ten drawings is "The Search for the Bull." The accompanying poem speaks of pushing back grasses in search and only hearing locusts chirping in the forest at night. These sounds are often heard in the film. When Kibong comes to the mountain temple, he is metaphorically searching for the bull. There is no bull in the first drawing, and it has not yet appeared in the film. The second drawing is "Discovering the Footprints," and the poem says "Deep in remote mountains they are found." The bull is still not depicted in the drawing. In the film, the ox first appears while Kibong is meditating. In shadows we hear sounds as if discovering traces of it as in the second drawing. Then, viewers begin to make out its eye, slowly coming to realize what is hidden on screen. We hear more restless sounds, see the ox free itself from a harness and walk out of a barn. We next see Kibong meditating again and another memory of home life from which he partially freed himself. At this point, we might wonder if the bull analogy applies to Kibong or Haejin. However, if we apply the original principle behind the drawings to the characters in the film, Haejin and the ox likely represent Kibong's awakening process.

The third drawing is "Perceiving the Bull." Tokuriki's drawing shows the boy monk who only sees the ox from behind and not in its entirety. Other drawings show a monk having seen the ox, chasing after it. This is depicted in the film when Haejin is lost in the forest and begins running after the ox. The film shot looks very close to the drawing. The bull leads Haejin out of the forest back to the temple. Metaphorically, insight leads the practitioner out of the forest of delusion. The fourth drawing is "Catching the Bull." The fifth is "Taming the Bull," showing a monk leading the bull by a leash. This is the final image in the film, when a monk that appears to be Kibong is shown in the distance leading the ox. This seems to be an unlikely ending. Because Kibong has returned to the secular world, we would not expect he has tamed the ox of insight. Since the scene concludes the film, we must consider that Kibong may have solved the *koan* given to him in the form of his master's cremation. The next image in the *Ox Herding Drawings* is called "Riding the Bull Home." Although Kibong is not riding the ox, he is leading it as he returns home. The seventh drawing is "The Bull Transcended." It shows a monk outside a hut in the full moon without a bull. Mr. Tokuriki's drawing looks particularly like Haejin back at the temple alone at night. The full moon is a well-known metaphor for Buddhist enlightenment. The eighth drawing is an empty circle titled "Both Bull and Self Transcended." When the master dies, there is only the sound of the ox. There is no sight of it. When Kibong cremates the master, there is an extreme close-up of the ox's eye that seems to be crying. The bird is also looking on.

Interestingly, the sequence does not end there with overcoming the self notion and awakening. The ninth drawing is called "Back to the Root, Returning to the Source." The tenth is "Entering Society, Extending a Hand." The first eight drawings can be considered steps of meditative progress. However, life does not end there. After awakening, the Buddha returned to help others along the path. Likewise, the *jataka*, stories of the previous lives of the Buddha, typically point to the importance of helping others. In Buddhism, a part of awakening and a sign that one has awakened is great compassion, known as **karuna**, for all beings. Wisdom (*prajñā*) and compassion are the two major characteristics of Buddhist life. They necessarily go hand in hand. Wisdom is represented in the first eight ox herding diagrams. Compassion is shown in drawings nine and ten. This also accords with the writing of Korean Seon master So Sahn, "If you attain the truth within your own mind, then even the senseless chitchat in the streets and markets are like the Dharma speech of a great teacher, and even a chirping bird or the wail of an animal express truth."[10]

A famous description of this says, "Before Zen, mountains are mountains. During Zen, mountains appear to be different. After Zen, mountains are mountains." A similar description says, "Before Zen, chopping wood and carrying water. After

Zen, chopping wood and carrying water." That mountains once again appear to be mountains can be seen by Kibong's return to life in the secular world. In both cases, though there is a return, things are not entirely the same. A transformation has occurred within, and Buddha Nature has been realized. Wisdom and compassion now inform the practitioner's actions in the world. The idea of "chopping wood and carrying water" is overtly depicted in the film. We see Kibong cutting dead wood at the beginning of the film. His blade slips and he cuts his finger. We see the ax drop and blood drip on the wood. His early problems with chopping wood and carrying water symbolize his issues with the secular world. Later, after studying Zen, he will return to the world and, once again, metaphorically and literally chop wood and carry water. However, he will be transformed and better able to do so. We should remember Kibong chopping wood, because when Hyegok gives him his *koan*, the master begins by saying, "Here is a log of wood with a crane's head, a dragon's back, and a lizard's breast engraved upon it. It has no name. It's your face before you were born." Huineng, the famous and important sixth Zen patriarch of Chinese Chan, in the same lineage as Korean Seon Buddhism, sold wood in secular life. Once while out gathering firewood he was awakened when he heard a priest speak a line from the *Diamond Sūtra*.[11] Afterwards he went to a mountain temple to study Chan. The fifth patriarch at the temple confirmed that Huineng had awakened and gave him his own robes, signifying the mind-to-mind transmission as well as the conference of the patriarchy from the fifth to the sixth leader of the Chan order. However, like Kibong, Huineng did not remain at the monastery but, instead, traveled south, eventually continuing the lineage there.

There is also an analogy in the film between the body after death and a piece of wood that burns as in cremation. When Kibong returns from the city after visiting his mother, the master scolds him, strikes him with his wooden stick on the back, and again asks him to answer the *koan*. In Chan, there are many cases of masters who suddenly shout or strike a student as an awakening technique, which is also related to sequences in the film *Fight Club*. The master ends this talk by dropping his stick at Kibong's feet. Kibong slowly lifts the stick with both hands and appears to contemplate it.

In addition to wood, trees and the forests appear prominently in the film. Other natural elements, especially earth/rocks, wind, water, and fire also appear. This is important for Kibong's *koan*. He must consider our original composition and what happens to the body after death. When Hyegok instructs him about cremation, Kibong replies that he does not yet understand reality. He asks the master who else would be able to show him. Hyegok replies, "Mountains, rivers, plants, universe. Here and there everything is in the same enclosure. To leave is to arrive. To arrive is to leave. Doesn't the wind blow as it wants? My body returns to its original condition." These sentences repeat many of the film's motifs. Kibong thinks of returning to the secular world and the master tells him there is no difference, no coming or going. Kibong also heard this from a fellow monk who had decided to return to the secular world. The monk speaks of the life of the Buddha, saying, "Was his flight an abandonment of the world? No, the departure was simply the process of returning. In fact he never left. He came back inside us all." Earlier in the film while the master is reading a scripture, he lets go of a page and comments there is no beginning or end. We find this same line at the end of the film *The Cup*.[12] Along these lines, the master calligraphically brushes the Chinese graph for "Buddha" on a sheet of paper. Kibong and Haejin hang it on a wall. When the master is near death, it falls off the wall, suggesting the Buddha is gone from the world. Yet we know from earlier dialogue the Buddha is in all things.

Viewers tend to see *Why Has Bodhi-Dharma Left for the East?* as filled with mysticism. However, once they understand the *Ox Herding Drawings*, the folklore related to the tooth, and other cultural symbolism, that perception falls away. The director said, "Zen is not a theology of supernatural revelation and one can scarcely find any religious dogma in it." He also said, "The film doesn't deal with God but with people who suffer—prisoners of the links created by birth and death. A film thus which relates to us all."[13] Perhaps the most mystical parts of the film come not from Buddhism but shamanism. A female shaman is dancing in the temple complex when the master dies. Another time, when Haejin is sleeping by the river, a shamaness rises from the river and moos like the cow, which we see on the hillside above. At times she appears to represent Haejin's lost mother. She also represents Hyegok. We see a close-up of her white shoes on steps outside a temple and later a close-up of Hyegok's white shoes on steps. After the master's death, Kibong puts his shoes under the temple, toes first, as if he will not use them again. Haejin later turns the shoes with toes pointing outward as if the master were in the temple, perhaps now in the form of Haejin.

With so much film time spent considering nature, the natural elements almost become individual characters. The director's presentation of these reminds us of other film-makers who have made great use of nature. In his childhood, Bae was especially interested in painting and cinema. The landscapes in this film show this dual interest. He was influenced by the films of Robert Bresson, who emphasized spiritual themes in film, and those of David Lean.[14] David Lean is known to have made films with great panoramic nature scenes, such as *A Passage to India*,[15] which also incorporates spiritual themes of India. Again, the film's emphasis on nature is equivalent to the final revelation in Hesse's *Siddhartha*. Master Hyegok further connects the natural elements to Kibong's *koan* by saying, "When the ties that hold the body together weaken, when the body gets scattered to be earth, water and wind, where does the master of my being go?" After Kibong cremates the master's body, he returns the ashes to the elements. He makes the fire and is overcome by the smoke as if by the master and his *koan*. Kibong's face, robes, and hands are completely covered with the ashes of Hyegok. Kibong takes the ashes and drops some in water. He puts some on tree leaves and drops ashes on the earth. He lets some blow in the wind, turning the bag of ashes inside out to blow a cloud in the wind. The master is returned to five elements: fire, water, wind, wood, and earth. This is related also to Kibong returning home, perhaps the answer to his *koan*.

Wind is important throughout the film. The sound of the temple bell comes through the air and is heard miles away. Several times in the film we hear a bell whether far away or close. Temple bells in East Asia are often bronze, large and heavy. They are sounded by striking the outside, in contrast to European bells with the clackers inside. Striking temple bells vibrates the air with a deep reverberation, resonant miles away. Hearing the sound arise around you is like being reminded of the ever-present and pervasive Dharma. Kibong strikes the temple bell and chants, "The sound of the bell overcomes passions. It increases wisdom and gives birth to enlightenment. It will release from Hell those who make the vows to seek for enlightenment and save people." This verse underscores the importance of both meditative practice and going back into the world to help others, the central theme in the film. Wind is again very prominent when Haejin burns master Hyegok's robes. From the robes, smoke curls to the temple ceiling. It seeps through every crack in the walk, completely permeating the building with the master's *koan* and rising beyond. Other scenes also feature wind, with the crematory smoke and steam rising from boiling water as when Haejin prepares the master's medicine.

There are numerous references to medicine in the film: Haejin rinsing his mouth, the master's burning medicine, Kibong's mother not seeing the medicine, Haejin feeding the sick Kibong medicine, the master saying his old body doesn't need medicine, and Kibong going to the city for medicine. In the *Lotus Sūtra*, and elsewhere, the Buddha is called the Great Physician because he knows what practices to prescribe in individual cases. The Dharma is his medicine. In Buddhist art and iconography there are images of the Medicine Buddha, who metaphorically administers remedies to life's problems. Likewise, Kibong's mother's blindness may indicate delusion in the secular world. Blindness (Sanskrit: *avidyā*) is a common metaphor for delusion in Buddhism. Earlier in the film we see Kibong with his mother, closing his eyes while facing outside the house as if blind. But even the harsh ascetic practice of the master has led to an illness. These examples point to the Middle Way between extremes of asceticism and renunciation. The path of the Buddha is known as the Middle Way.

Following the awakening progress of Kibong in the film, it is possible that the viewer might ignore Haejin's attainment. However, it is Haejin who receives the master's robes and burns them. Haejin is also the one who seeks the ox and finds it. He has a vision of being drowned in water by children of the secular world, being different from them and perhaps letting his worldly self-image die in the water. Most impressive is Haejin's drifting in the water, leading him farther into nature just as following the ox does. Becoming frightened by the screech of the bird, he falls into the water and loses consciousness. His fabricated self is no longer leading him around by desire and aversion. He has let himself go at the will of nature, returning to the source. When he gets out of the water is when he perceives the ox of Buddha Nature. In contrast, Kibong has what seems to be an illness-dream, seeing himself in the raging river holding on for his life. He then envisions the old master in the river letting go, apparently of life. There is also a shot of Kibong meditating on a rock in the river while balancing a rock on his head. This puzzling image does not represent a practice of Seon meditation. Instead, it is a cinematic reference to the Seated Stone Buddha of Gwanbong Peak in Korea, which appears to be wearing a Korean bamboo hat made from a stone. Dated to the ninth century CE, the stone carving depicts the Medicine Buddha in a meditative position holding a container of medicine.[16]

In addition to the parts played by the five natural elements, animals appear prominently in the film. The bird witnesses important events throughout. Less obvious are other animals. For example, there is a frog shown while the master is talking. A frog is emblematic of Chan practice because it looks vaguely like it is sitting patiently in meditation. The famous Japanese Zen master Dōgen is associated with a frog, as is Bashō, the renowned haiku poet and Zen monk.

Whose mind does the ox represent? At times, it appears to be Kibong's and at times Haejin's. The director says the film was like a *koan* to him. Is it to be a *koan* for us, as well? If so, the ox may represent the viewers' minds as we progress in understanding through the film. Sometimes the master and Kibong appear to be talking to us, the audience, no one else is around. Bae also said he hoped to build a temple through his film.[17] It took the director four years to make the film, perhaps as if he were working on a *koan*. Bae was producer, director, screenwriter, cinematographer, and editor of the film. What is the duration of time in the film? The flashback scenes make it difficult to determine. When Kibong is at the temple complex off the mountain, we see him in a new, pressed, and creased robe. In the mountain temple, his robe needs repair. This shows both the passing of time and the contrast between the temple complex with well-kept grounds and the mountain temple with broken paper on the doors. We are given another vague timeframe when we learn master Hyegok took the orphan child to the monastery five years before Kibong went there. Perhaps there is a deliberate confusion of time in the film, mimicking time distortion in some Buddhist scriptures, such as the *Lotus Sūtra*.

It is Haejin who is entrusted with the master's robes as a symbol of succession, as the new master in Seon tradition. Haejin burns the robes, illustrating his detachment and his grasping of the *koan* the master gave Kibong. In the *Platform Sūtra*, after the sixth patriarch, Huineng, received the fifth patriarch's robe, he throws them down on a rock, saying, "I came for the Dharma, not the robe." Interestingly, master Hyegok had requested to be cremated while wearing his robes, perhaps an indication of his own rejection of the tradition. Burning the robes, smoke rises and swirls, the bird calls while Haejin gets water outside. Haejin is no longer afraid and the bird flies away. Haejin has gained control of his mind of fear. His attachments have flown away like the bird. The bird flying away is also like Kibong leaving. Is it Haejin who has awakened? Earlier he called to Kibong in the wilderness as if to join him in his chase of the ox. He also calls out as Kibong leaves the temple for the secular world. In both cases, Haejin has replaced the master in this role of calling to Kibong. Haejin has been watching the master and listening to the instructions he gave Kibong. As the master instructs Kibong in the rushing water, Haejin is on the hillside listening. The film leads us to a question that has been asked by Korean Soen Buddhists: Can a person who became a monk early in life without so many connections to the secular world, and having always been celibate, awaken while one who becomes a monk later in life after having a family cannot?[18] In the past, Korean and other countries' Buddhist temples often took in and raised orphaned children. In modern times, this practice largely stopped when orphanages were established.

When Haejin finds his discarded tooth the master asks him, "What is the connection between the non-difference of self and other?" This may also be a reference to the difference between Haejin and Kibong. When the master gives instructions inside the temple, he walks past Kibong to Haejin, brushing Haejin's shoulder with his own. As in *The Cup*, the apparently worst student, the one who has killed a bird, may turn out to be the best. As Shunyru Suzuki explains in *Zen Mind, Beginner's Mind*, the person who can sit the longest isn't necessarily the best practitioner, just as the worst horse might be the best horse.[19] In the final scene, in the distance, Kibong appears to be leading the ox, or is it an older Haejin leading it? Maybe it doesn't matter which one it is. Throughout the film, Kibong's attainment is represented in the actions of Haejin. Like all of us, the two are intricately related, a fact Buddhists call dependent origination. In that case, Haejin's calling out the Kibong is Kibong calling out to himself.

The question remains whether Kibong's return to society is a sign that he has progressed in Seon attainment or rejected it. If it is a rejection, this may reflect recent events in Seon history. Modern Korean Buddhism was shaped by the Japanese occupation of that country (1910–1945). At that time, the old Seon tradition of celibate monasticism was effectively destroyed by Japanese rulers, who reshaped Korean Buddhism according to models from Japan. Japanese monks who associated with the wartime government gained financially from it. These monks were not celibate, but married and running temples as family businesses free from taxes. The occupational government put these monks in charge of the official offices of Korean Buddhism, deciding which temples would be funded, who would serve as heads of temples, who would be ordained, etc. Likely affected by the family values of Confucianism, these government-aligned monks encouraged married monasticism in Korea through finances and temple positions. The Korean monks loyal to them in turn promoted the same among their Korean understudies. Celibate monasticism declined dramatically and many returned to secular life. Only in recent years, through much political protest and by enduring violent attacks, did the celibate monks regain some temples in Korea. Today, the legacy of the struggle between married and celibate monks continues.[20]

If by the end of the film Kibong has awakened, his attainment is expressed in a similar manner found in Zen stories of others who have done so, subtly. After Kibong cremates his master, he sits on rocks looking at the sunrise and the mountains. In the end, it does not matter whether we choose to believe Kibong awakened and completed the ninth and tenth stages of awakening as depicted in the *Ox Herding Drawings* or if he ultimately rejected the way of Seon mountain asceticism. Because, according to Zen writings and numerous related scriptures, awakening and delusion are the same and neither ultimately exist at all.[21] Awakening and delusion are categories constructed by the mind to deal with the world but are based on limited and inaccurate knowledge. For this reason, the *Heart Sūtra* says, "Form is no different than emptiness. Emptiness is no different from form." The secular world of birth and death (**samsara**) is the same as extinction (nirvana). How are we to realize this, since we consider the two categories through the lens of preconceptions? The director said, "I would like the audience to see the film without preconceived knowledge or ideas."[22] Is this either possible or desirable? Doing so might require a Buddhist method for film viewing.

Further Reading

Cleary, Thomas (trans.). *The Platform Sūtra of the Fifth Patriarch. The Sutra of Hui-Neng: Grand Master of Zen* Boston: Shambhala, 1998.

Reps, Paul. *Zen Flesh, Zen Bones.* New York: Anchor Doubleday, 1961.

Suzuki, Shunryu. *Zen Mind, Beginner's Mind.* NY and Tokyo: Weatherhill, 1988; Boston: Shambhala, 2006.

Further Viewing

A Little Monk (Kyung-jung Joo, Korea, 2002). This film seems to be a response to *Why Has Bodhi-Dharma Left for the East?* In this one, however, there is a feeling that nothing is gained by remaining in an isolated meditation center.

Passage to Buddha (Korean title: *Hwaomgyong*, also called *Hwaomkyong*) (Sun-Woo Jang, Korea, 1993). A boy travels seeking to understand life. This film is based on similar events in the *Avataṃsaka Sūtra.* Some say this is the best Korean film on Buddhism to date.

Master of Zen (Cantonese title: *Da mo zu shi*) (Brandy Yuen, Hong Kong, 1994). A cinematic depiction of the life of Bodhidharma.

Notes

1 Dumoulin, Heinrich. *Zen Buddhism: A History*, p. 68.
2 *Chan* or *Channa* is a transliteration meant to sound like "*dhyāna.*" "Zen" is the Japanese pronunciation of the Chinese graph for Chan.
3 Fischer-Schreiber *et al.*, *The Encyclopedia of Eastern Philosophy and Religion*, pp. 38–39.
4 *Ibid.*, p. 39.
5 *Samyutta Nikaya* 12.15. See Chapter 4 in this volume for further explanation.
6 http://cdn.shopify.com/s/files/1/0150/7896/files/BodhiDharmaPK.pdf?1009.
7 *Mahaparinibbana-sutta* 2.33; 6:10; The *Mahaparinibbana-sutta* is the sixteenth scripture in the *Digha Nikaya*, or *Collection of Long Discourses* of the Pāli Canon.
8 Leonard Cohen's "Ballad of the Absent Mare" (Columbia, 1979) is also based on the *Ox Herding Drawings.* Cohen spent time at the San Francisco Zen Center and elsewhere practicing Buddhism.

9 Paul Reps, *Zen Flesh, Zen Bones*, p. 134.
10 So Sahn, *The Mirror of Zen* in Addiss, *et al.*, p. 231.
11 *The Platform Sūtra of the Fifth Patriarch.*
12 See Chapter 7 in this book.
13 http://cdn.shopify.com/s/files/1/0150/7896/files/BodhiDharmaPK.pdf?1009.
14 *Ibid.*
15 Released in 1984.
16 The statue is located on the southern peak of Mt. Palgongsan, called Gwanbong Peak.
17 http://cdn.shopify.com/s/files/1/0150/7896/files/BodhiDharmaPK.pdf?1009.
18 We can see this in Ven Jiheo's *Diary of a Korean Zen Monk.*
19 *Zen Mind, Beginner's Mind* by Shunryu Suzuki, p. 29.
20 See Chanju Mun, *Ha Dongsan and Colonial Korean Buddhism: Balancing Sectarianism and Ecumenism.*
21 For example, see the *Prajñāpāramitā Sūtra.*
22 http://cdn.shopify.com/s/files/1/0150/7896/files/BodhiDharmaPK.pdf?1009.

6
THERAVĀDA BUDDHISM, SOCIALLY ENGAGED BUDDHISM

The Burmese Harp

The Burmese Harp (*Biruma no tategoto*, Kon Ichikawa, Japan, 1956) is not about Theravāda Buddhism. It neither offers a realistic picture of the people of Myanmar (Burma)[1] nor Japan's World War II war campaign in Southeast Asia. But the film gives us the opportunity to ask and answer some basic questions about Theravāda Buddhism in the past and present and to look at the recent headline-making political activities of monks in that country.

1. Basic Plot Summary

The film opens with landscape scenes of Burma. We see barren rocks and hear narration about the impact of World War II on the hearts of Japanese people. There are shots from above of the mountains with sounds of artillery. There are tired Japanese soldiers marching, coming to rest on the forest floor at the border of Burma and Thailand. Though exhausted and hungry, the soldiers' morale is boosted when the captain (Rentarō Mikuni) asks Corporal Mizushima (Shōji Yasui) to play a song on his 13-string Burmese harp, known as a *saung*. The captain is a music school graduate and Mizushima, the main character in the film, has taught himself to play the harp. The captain leads the troops in a song about looking to the sky with desolate hearts. Mizushima puts on Burmese clothes and is sent ahead to scout. He is to play signals on the harp indicating if there is danger or it is safe to pass. Alone and unarmed in the forest, he is forced by bandits to exchange his clothes for a banana leaf skirt. Afterwards he plays the signal that all is clear. When the soldiers see Mizushima wearing banana leaves, they jokingly comment he looks natural and say the bandits must have been polite since they left him the skirt.

The men march on and reach a village. There they eat and drink with the local people inside a large hut. After a time, the villagers leave the hut and suddenly the men realize the British army is in the surrounding forest. However, the Japanese soldiers and the viewers are unaware the war has ended with Japan's surrender. The British troops hope to take the men into custody without further violence. Meanwhile, the Japanese soldiers scheme to recover their rifles from outside the hut and engage in battle. Their plan is to pretend to be drunk, to place Mizushima and his harp on the weapons cart and roll it into the hut while singing. Fearing for their lives, they carry out the plan while singing *Hanyū no yado*, the Japanese version of *Home Sweet Home*. They make it back inside the hut and ready their weapons. But just as they are about to fire, the Japanese soldiers are baffled to hear the British soldiers now singing *Home Sweet Home*. The British, along with Indians in turbans, emerge from the forest beneath a full moon, still singing loudly. Inside the hut, Mizushima begins to accompany the voices on his harp. Eventually the Japanese soldiers also join the chorus and no shots are necessary.

In the next scene, the Japanese soldiers are in a British camp. The captain sumons Mizushima and requests he go on a mission to contact another group of Japanese soldiers who are still fighting in the mountains. He is to inform them the war is over and they should surrender. The captain tears off his own officer's insignia to indicate it is not an order, and asks Mizushima if he is willing to go in order to save the soldiers. Mizushima is instructed to meet with his group later in the town of Mudon. Mizushima agrees and sets out as the others wish him well. When he arrives at the mountain a battle is underway. The British stop shelling and allow Mizushima only 30 minutes to persuade his countrymen to surrender. He climbs the rocky mountain and is fired upon at first by the Japanese soldiers. Seeing he is Japanese, the men stop firing and take him inside a cave, believing he came to fight with them. Mizushima informs the men of the outcome of the war, but they refuse to surrender. Drunk on sake, they call him a coward and strike him. He argues for them to surrender, but they are also intoxicated by war. The time limit expires and the British begin shelling again. Mizushima is wounded and loses consciousness. When he regains consciousness, he sees dozens of dead Japanese soldiers, killed for no reason. He stumbles over their bodies and rolls down the mountainside, again losing consciousness.

When Mizushima wakes up again, he is in the care of a Burmese Buddhist monk (**bhikkhu**). Sometime later he bathes in a river and his clothes are stolen. Now he only has tattered Buddhist robes to wear. Dressed in this way, he begins a long walk to the town of Mudon, where his captain said he would be. Mizushima limps across barren fields for a long time, barefooted and bleeding. He falls to his knees, whispering to himself, "I'm starving." Local peasants happen by and take him for a Buddhist monk doing austerities. They offer him balls of rice and bow to him. Mizushima devours the food and continues to trudge south. Later he comes upon the scene of dead soldiers being eaten by vultures. With much labor, he drags the bodies into a pile and cremates them. He piles rocks on the mound of ashes and salutes it. There are more bodies and he can only salute as he passes. Walking on, he is startled to come upon another large pile of dead soldiers. He puts his hands over his eyes and runs past to the edge of a river. A boat arrives carrying a Buddhist *bhikkhu*. The *bhikkhu* seems to mistake him for a fellow cleric and offers him a ride to Mudon. There he spends the night in a monastery. That night he sees a British funeral for unknown Japanese soldiers and painfully remembers all of the bodies he had passed. With sudden resolve, he leaves the monastery, returning to the war dead to bury their bodies. Still dressed as a *bhikkhu*, he passes his former military unit. The soldiers are unsure if it is Mizushima and he continues on without a word. They are unable to approach him because they are in British custody.

Thereafter, he works hard burying the decaying bodies, attracting the attention of local people. Seeing his tenacity, they begin to help. He folds his hand toward them and continues to work. While digging, he finds a large ruby. The local people interpret this as the souls of the dead and Mizushima prays. In the next scene, the soldiers are at the pagoda in Mudon when they hear *Hanyū no yado* being played on a harp. They run and get a distant glimpse of Mizushima but still cannot be sure it is him. Again, during a Buddhist funeral precession for British soldiers, the captain believes he sees Mizushima because one of the *bhikkhus* carries a box of ashes. The captain identifies this as a Japanese Buddhist custom. He later goes to the British war dead repository, opens the box, and finds the ruby inside.

In hopes of bringing him back, the soldiers train a parrot to say, "Mizushima, return to Japan with us." They ask a local woman to give him the parrot. She replies he is a traveling high *bhikkhu* but she will try to give it to him. Later, Mizushima comes near the fence of the soldiers' compound and plays *Hanyū no yado* as they sing. He bows and walks away as they call to him to come back to Japan. Mizushima sends another parrot and a letter back with the woman. The parrot says, "No, I can't go back with you." The soldiers board a ship back to Japan without him. On board, the captain reads the letter aloud. In it Mizushima explains that, although he longs to return to his country, he had decided to stay to bury the dead, to help alleviate the pains of life experienced by others, and to create a place where the dead can rest. He says he has taken a Burmese master and will train himself for these tasks, not knowing if he will ever return to Japan.

2. Buddhist Themes in and Related to the Film

Theravāda is the predominant type of Buddhism in most of Southeast Asia, including Sri Lanka, Myanmar, Cambodia, Laos, and Thailand. It contrasts to Mahāyāna Buddhism, which is the main type in East Asia: China, Japan, Korea, and Tibet. Theravāda Buddhism is called the Way of the Elders. After the time of the Buddha, Buddhism split into a variety of traditions, some of which further spilt. Theravāda is considered the oldest surviving Buddhist tradition and therefore the closest to early Buddhism. Theravāda *bhikkhus* preserve the tradition of *Vipassana*, Insight Meditation, which they say is the very meditation method used by the Buddha to achieve awakening. *Vipassana* teaches the practitioner to concentrate "bare attention" on bodily functions, beginning by following breaths while thinking, "I'm breathing in. I'm breathing out." This meditation is aimed at taking control of one's mental activities and overcoming the illusion of the self.

Vipassana is strengthened by the *Abhidhamma*, important writings on the nature of experience. Buddhist scriptures are traditionally divided into three groups known as the **tripiṭaka** or three baskets of teachings. The three baskets are the sūtras, the *vinaya* or collections of vows, and the *Abhidhamma*. The *Abhidhamma* scriptures analyze sensations such as sight, being the perception of light through sense organs that interpret and relay it further to the mind. The mind acts on this information in certain ways and forms judgments also based on sources that are scrutinized. The *Abhidhamma* writings consider numerous perceptions and the resulting internal synthesizing processes. It concludes, as the Buddha had: all things are interdependent and there is no self as we assume. Therefore, for those prone to such reasoning, this extremely analytical method may be useful in ultimately overcoming attachments to and reliance on reason. Theravāda *bhikkhus* also honor the *Metta Sutta, Discourse on Loving Kindness.*[2] The *Metta Sutta* records the Buddha's teaching on loving all creatures. Reciting it and meditation on it helps us become infinitely compassionate. The scripture says:

> Even as a mother protects with her life
> Her child, her only child,
> So with a boundless heart
> Should one cherish all living beings:
> Radiating kindness over the entire world[3]

Theravāda Buddhists deal with conditions in the modern world by utilizing these ancient principles. Based on Loving Kindness, they have developed the principles of **socially engaged Buddhism**, as have Mahāyāna Buddhists. The term "socially engaged Buddhism" was first used by Vietnamese monk Thich Nhat Hanh (1926–present). Thich Nhat Hanh is a world-renowned peace activist and was nominated by Dr. Martin Luther King, Jr. for the 1967 Nobel Peace Prize. The principles of socially engaged Buddhism are closely related to *The Burmese Harp*. Socially engaged Buddhists have led struggles for environmental responsibility, for social justice and equality. Although Mahāyāna scriptures such as the *Lotus Sūtra* criticize other Buddhist traditions for not being socially responsible, as is the ideal Bodhisattva, this clearly cannot be applied to modern Theravāda Buddhists. The Buddhists of Myanmar, the setting of the film, have been in the forefront of the news on these struggles. Also as a part of socially engaged Buddhism, recently *Vipassana* has been taught beyond monasteries, in prisons of India and the United States. This is documented in the films *Doing Time, Doing Vipassana,* and *Dharma Brothers.* Prisoners who are taught derivatives of the "Burmese Method" of *Vipassana* report a new sense of understanding of their crimes and develop remorse based on human interdependence. They also find solace behind bars in the practice.

The Harp of Burma (Biruma no Tategoto) is a best-selling novel written in 1946 by Takeyama Michio.[4] It was made into movie versions twice.[5] In 1957 it was nominated for an Academy Award for Best Foreign Film. It is widely known in Japan and particularly loved by the generation that can remember World War II. The main factor in this popularity is likely the story's expression of feelings about the senselessness of war and the aftermath for Japan. The book was written at a time when Japanese people were struggling to understand the meaning of military defeat and how their country could revive from a state of devastation. It depicts basic human values as universal even in the face of obsessive militarism. This was particularly topical when individual loyalties to the group and country had been shaken and reshaped in terms of the world. The film examines this in light of Buddhist compassion for all beings. The story also leads us to reflect on modernization and what we have lost in the process. By extension it brings up the question posed in the book *Pruning the Bodhi Tree*: has Mahāyāna Buddhism, as developed in Japan, departed from the true path of Buddhism exemplified by the Way of the Elders (another name for the Theravāda)?[6]

The ideal Theravāda *bhikkhu* of high attainment, such as Mizushima, is known as an *arahant* (Sanskrit: *arhat*). The word *arahant* may be taken as meaning "the destroyer of the enemy," which would be Mara, illusion. More commonly it is thought to mean a worthy one. *Arahants* are free of future rebirths because they have overcome cravings and aversion. They destroy illusion by practicing virtues including giving (*dāna*), by friendliness (*mettā*), by developing compassion for others (*karuna*), by being appreciative (*mudita*), and by developing equanimity (*upekkha*).[7] All of these traits are considered factors leading to liberation. Those who think Buddhists simply withdraw from society to meditate on mountainsides while the world dies are seriously misinformed about the basics of Buddhist theory and historical practices. Mahāyāna Buddhists including those of Japan have similar values linked to the ideal life of the Bodhisattva. However, Japanese Buddhists also have a long history of engagement in violence and support of wars. During World War II, Japanese Zen Buddhist monks supported the Imperial war, giving pro-war talks that reinterpreted such Buddhists ideas as self-sacrifice.[8] Mizushima stays in Burma to become a Buddhist instead of returning to Japan. Doing so implies that Japanese Buddhism has roots in goodwill but has departed from them in the modern world. Right or wrong, this point of view is also made in the film in the implication that modern Japanese people have parted from the better ways of earlier times, and Japan changed to a less beautiful land of modern cityscapes.

When Mizushima suddenly decides to leave Mudon and remain as a Buddhist in Burma, this is his Great Departure, like the Buddha's. Also like the Buddha's departure, it is prefaced by seeing suffering, death, and a Burmese Buddhist who nurses him back to health. This is analogous to the Buddha's Four Sights that transformed his life. The suddenness of Mizushima's departure is also like that of the Buddha. In the life of the Buddha, the urgency of his path is explained by the immediacy of suffering and death.

The themes of rustic people and unspoiled forests are united with the idea of a harmonious power in music. The film portrays a mysterious quality in music capable of transcending the limitations of historical appearances. It is through this magic of music that we are made aware of the universal good in humankind, which is depicted as the soul in the ruby and Buddha Nature. Music functions in the film exactly like the Dharma, it brings peace and equanimity across all assumed human boundaries. The humanizing power of music is so important to the troops that when the sergeant is accused of having a tin ear, he calls them to order in an angry tone. More than militarily, Mizushima's harp can sound an alarm or indicate all is clear, as it does when his friends see him in robes through the camp fence. This same power of music to convey Buddhist truth is spoken of by Zeami (*c.* 1363–*c.* 1443 CE), the famous composer and theorist of Japanese Nō drama of the Middle Ages. In *The Burmese Harp*, in a sense, Mizushima is like a shaman and his harp like a magical instrument. Through music the viewers come to see him and his homemade Burmese harp as the very soul of the Japanese soldiers. This is revealed in many ways including his accidental discovery of his (and everyone's) Buddha Nature. In much the same way, he chances upon the ruby beneath a layer of dirt. It is important that Mizushima is not formally trained in music. His ability is natural like the ruby and like Buddha Nature. In Japanese language, *tama* means both "jewel" and "soul or spirit." This double entendre is recognized in Japanese shamanism and in Shintō religion. For example, the expression "the jewel dropped into the mouth" means the voice of a **kami** (spirit) speaking through the mouth of the shaman. The film opens and closes with the same words written on the screen: "The soil of Burma is red and so are the rocks." In part, this makes us think of the country as bloody and war-torn. More important may be the lines of connection with the ruby, the soul of the people, and Mizushima, who comes to be identified with the land. To begin this identification, we are told he looks exactly like the people of Burma except for his clothes. The implication is that, although the Japanese have adopted modern ways, at heart they are like the peaceful people of Burma as imaged in the story. And like the hearts of Japanese people, Mizushima struggles to understand human suffering and death, the problem Buddhism addresses. In the context of the story, the Burmese live as Buddhists. While war and death are the illusory faces of life, an enduring eternal spirit resides as the land and the people. This eternal spirit is Buddhism or Buddha Nature.

As we follow Mizushima's journey, we see his transformation from soldier to the holiest of *bhikkhus*. At first he seems like an impostor, a soldier in disguise. But the Burmese bow in respect for him. They recognize his spiritual transformation even before he does, because they are, allegedly, closer to the natural state he seeks. Mizushima walks across the land very much on a spiritual pilgrimage. Pilgrimage is an important part of many Buddhist traditions. A Buddhist pilgrim visits famous historical sites, typically where the Buddha or a Buddhist saint performed an important act. By participating in pilgrimage, Buddhists relive the life of the Buddha and reap the rewards the Buddha received. There are a number of pilgrimage destinations in Myanmar, including the world-renowned **Shwedagon Pagoda**, also called the Golden Pagoda. Shwedagon Pagoda is said to enshrine eight hairs of the historical Buddha and relics of three other past Buddhas. An important part of early Buddhism that entered both the Theravāda and Mahāyāna is reverence of stupas. A **stupa** is a mound of earth that enshrines a Buddhist relic. Most typically, the relic is the remains of the Buddha, such as a single finger joint. In ancient times, King Aśoka (304–232 BCE) conquered and united India. Afterwards he converted to Buddhism, making the Buddhist precepts the law of the land. He divided the remains of the Buddha's body, built stupas around India above some of these relics, and sent other relics to neighboring countries where rulers did the same. In honor of the Buddha, monks and lay followers would make pilgrimages to the sites of these stupas, circumambulate them clockwise, chant and pray. This became an established part of some Buddhist traditions. The appearance of Buddhist stupas vary among countries. Indian stupas are mounds of dirt covered with stones or bricks. Burmese stupas are domes, while China and Japan each have their own version of pagodas, which are also Buddhist stupas. In *The Burmese Harp*, Mizushima is on such a pilgrimage to burial sites where he will cremate the remains of people. It is a pilgrimage that will transform him. When he first cremates the bodies of Japanese soldiers, he makes a mound of earth, places rocks on it, and salutes. All of this is quite similar to Buddhist observances at stupas. We also witness a number of funerals and Mizushima inside the famous recumbent Buddha in Mudon, another pilgrimage site. The recumbent Buddhas, mainly of Southeast Asia, depict the Buddha laying auspiciously on this right side at the time of his *parinirvana*, bodily death. Mizushima, already connected to death in various ways, is inside the hollow body of the recumbent Buddha as the soldiers sing outside. From the heart of the Buddha he plays the harp and the magical music of the Dharma issues forth. At first the others do not know where the sound comes from, then they realize. This is similar in concept to Japanese temple bells. The heavy bronze is struck from the outside, vibrating the air miles away like the Dharma all around us. Inside, he is as the spirit of the Buddha and the soul of the dead. Mizushima runs toward the head inside the recumbent Buddha. He looks out on his former group through a hole for an eye of the Buddha. The eye of the Buddha is mentioned in scriptures, meaning meditative vision. It is with this new insight that Mizushima looks upon his friends with compassion and cries. Although the story does not mention it, there is also a Theravāda practice of meditating on the decay of corpses. The idea in doing this is to become free of attachment to the body and realize the transience of our condition.

One cinematic way we see the connection between Mizushima and the land is by using long shots showing panoramic views. This same technique is used in *Why Has Bodhi-Dharma Left for the East* to connect Buddhist attainment with the natural environment. On his way to Mudon, for example, Mizushima comes upon a startling number of unburied bodies along the beaches and mountains of Burma. The camera places him alone in the larger context of the otherwise beautiful landscapes of the country, signifying his development as an individual and his place as part of the more natural Burmese countryside. We see this again in the final scene as he walks further away from the camera, becoming the landscape itself. In stark contrast, his fellow soldiers are framed behind barbed-wire fences and always as a group. On board the ship back to Japan the soldiers nestle together on the confinement of the deck. As the captain reads Mizushima's letter, the camera pans toward the expanse of the ocean, emphasizing the broadness of his statements and what he has become. During two singing sequences there are long shots over villages lighted by the full moon. A full moon is a symbol of Buddhist awakening in Buddhism.

The novel clears up several features in the film. In the third chapter of the second section of the book, the narrator says,

> We were much impressed by the way the people of this country respect the priesthood. Their almsgiving is no mere act of charity but one of gratitude to those who do penance for the salvation of all living beings. They don't just hand over their gifts; they kneel and offer them.[9]

This devoutness is observed throughout the book. Without it, Mizushima would likely have starved. It is at the moment he gives up and falls to his knees that he is saved by the devoted. In the same chapter, the narrator describes an ongoing discussion the soldiers have about which is more profitable: to be raised as the Burmese, whose young men all spend a portion of their youths as *bhikkhus*, or to be raised as the Japanese, whose young men all spend a portion of their youths in the military. The discussion veers close to becoming a dialogue on tradition versus modernity, on whether following traditional values or seeking to move forward is the better path. As Takeyama writes, "But which of these attitudes, of these ways of life, is better for the world and for humanity? Which should we choose?[10] Along these lines, the narrator later says, "We Japanese have not cared to make strenuous spiritual efforts. We have not even recognized their value. What we stressed was merely a man's abilities, the things he could do—not what kind of man he was, how he lived, or the depth of his understanding."[11] In the letter in the final portion of the novel, Mizushima explains himself and his transformation: "As I climbed mountains and forded rivers, and buried the bodies I found lying smothered in weeds or soaked in water, I was harassed by tormenting questions. Why does so much misery exist in the world? Why is there so much inexplicable suffering? What are we to think?"[12] The questions raised in Mizushima's mind about suffering are questions central to Buddhism. The quest for the answers to these questions, however unanswerable, is what leads Mizushima to make the choice to stay in Burma. Buddhists seek awakening through the destruction of desires and selfless acts for others. Fifty years after the film, how has this played out in Myanmar?

Recent Events in Myanmar

In September 2007, Buddhist monks led the largest protest against the military government of Myanmar that country had experienced since the popular uprising of 1988, when 3,000 people were reportedly killed. Since then, many Americans have been puzzled and excited by news of events in Myanmar. Images of monks with megaphones and raised fists challenge typical understandings of quiet and peaceful Buddhists as portrayed in *The Burmese Harp*. Leading up to the events of September 2007, a month earlier the government doubled the price of gasoline, triggering corresponding rises in the price of public transportation, rice and cooking oil in the impoverished country. Deep social economic suffering in Myanmar is well documented. In 2006, the UN Development Programme's Human Development Index, citing a high infant mortality rate, short life expectancy, the serious threat posed by the HIV/AIDS epidemic, tuberculosis, and malaria, ranked Myanmar 130 out of 177 countries in terms of development. In May 2007, the International Committee of the Red Cross (ICRC) issued a rare criticism by accusing the Myanmar government of abusing the rights of the people. The new burden imposed by the gasoline price hike was likely felt to be intolerable by many. Within days of the price increase, a pro-democracy demonstration of about 400 people took place in Yangon (also called Rangoon), the former capital and largest city of Myanmar with a population of six million. While the government quickly suppressed the protest, arresting numerous activists, smaller demonstrations continued around the country with the participation of a modest number of monks. On September 5, the military forcibly stopped a rally in the town of Pakokku, injuring at least three monks. This provoked public and monastic outrage since an estimated that 89 percent of the Myanmar population is Buddhist and the hundreds of thousands of clergy members hold high status in society.[13] At some point in life, most males in Myanmar become monks for at least a three-month period, usually as a child or just before marriage in order to learn social morals. Thus, the public has a very close connection to the 400,000–500,000 professional monks in the country of around 50 million people.

The next day, monks in Pakakku made a drastic if not heretical move by taking government officials hostage for a short time, demanding that the government issue an apology by September 17. After the deadline passed with no apology, monks began protesting daily around the country, their numbers increasing to tens of thousands. While we might wonder why Buddhist monks feel the need for an apology from the laity, it is interesting to note that many reviewers have criticize *The Burmese Harp* for not apologizing for the war or at least acknowledging Japan's guilt in it. Instead, the film is seen as a part of an early postwar attempt to tell the war from the point of the Japanese as part of a larger world community of victims. The historical specifics of the war do not appear in the film, only the larger cruelty of it.

In the novel, the soldiers argue over the woes of technology in their country compared to the naturalism of the Burmese people. One comments, "The Burmese never seem to have committed our stupid blunder of attacking others."[14] In defense of the story, this is an admission of Japanese guilt. On the other hand, while the Burmese may have never been involved in world conquest, they have not been always been the peaceful people portrayed in the film.

At the time of the protests, Burmese *bhikkhus* also refused to accept alms or perform religious services for members of the military and their families. In Myanmar, non-monastic Buddhists participate in the religion largely by earning merit for good fortune in this life and a better future birth by contributing materially to the wellbeing of monks.[15] This is why we see in the film Burmese peasants stop and give rice to Mizushima, who they see as a holy *arahant*. The system of merit and demerit (karma) is believed by hundreds of millions of Buddhists worldwide. It provides an explanation for why a person is born in a particular situation. For example, the justification for an individual maintaining the wealth of his or her family in an overwhelmingly impoverished country, an individual's right to rule the country, or, conversely, a baby being born with cancer, are all routinely explained by past-life karma accrued by earning merit or demerit. For this reason, it is of utmost importance to earn merit in this life. This contrasts to the idea in the Chan/Zen/Seon tradition of Mahāyāna Buddhism that there is no merit, as stated by Bodhidharma.[16] The Myanmar monks' refusal to accept alms from the military and their families affectively denied them access to the merit system and so, according to the belief, to wellbeing. This seems to raise questions concerning Buddhists taking vows to save all sentient beings or to provide spiritual aid to any person seeking it. However, Theravāda Buddhist scriptures stipulate that monks should refuse alms in certain cases. According to the *Pattanikujjana Sutta*, the Buddha said, "Monks, the bowl should be turned upside down for the lay devotee who is endowed with eight qualities: (1) if he tries for non-gain of monks, (2) if he tries for ill-being of monks, (3) if he tries for non-residence of monks, (4) if he reviles and abuses monks, (5) if he causes monks to break away from (other) monks, (6) if he speaks ill of the Buddha, (7) if he speaks ill of the Dhamma, (8) if he speaks ill of the Sangha. I allow you, monks, to turn the bowl upside down for the lay devotee who is endowed with these eight qualities."[17] The upside-down alms bowl became an international symbol of protest against the military dictatorship of Myanmar. At the time of the protests, donated food from military families was left to rot in the streets. Despite widespread hunger in Myanmar, the population would not touch it. This attests to both the popular support of the political cause of the monks and the belief in their spiritual efficacy. But we must wonder how the failure to distribute the food in some way reflected on the monks in the eyes of the world.

The most famous political figure of Myanmar is Aung San Suu Kyi (1945–present), who was awarded the US Congressional Medal of Honor in 2008. At Shwedagon Pagoda in 1988, she addressed a crowd of 500,000, demanding democracy for her country. Following this, the 8888 movement occurred (August 8, 1988) and thousands were killed in anti-government riots. As a result, the State Law and Order Restoration Council (SLORC) was formed and thousands were arrested. Shortly afterwards, Burma was renamed Myanmar. In 1989, National League for Democracy leader Aung San Suu Kyi was put under house arrest. In the 1990 general election, she was elected Prime Minister of Myanmar but her house arrest prevented her from taking office. In numerous articles and statements, she has consistently voiced her support for Buddhism and democracy in her country. After pressure from US officials, the Myanmar government, hoping to attract American business investments, released her from house arrest in November 2010. Today, she continues her political activism in her country but has recently suffered from a number of health problems.

Further Reading

Boyce, Barry (ed.). *The Mindfulness Revolution: Leading Psychologists, Scientists, Artists, and Meditatiion Teachers on the Power of Mindfulness in Daily Life.* Boston: Shambhala, 2011.
Kornfield, Jack. *Living Dharma.* Boston: Shambhala, 2010.
Hubbard, Jamie. *Pruning the Bodhi Tree: The Storm Over Critical Buddhism.* Honolulu: University of Hawaii Press, 1997.
Takeyama Michio. *The Harp of Burma (Biruma no Tategoto).* Rutland, Vermont and Tokyo: Charles E. Tuttle Co. Publishers, 1966.
Victoria, Brian Daizen. *Zen at War.* Oxford: Rowman & Littlefield, 2006.

Further Viewing

Burma VJ: Reporter (Anders Østergaard, Denmark, 2008). A documentary about the protests in Burma, made from smuggled footage.
The Dhamma Brothers (Andrew Kukura and Jenny Phillips, USA, 2008). A documentary about doing Mindfulness Meditation in an overcrowded maximum-security prison in Alabama.
Beyond Rangoon (John Boorman, USA, 1995). A drama and action film about an American doctor, played by Patricia Arquette, stranded in Myanmar during the 8888 massacre.

Notes

1 In 1989, the Burmese military government officially changed the English version of the country's name from Burma to Myanmar, and the capital city from Rangoon to Yangon. These changes reflect the local names. Some groups opposing the government refuse to recognize the name changes.
2 *Saṃyutta Nikāya* 1.8.
3 *Ibid.*, See: http://dharma.ncf.ca/introduction/sutras/metta-sutra.html, accessed 8/18/12.
4 Available in English under that title.
5 Originally made in 1956 and remade in a color version in 1987. Both were directed by Kon Ichikawa.
6 Hubbard, Jamie, *Pruning the Bodhi Tree: The Storm Over Critical Buddhism.*
7 See, for example, the *Nissaraniya Sutta: Means of Escape* in the *Anguttara Nikaya* 6.13.
8 See *Zen at War* by Brian Daizen Victoria.
9 Takeyama, p. 45.
10 Takeyama, p. 47.
11 Takeyama, p. 129.
12 Takeyama, pp. 129–130.

13 https://www.cia.gov/library/publications/the-world-factbook/geos/bm.html, accessed 7/30/13.
14 Takeyama, p. 48.
15 This idea of buying good fortune compares roughly to the Christian notion of giving tithe.
16 See Chapter 5 in this volume.
17 From the *Pattanikujjana Sutta* in the *Aṅguttara Nikāya*, sutta 87:7, numerals added. Translation and discussion by Martin Kovan, "The Burmese Alms-Boycott: Theory and Practice of the *Pattanikujjana* in Buddhist Non-Violent Resistance," originally presented at the International Association for Buddhist Studies Conference, Taiwan, June 20–25, 2011.

7

TIBETAN BUDDHISM

The Cup

1. Basic Plot Summary

The Cup (Khyentse Norbu, Bhutan, 2000) is about traditional Tibetan Buddhism struggling to survive outside its homeland in modern times. The story follows a group of monks at a Tibetan temple in exile in India (although it is filmed in Bhutan). Some of the monks' near obsession with World Cup soccer brings into question their goal of giving up worldly attachment and becomes a part of their teachers' reorientation of traditional methods. At the beginning of the film, two boys arrive at the temple from Tibet and hope to be accepted as monks there. One is Nyima (Pema Tshundup), who is around 12 years old. The other is his uncle, Palden (Kunsang Nyima), who is perhaps 18. The boys' families sent them to study in India to escape increasing repression of Buddhism by the Chinese in Tibet. The man who brought them to the temple regularly helps Tibetans escape Chinese control. On this trip he presents the abbot of the monastery with a pair of earrings, saying the girl who had worn them died in an uprising at Lhasa, capital of Tibet and site of the home temple of the Dalai Lama and of Tibetan Buddhism.[1] Her mother wanted the monastery to have the earrings as a donation. He also gives the abbot a watch, which belonged to Nyima's mother. She sent it in case the boy needed money. The abbot gives the watch to Nyima and tells him to keep it. The boy is clearly sad to have left his mother behind and the watch is the only physical reminder he has of her. The abbot also tells the newcomers that India is the most densely populated land on earth and yet the Indian people have welcomed Tibetans. Therefore, they should study hard in this new country. The boys are then sent to receive their ordination.

Meanwhile, outside in the temple courtyard, young monks are playing soccer with a Coke can. When the head monk, Geko (Orgyen Tobgyal), comes by, they scatter quickly. It is clear that the young monks are not allowed to play soccer. The Coke can is an obvious symbol of the modern world. We also see the young monks writing graffiti on a wall, again running when Geko comes. Soon the two new arrivals enter an ordination room where monks are chanting. The abbot ceremoniously unfolds a paper revealing their new Buddhist names. Behind him, among the chanters, a young monk named Orgyen (Jamyang Lodro) throws another kind of rolled paper to a monk. The paper says "Brazil vs Argentina." Geko sees the monks playing instead of chanting and assigns them the task of shaving the heads of the new initiates. As they are being shaved, the monks who have been living in India begin to talk about soccer. Orgyen asks the new arrivals if it is true Tibetans only bathe once in their lifetimes. Palden replies that they bathe every New Year. Although Orgyen is of Tibetan heritage, he has been raised in India and knows very little about Tibet. Yet he tells the newcomers they have a lot to learn. Orgyen announces he is going to bathe. He then boldly throws off his monk's robes, stripping down to his boxer shorts and tank-top T-shirt that says on it "Ronaldo," the name of his favorite soccer player. Orgyen flexes his muscles like an athlete and says he hopes France wins the World Cup because they are the only country that fully supports Tibet. Another monk asks about the US team, but Orgyen says the monk only likes the US because an American sponsor sends him three dollars each month.

At morning prayers, many of the monks are sleepy. Some of them were out late the night before watching soccer matches at a local business. During the prayer service, the monks play pranks on one another. One sows another's robe to a rug and when he stands, he drags it behind him. At meal time Orgyen makes a bet with another monk that France will win the next game. The newer monks from Tibet are not interested. We see writing scribbled on the wall outside saying "Long live Paraguay!", "Victory to Germany," and "Free Tibet." Their interests seem to span this spectrum. The new monks ask why the games must be watched at night. Orgyen replies it has something to do with the earth not being flat, adding, you wouldn't understand because you're from Tibet. Again he feels that being raised in India has given him a better understanding of the world than traditional Tibetans have.

That night, several young monks sneak out of the monastery in order to go into town and watch soccer. In front of a television, Orgyen jumps up cheering and a scuffle breaks out. The monks become rowdy and are kicked out. When they return to the monastery, Geko is waiting for them. He comments to Palden about how quickly he had been corrupted, implying the same of Tibetan Buddhism outside its country. Geko scolds them and says he will have to tell the abbot. Upon hearing about this, the abbot asks if the boys knew that Geko had informed him, the abbot. Since they did not, the abbot tells Geko to act as if he had not told him; otherwise, he would never be able to discipline them. The abbot also asks what kind of game soccer is. Geko says it involves two civilized nations fighting over a ball. The abbot says, you must be joking and asks if there is any violence or sex. Geko says there is only violence sometimes. When the abbot asks Geko how he knows so much about the subject, Geko smiles. This is the first indication in the film that Geko too had been interested in soccer and perhaps had been as mischievous as the young monks. Yet he turned out to be a responsible senior monk, implying interests in the new ways of the world had not ruined Tibetan Buddhism. The abbot likely realizes this. Geko excuses Palden for his part in sneaking out because he was new. He punishes the others by assigning them cooking duties for a month.

While in the kitchen, Orgyen has an idea about soccer. He convinces the others to ask the abbot if they might be allowed to watch the World Cup final at the monastery. They will tell the abbot they are willing to study extra hard and stop fooling around so much if it be allowed. They first go to Geko with this. Geko in turn goes to the abbot and says he has a request to make, taking responsibility and supporting the boys. The abbot has been looking through luggage trunks he keeps packed and replies, "Look how silly I am. I thought we would return to Tibet soon. I was going to show postcards of America with 100-story buildings . . . I should give up this attachment of homeland." In this frame of mind, Geko asks the abbot about bringing a television to the monastery. The abbot asks what the winner of the game receives. As Geko replies, "A cup," the abbot raises a cup to his lips and drinks. Both smile.

Receiving the abbot's approval, Orgyen sets about raising money from the monks to rent a television and satellite dish. After raising the standard amount, they learn from the rental business that they need more money since it is World Cup final night. Orgyen returns to the temple and pressures Palden into asking his nephew Nyima for his mother's watch. Nyima sadly hands over the watch, which they take to the rental store, and then return with the television. As the game is being played, Orgyen finds he cannot enjoy it because he is concerned about Nyima, who is sitting across the room and is very upset at having given up his mother's watch. At one point during the game the power goes out briefly. A monk stands up with a flashlight and begins to tell a story about a rabbit using shadow puppets. He is interrupted when the power is restored and a monk says, "To hell with rabbits, let's watch football!" Orgyen leaves the room during the match and Geko follows.

Geko finds Orgyen in his room looking through all of his possessions to find items to sell in order to retrieve Nyima's watch. Orgyen has for the first time overcome his complete self-interest in concern for another. Geko tells him, "You're so bad at business, you'll make a good monk." Geko also assures Orgyen, he, and the abbot will pay to have the watch returned to Nyima. In the final scene, Nyima has his watch back and asks about the end of the rabbit story. The monk replies, "What's all the fuss about endings," meaning the end of the film as well.

2. Further Connections with Buddhism

One thing that makes *The Cup* particularly interesting for our purposes is that the director is a Buddhist master, having the honorific title "*Rinpoche*," literally "precious one." The film is about Buddhism, but is Khyentse Norbu acting also in the role of a *Rinpoche* by making the film? That is, can this film help the viewers realize Buddhist truths? When the shadow puppet rabbit story is rejected for the television, does this suggest the old ways of transmitting Buddhism are given up for newer media like the present film?

In Tibet, Buddhism developed in a specific way found nowhere else in the world. While relying on Mahāyāna principles accepted widely throughout East Asia, the social and political history of Tibet influenced interpretation and monastic organization. There are four types of Buddhism in Tibet. The tradition portrayed in the film is the one the Dalai Lama leads, called Gelug or "Yellow Hats." The word *Lama* is similar to guru. It is a designation for a Tibetan Buddhist teacher. *Dalai* means "Great Ocean." The current Dalai Lama, whose name is Tenzin Gyatso, is considered the 14th in a lineage of reincarnations or manifestations of the Bodhisattva of compassion, Avalokiteśvara. He is said to have been born many times in order to continue his **Bodhisattva Vow** to save all sentient beings from suffering. In *The Cup*, a letter arrives telling the monastery that Palden and Nyima are coming. The letter says that, in Tibet, it is now illegal to even possess a picture of the Dalai Lama. We also see this in the film *Windhorse*, which also depicts Lhasa women losing their lives in struggle with the occupying Chinese, as mentioned in *The Cup*.[2] Just before the letter arrives, we see the abbot with a picture of the Dalai Lama.

The People's Republic of China invaded Tibet in 1949 and took control of it in 1959. When the Chinese took control, the Dalai Lama fled the country and became the leader of the Tibetan government-in-exile headquartered in Dharamsala, in northern India until the time of his retirement from political office on March 14, 2011. In *The Cup*, two girls from Tibet hope to come to the monastery in India to be closer to the Dalai Lama. The Dalai Lama is still consider by many Tibetans the principal spiritual guide of the country and, being a manifestation of Bodhisattva Avalokiteśvara, a supernatural being with divine powers including insight into the nature of reality beyond that of ordinary people. While this aspect of the Dalai Lama's persona is typically unacknowledged in his American and European appearances, it is nevertheless an important part of the tradition. The animated spoof of him appearing in an episode of the *The Simpsons* depicts him flying away at the end, exaggerating but not fabricating the idea that he has supernatural abilities.[3] The Dalai Lama was awarded the Nobel Peace Prize in 1989. Afterwards his public image became well known in Europe and America. Abroad he is often called His Holiness or H.H. the Dalai Lama in the manner of a Catholic pope, in order to express the reverence contained in the term "Dalai Lama" in Tibet. He is the subject of several popular film dramatizations, including *Seven Years in Tibet* and *Kundun*.[4]

Tibetan Buddhism is a type known as Tantric Buddhism, esoteric Buddhism, or *Vajrayāna*. The word "Tantric" has come to be associated in English with sexual practices. Tantric Buddhism sometimes uses drawings of sexually united beings to indicate the unity of all mental dualities. On the temple walls in *The Cup*, viewers

FIGURE 7.1 *Vajra*

can see some of these images on a type of banner known as *thangka* paintings. The scriptures containing instructions on how to unite mental dualities and achieve awakening are called *tantras*. We see the abbot reading these in the film.

While the word "esoteric" implies secrecy, esoteric Buddhism is open to all people.[5] Initiation and personal training is required. We see initiation in the film when Palden and Nyima enter the room with chanting monks. *Vajrayāna* means "the way of the *vajra*," a ritual instrument that symbolizes a diamond that cuts through delusion. It is typically a metal piece with pointed ends held in one's hand as in Figure 7.1. However, *vajra*s can be found in numerous sizes, such as large wooden decorations on temple roofs. The abbot holds a *vajra* in the film during ceremonies.

Like other varieties of Tantra, Tibetan Buddhism places importance on practices that involve the "Three Mysteries": **mudras**, **mantra**, and mandala. These are mysterious in that they lead to awakening. Meditation using these three devices is considered the quickest path to the goal, in contrast to non–Tantric or esoteric practices of other traditions of Buddhism that may require many lifetimes. A mudra is a highly symbolic finger gesture. Any way that you may have tied your fingers together in play as a child may well be a mudra. Although there are hundreds of possibilities, **108** mudras, the sacred number in Buddhism and other Indic religions, are most often used. Drawings of Buddhas and Bodhisattvas usually depict them forming mudras representing ideas such as meditation, teaching, wisdom, or fearlessness in religious practice. Beginning early in the film we see the abbot and others weaving their fingers together to form various mudras.

A mantra is a sound or series of sounds pronounced ritually for spiritual power. There are mantras specific to each Buddha and Bodhisattva and also mantras expressing significant ideas. A famous example of a mantra in Tibetan Buddhism is "*om mani padme hum.*" This literally means "the jewel is in the lotus," a sexually implicit image of the unity of all reality. Like this one, mantras are usually in Sanskrit. Even though the practitioner may not understand its meaning, the mantra is left in Sanskrit and not translated. The Sanskrit sound is considered most effective for power, more so than the meaning of the mantra. Some Buddhists claimed to have performed miraculous deeds using mantras, such as bringing rain or cursing someone. The film opens with the sounds of mantras and we hear them throughout. Tibetan monks developed a kind of deep, guttural throat chanting, which provided science with the first example that human voices can make more than one sound at a time. Tibetan throat-chanting monks tour widely demonstrating their type of mantra singing, which is religious practice.

Mandala literally means "a circle." It is usually a painting depicting a main Buddha surrounded in the center of a large lotus flower by other Buddhas and Bodhisattvas, each sitting on a petal of the flower. A mandala can be used as decoration, as we see on the walls in the temple. In meditation, it is an object of concentration. The central Buddha often depicted in Tibetan mandala is not the historical Buddha Siddhartha Gautama, but **Vairocana**, a theoretical representation of the universal teachings of the Buddha, the Dharma. Vairocana is used as a meditative image, representing the perfect creature that the practitioner would like to become, that is, an awakened being. The Buddhas and Bodhisattvas on the lotus petals are also used for concentration or visualization purposes. Each represents an attribute of Vairocana's perfection, such as wisdom and compassion. Sitting in meditation in front of the mandala, the Tantric Buddhist visualizes one of the figures representing a characteristic to be achieved. The practitioner forms the mudra associated with that figure and chants the mantra of that Buddha or Bodhisattva. Eventually, after perfecting all of the attributes, the practitioner becomes Vairocana, a Buddha. The colors of the mandala are also of symbolic importance. Vairocana is depicted as white, representing perfect purity. He is also the aggregate of the colors of the surrounding Buddhas, each of whom sit in a cardinal direction and are red, yellow, green, and blue. Recently Tibetan Buddhists have toured various countries, building sand mandala. Using colored sand, monks work for three days constructing a mandala for public viewing. Afterwards, they return the sand to nature, showing the transience of life, as of the art they created. The colors of the mandala may have been used as the color template the director used to make the film. More importantly, the film may become the modern version of a mandala. Film is able to depict and convey ideal qualities of Buddhism for visualization by a large audience or individually.

As seen prominently in *The Cup*, Tibetan Buddhists robes are maroon, yellow, and sometimes red, with blue piping on the sleeves. This contrasts with the traditional saffron colored robes in India. Maroon and red were adopted because they were much cheaper colors to use at one time in Tibet. In Taiwan and Korea Buddhism, monks and nuns wear gray robes. In Japan they wear black or white.

When Palden and Nyima arrive at the temple, we see them offer the abbot white strips of cloth called *khata*. *Khatas* are typically made of cotton or silk and look like long scarves. Sometimes they are inscribed with mantras or designs of the eight auspicious symbols of Tibetan Buddhism. *Khatas* are often white, the color of Vairocana, representing purity. They are also seen in the other colors of the mandala—blue, red, green, and yellow.

Offering *khata* is one of the best known customs of Tibet. It is a sign of one's love or respect for another. At holy sites, to esteemed monks, teachers, dignitaries, and elders, a *khata* is offered with hands folded near one's forehead. A bow is made respectfully with the head bending over joined palms. This hand gesture known in religions around the world as a symbol of prayer is called the *Añjali Mudrā* and was used in ancient India as well as for the standard greeting in India today.[6] The *khata* is not draped around the honored person's neck but placed nearby. Typically, the person receiving it gives it back as a blessing. In *The Cup*, the abbot returns a *khata* to the driver bringing the new students. A *khata* offered to the Dalai Lama and received back will be cherished as a talisman. *Khatas* are also placed over statues, *thangka* paintings, pictures of reincarnated Rinpoches and altars. They may be flown or put on Prayer Flags before they are hung.

Colored Prayer Flags inscribed with verses or wishes are placed in the wind and the flapping is seen as continuous praying. When Geko takes soccer team pennants from the young monks he sarcastically asks if they are Prayer Flags. A similar idea is connected to Tibetan Prayer Wheels. The older fortune-reading Lama (Godu Lama) and others in the film spin Prayer Wheels—for example, when he is on the roof with the satellite dish. The satellite dish seems to be a larger version of his Prayer Wheel. The outside of a Prayer Wheel may be inscribed with a mantra. Spinning it symbolically repeats the mantra again and again. In the same way, a mantra may be written on paper and placed inside the Prayer Wheel to be spun in repetition.

As with the number of mantra used, Buddhist Prayer Beads also have 108 beads. We see Prayer Beads throughout the film. For example, when Geko goes for a fortune reading, the older Lama rubs Prayer Beads in his hands. As in Japanese Buddhism, some feel the sound of the beads being rubbed is auspicious, and gets the attention of spirits. The 108 beads are sometimes thought to represent the number of defilements we have. Prayer Beads assist us in overcoming them one at a time.

There are eight auspicious symbols of Tibetan Buddhism. Many of these are seen throughout *The Cup*. They are:

1. a Conch Shell
2. a Lotus Flower
3. a Wheel of the Dharma
4. a Parasol
5. an Endless Knot
6. a Pair of Golden Fish
7. a Banner Proclaiming Victory
8. a Treasure Vase.

At the beginning of *The Cup*, we see two monks in yellow hats, a symbol of the Gelug sect, blowing conch shells. In ancient Indian epics conch shells are blown like bugles in battles.[7] Their sound is believed to drive away evil spirits and prevent natural disasters. In Tibetan Buddhism they are used to call together religious assemblies. During rituals they are used both as musical instruments

FIGURE 7.2   Scene near the beginning of *The Cup*

and as containers for purifying water. Among the eight auspicious symbols, the conch shell stands for the Buddha's teaching, which spreads in all directions like its sound. The two monks sounding conch shells at the beginning of *The Cup* may be announcing a religious service inside the temple. More importantly, they declare to the viewer that the teachings of Buddhism is about to begin through the medium of the film. The monks stand with the shells on either side of a Wheel of the Dharma (*Dharmachakra*), flanked by two deer. A wheel is also an ancient symbol of India. In the Tibetan version and some Indian depictions, the wheel has eight spokes, indicating the Eightfold Path of Buddhism. In Tibet the Wheel of the Dharma represents spiritual change and overcoming the obstacles of illusions. In the center of the Wheel is a symbol with three segments known as a *gankyil* or Wheel of Joy. It can represent the **Three Jewels of Buddhism**: the Buddha, the Dharma, and the *sangha*, the overcoming of the three poisons: passion, aggression, and delusion, or primordial energy. It also represents the energy of Snow Lions, the mythical creatures on the top of the pillars above the heads of the monks in Figure 7.2. Snow Lions represent fearlessness and are a national symbol of Tibet. The deer beside the Wheel of the Dharma indicate Deer Park, where the Buddha first put the Wheel of the Dharma into motion, that is, taught Buddhism. The Wheel is poised on a lotus flower, also one of the eight auspicious symbols.

We see a parasol in the final scene as a monk walks down a road in the distance. A parasol is an old symbol of royalty in India. It was held over the heads of kings and other important people for protection. In Indian art it came to indicate both royal and religious persons. Buddhist stupas also have stylized umbrellas on top. The parasol is like the Bodhi Tree that was over the Buddha during awakening. For this reason, the parasol can represent wisdom. It can also represent compassion, since it provides protection from the elements.

Several times in *The Cup* we see tsampa, a staple food of Tibet. Tsampa is roasted barley, wheat, or rice flour often mixed with salty butter tea. When Palden and Nyima arrive at the temple they are given a heaping pile of tsampa in butter tea. Butter tea is traditionally made from yak butter. Drinking it is a regular part of Tibetan life. Tsampa is also used in many Tibetan Buddhist rituals. Geko builds a small stupa of tsampa and throws some into the air. Throwing tsampa in the air may predate Buddhism and is also a custom during weddings. It indicates happiness. On the bottom of the cups of butter tea, the viewer sees a swastika. This is an ancient design from India representing the pattern of the cosmos. It was adopted into Buddhism as an auspicious sign.

According to the director's commentary included on the DVD release of *The Cup*, the arrival of the older novice, Palden, was real. He had just arrived in time to be filmed. His tonsure, the ritual shaving of his head, was also real in the film. He later returned to Tibet and was imprisoned. The monk who played the younger novice Nyima, grew up, moved to New York, and defrocked. This is not uncommon. People become monks and nuns for various reasons, including escape from worse social conditions at home. Once Asian monks arrive in America, giving up monastic life is one of the options to be considered.

The director's commentary also tells us the actual horseplay that goes on in monasteries was greatly toned down for the film because the viewing audience would not believe the real extent of it. The actor playing the older of the playful monks, Neten Chokling, later became a film-maker and directed *Milarepa,* about Tibet's great mystic monk by that name. Jamyang Lodro, who played Orgyen in *The Cup*, grew up and rose in the temple hierarchy. We can't help but wonder if the film influenced him to think about his actions. Orgyen Tobgyal, who played Geko, is famous for being strict. The old car in this film is his. His part as Geko, who knows about soccer, is modeled after the director. The commentary says the story was based on a true event and that today most monasteries have televisions.

Students viewing *The Cup* in the classroom are surprised by the antics of the young monks. This goes against two common conceptions we have of Buddhists: that they are continually meditating and that they are awakened. By challenging these conceptions, the film helps demystify monastic life. Typically young Buddhists are students of Buddhism, not Buddhas. Few will be Buddhas. Hermann Hesse's *Siddhartha* asks how many of the Śramamas will attain nirvana. This question is applicable here as well. The students are sometimes also working or engaged in other aspects of life.

Beginning with the realization that Buddhist life is not what we believe, *The Cup* may also help us examine the implications of these perceptions for our lives. For example, we may feel the young monks in *The Cup* should be more devoted to Buddhist training. However, according to Buddhism, we should be less concerned about holding high standards for others, and more so concerning ourselves. In the documentary *Words of My Perfect Teacher,* about director Khyentse Norbu, there is a segment showing a Tibetan *tulku*, an enlightened Lama who is reborn for the wellbeing of people. The *tulku* is young and living in California. He offers to sell his title of *tulku* to the highest bidder on eBay. Seeing this, viewers are probably shocked. Perhaps the main point in *The Cup*, spoken of by the abbot at the end of the film, is that according to Buddhism we cannot change the world. Instead, we should concentrate on cultivating our own lives and thereby help the world.

Why do we think the kids in *The Cup* shouldn't ignore Buddhist teachings? If we think they should be devoted to what they have committed themselves to, we too should be better devoted to the studies we've committed to. Why shouldn't the *tulku* sell his title on eBay? Do we value the preservation of indigenous cultures, even potentially "bad" ones, above the melting-pot ideal of American culture? If so, we are approving of a world caste system, believing that people should remain what they are born into. We don't seem to believe that about ourselves when we are born into poverty, for example. Do we feel outraged at the *tulku* because we think he is a legitimate heir to a Tibetan Lama institute and he is wasting his awakening potential? If so, this may be our most hypocritical judgment. According to Buddhism, each of us is the legitimate heir of the Buddha. Every moment we are not pursuing awakening, we are in effect selling our inheritance on eBay or for minimum wage. In contrast, when we have our minds in order, all things are in order. This is the point of study and of *The Cup*.

Near the end of the film, the abbot quotes Shantideva. Shantideva's best known book is a prose writing called *Guide to the Bodhisattva's Way of Life* (Sanskrit: *Bodhicaryavatara*). The abbot applies the quote to the focus of the film, how Tibetan Buddhism is to deal with modern social reality. Shantideva says the following.

(12) Unruly beings are as (unlimited) as space:
    They cannot possibly all be overcome,
    But if I overcome thoughts of anger alone,
    This will be equivalent to vanquishing all foes.

(13) Where would I possibly find enough leather
    With which to cover the surface of the Earth?
    But (wearing) leather just on the soles of my shoes
    Is equivalent to covering the earth with it.

(14) Likewise it is not possible for me
    To restrain the external course of things;
    But should I restrain this mind of mine,
    What would be the need to restrain all else?[8]

After the abbot speaks this message, there is a shot of a silver cup on an altar in the temple. The offering cup as been transposed for the World Cup, which has now become a part of monastic life. Even the World Cup has taught an important Buddhist message about selflessness. This shows that, although locations and conditions change, the essential ideals of Buddhism are adaptable. At the same time, the medium of film and motif of soccer has been used to teach this message to the viewers, who were also exposed to many aspects of Tibetan Buddhist life.

As with Orgyen, sometimes the worst student is the best student. The Buddha uses a metaphor of four types of horses to describe four kinds of students. The best horse will run fast or slow, turn right or left, with the rider's will, without the use of a whip. The second best runs as well as the first at the sight of the whip. The third responds when it feels pain on its body. The fourth responds only when the pain penetrates to the marrow of its bones.[9] In *Zen Mind, Beginner's Mind*, Suzuki Shunryu comments on this parable:

> When we hear this story, almost all of us want to be the best horse. If it is impossible to be the best one, we want to be the second best. This is, I think, the usual understanding of this story and of Zen [. . .] This is not the right understanding. If you practice Zen in the right way it does not matter whether you are the best horse or the worst one [. . .] When you are determined to practice zazen with the great mind of Buddha, you will find the worst horse is the most valuable one.[10]

There is also a Buddhist metaphor of four kinds of cups that illustrates four kinds of students. Instruction is symbolized by water being poured. The first cup is upside down, representing a student who does not pay attention. Water cannot be poured in. The second cup is right side up, but has a hole in the bottom. We hear what's being taught, but do not digest it or take it to heart. The third cup is right side up and doesn't have a hole in it. But the inside of the cup is covered with dirt. When the clear water of instruction is poured in, the dirt makes it cloudy just as we distort what we hear by interpreting and editing it to fit into our preconceived ideas or opinions. We typically try to match what we hear with how we already understand things. Anything new that does not match our opinion is resisted, ignored, or disregarded. The film introduces us to realities of temple life that do not match our preconceptions. The fourth cup represents the ideal way to be a student. It is upright and receives the water of teaching. It has no holes and retains what is taught. It is clean and open to learning new ideas.[11] This cup is pictured at the end of the film. Orgyen has progressed from being the worst cup to being the best; and perhaps the audience is being implored to do likewise.

Further Reading

Beer, Robert. *The Encyclopedia of Tibetan Symbols and Motifs*. Boston: Shambhala, 2009.
Shantideva and Padmakara Translation Group (trans.). *The Way of the Bodhisattva*. Boston: Shambhala, 2008.
Powers, John. *Introduction to Tibetan Buddhism*. New York: Snow Lion, 2007.

Further Viewing

Samsara (Pan Nalin, France, 2001). The story of one man's struggles in renouncing the world for the sake of awakening.
Travelers and Magicians (Khyentse Norbu, Bhutan, 2003). A modern Tibetan man hopes to move to America. On his way, he travels with a Buddhist monk and discovers a part of Tibetan culture.
Milarepa (Neten Chokling, Bhutan, 2006). An enactment of the story of the early life of the Tibetan saint Milarepa.

Notes

1 The word "abbot" is conventionally used in English for an Asian Buddhist position that does not easily correspond to that of Catholicism, from which the word was adopted. The same is true in calling Buddhists "monks," "nuns," and "priests" instead of *bhik-khu* (Pāli) or *bhikṣu* (Sanskrit) and *bhikkhuni* (Pāli) or *bhikṣuṇī* (Sanskrit). In Buddhism generally, there is no difference between a "monk" or "nun" and a "priest."

2 See Chapter 9 in this book.

3 *The Simpsons*, episode 332, season 15, "Simple Simpson," directed by Jim Reardon, USA, 2004.

4 *Seven Years in Tibet* was directed by Jean-Jacques Annaud and released in 1998. *Kundun*, released in 1997, was directed by Martin Scorsese.

5 This can be compared to the organizations in *Fight Club,* as well.

6 The gesture appears on seals from the Indus Valley dated around 2000 BCE.

7 In the *Bhagavad Gita*, Arjuna delays his blowing of the conch shell while Krishna explains yoga and ultimate reality.

8 *Guide to the Bodhisattva's Way of Life*, Stephen Batchelor (trans.), vols 9–14, pp. 45–6.

9 In the *Numerical Discourses* (Pāli: *Anguttara Nikaya*), *Book of Fours* (*Catukka Nipāta*), twelfth chapter: "The Horse Trainer Chapter" (*Kesi Vagga*). See http://www.metta.lk/tipitaka/2Sutta-Pitaka/4Anguttara-Nikaya/Anguttara2/4-catukkanipata/012-kesivaggo-e.html, accessed 8/18/12.

10 *Zazen* means "seated meditation." Suzuki, Shunryu, *Zen Mind, Beginner's Mind*, p. 38.

11 http://www.bauswj.org/baus/newsletter/2003/nl86_4types_students.html, accessed 7/30/13.

8
JAPANESE SHIN BUDDHISM
Departures

1. Basic Plot

The opening sequence of *Departures* (*Okuribito*, Yōjirō Takita, Japan, 2008) mixes the gravity of a funeral service with a strangely comic moment, creating an uneasiness that remains pervasive throughout the film. As the family looks on, a mortician wipes the body of a deceased person with a cleaning cloth beneath a draping sheet. Suddenly, he stops in visible tension, stunned at discovering the male organs of the presumed female corpse. The film then flashes back to the story of how this man has become a mortician. We watch as, no sooner has he, Daigo Kobayashi (Masahiro Motoki), finally landed what he believes to be his dream job as a cellist that the orchestra is dissolved. At home that evening, his wife Mika (Ryōko Hirosue) enters with an octopus that a fisherman who lives next door has given them to eat. The newly unemployed Daigo reluctantly admits to his wife that they are in deep debt for his expensive cello. Mika's worry deepens and she goes to prepare supper. In an instant, the silence is shattered and the anxiety increases as she screams from the kitchen. The octopus is alive and slithering across the floor! The couple can only watch, at a loss for what to do. Should they kill it and eat it as planned? In some way the octopus seems to mimic their struggle. They decide to give it a chance and take it to a nearby river that flows through the city. However, to their disappointment, the octopus only floats lifelessly as it spreads out and drifts on the surface of the water. Watching this, Daigo abruptly announces that he wants to quit playing the cello for a living, and move back to his hometown Yamagata in rural northern Japan. Mika agrees. The next day, Daigo sells his cherished cello to a music store and prepares to leave the city.

In Yamagata, Daigo and Mika move into a small, rustic house, the only thing his mother left him when she died two years earlier. Sadly reminiscing, Daigo tells

Mika that his father abandoned the family for another woman when he was 6 years old. Throughout the film, however, there are indications that his father continued to care about him and that he did not live with another woman for long.

Daigo begins to search the local newspaper for a job. In the midst of skimming through the pages, his face suddenly changes and he exclaims, "This is it!" Although he does not understand what the job is, he is convinced that it must be for him. The ad seeks a person that "helps out with journeys," offering high pay and short hours. With only this understanding, he goes to apply at the address with résumé in hand.

There, Daigo meets the company boss Ikuei Sasaki (Tsutomu Yamazaki), who casually asks only one question: "Can you put in long hours?" When Daigo affirms this, the boss says simply, "You're hired." Surprised, Daigo pensively asks what the position is and learns he is to be an "encoffiner," a funeral professional who prepares bodies for cremation and helps the spirit of the deceased enter into the next life. The advertisement to help out with journeys was a misprint that should have read "helps out with departures."[1] The company fills a small niche for society, providing a service once handled by families and not offered by funeral homes. Daigo is hesitant but the boss tells him to give it a try and, if he does not like it, he can quit. He pays him much-needed cash in advance. Daigo returns home with groceries and only tells his happy wife othat the job involves ceremonies. We soon learn it is considered unclean and taboo in Japanese culture to work with corpses and Daigo must keep it a secret from his wife and neighbors. The next morning he is sent on his first assignment. He is to assist the boss in producing a training film on preparing a corpse. Reluctantly, Daigo becomes a model in the film, acting the part of the corpse. After this, he is called for his first job as the mortician's assistant, accompanying the boss to a home where he is shown by police to a badly decomposed body. Daigo tries to fight back nausea but is overcome by the sight and smell. Later, as he is returning home on a bus, people around him can smell death and decomposition on him. At home his wife serves chicken sashimi. But now seeing food as the bodies of dead animals, Daigo becomes ill and cannot eat. In a state of dejection, he searches through the house and discovers the cello he often played as a boy. Wrapped in a piece of sheet music in the cello case, he also finds a rock his father had given him. His father had told him it was a rock letter, explaining that the shape of the rock related something of his feelings at the time.

Daigo considers quitting his new job, again while standing by a river. From deep thoughts he is startled to see the boss driving on a nearby road, calling to him to come to work. Daigo asks the boss if he had just coincidentally been driving by. The boss answers flatly that it is all fate and his God-given job. Daigo reluctantly accompanies him to the next job and is soon observing as the boss carefully handles the corpse of an older woman. The boss applies makeup to her face as her family looks on. Clearly, the family is relieved greatly that he has transformed her appearance to one more recognizable, and it appears he has prepared her for an afterlife. In this atmosphere Daigo comes to see his job is to act as a gentle gatekeeper between life and death, as well as a liaison between the departed and the family. He begins to take pride in this and finds in the job a spiritual light he had not previously known.

Daigo later goes on a call by himself and people are impressed by the care he takes encoffining; but, neighbors begin to hear about his position. A childhood friend passes him on the street and tells him to get a proper job, while shuffling his family quickly away. Returning home, Daigo finds his wife watching the training video in which he plays a corpse. Upset, she firmly tells him to quit the job immediately. Far from understanding his newly found respect for the position, when he reaches for her she screams, "Don't touch me! Filthy!" Afterward she announces she can no longer be with him and returns to her parents.

Daigo tries to quit his job, but the boss shares the story of how he had become a mortician himself. He explains his own wife had been his first client and how the experience had transformed him. He also shares his view on the human condition, saying that if we have to eat the living to live, it might as well taste good. As Daigo listens, he senses the pathos of life and the inevitability of death. He begins to lose his sense of self-importance and feels that he should do what he can to make life and death easier for others.

We see seasons change in the film as cello music plays. We see Daigo enjoying food with his coworkers in a way he had previously been unable to do. Through working with the deceased and their families, he begins to uncover the wonders and joys of life and living.

One day Mika returns and informs Daigo she is pregnant. She says he should quit his job so that their child will not be teased or bullied in school. Suddenly he is called to attend to the corpse of an older local woman with whom they had been friends. Mika accompanies him, watching as Daigo compassionately prepares the body. She notices the comfort this dignified act brings to the family. For the first time she realizes there is depth and significance to his job that transcends the social stigma associated with it. In this way she comes to accept and approve of his position. Afterward, Daigo learns that his father has just died and is about to be encoffined. Daigo still holds a grudge against his father for abandoning his family and says he will not go to the funeral; however, his coworker begs him to go, saying she had also abandoned her child at 6 years old because of a misjudgment and the social stigmas that would have been involved in trying to return. Daigo asks in anguish if everyone in the world is irresponsible. Together with Mika he decides to go to the funeral. There the encoffiners are treating the corpse without respect and Daigo takes over, preparing his father's body. This act softens him to his father's abandonment and opens him to the idea that all people suffer the same end regardless of their actions. As the boss says, Buddhist, Christian, Muslim, Hindu, we handle all religions here. Having come to terms with his father, if only after his death, Daigo later offers a rock letter to his unborn child within Mika, just as his father had done to him.

2. Buddhist Themes

Okuribito is loosely based on the book *Nōkanfu nikki*, published under the English title *Coffinman: The Journal of a Buddhist Mortician*. The book is the diary of the "encoffiner" or mortician Shinmon Aoki, from the snowy northern part of the large island of Honshu. We learn through the book that the majority of the people in this area are believers in **Shin Buddhism**. Yamagata prefecture also has one of the older populations in Japan, underscoring the importance of funeral services. Today, Shin is the most popular form of Buddhism in Japan. It is a devotional type of Buddhism concerned with a person's salvation in Pure Land heaven after earthly death. The book deals with deaths in the Shin community, focusing on related beliefs and customs. The opening scene in the film shows headlights approaching in falling snow. This is repeated later in the movie. Likewise, the first chapter in the book is called "Sleet." It makes clear the connection between the cold climate and death. It links the light we see in life, the light of **Amida** Buddha, and the light people report seeing at death, those who have been revived in a hospital, for example. It relates the white of snow and light to purity, the Pure Land, and the white death robe placed on a corpse. In this way, layers of symbolism appear in the book and somewhat in the film, particularly in relation to Shin Buddhism. The Japanese pronunciation of the name "Amida" is derived from the Sanskrit *Amitābha*, meaning "Infinite Light."

Devotional Buddhism existed in Japan long before it became the two large and distinctive traditions there today, the Pure Land Tradition (Jōdoshū) and the True Pure Land Tradition (Jōdo Shinshū). In the Nara (710 to 794 CE) and Heian (794 to 1185) periods, repeating the name of the savior Buddha Amida was sometimes practiced with emphasis on the number of repetitions. According to the belief, the more times the faithful called on Amida, the more likely they were to be taken to paradise after death. However, the powerful established Buddhist traditions considered this a lesser practice that, although legitimate, was most suitable for those of inferior ability. After the periods of aristocratic rule with corresponding court priests, battles erupted around the country. The strongest warrior leaders gained control of the nation and the political center shifted from Kyoto to Kamakura. In the new unstable climate, Japanese people became convinced the world had entered *mappō*, the degenerative age of Buddhism when people could no longer understand the ideas of the Buddha, much less put them into practice for overcoming suffering. All that seemed to remain was prayer and faith that Amida would take individuals to the Pure Land after death.

Historians have divided Japanese Buddhist traditions into two broad groups. Those that advocate meditation, the study of sūtras, or engagement in other practices for awakening are classified as traditions of *jiriki*, self-power. Those that focus on devotion to a savior practice the traditions of *tariki*, other-power. The other-power in the case of Shin is that of the Buddha Amida. Although it may seem at first glance that this defies the spirit of Buddhism, Shin Buddhists point out that belief in one's own power is egotistical. If Buddhists truly want to destroy the ego, they must give up the notion that it is powerful and capable of salvation. In the book and film we find repeated emphasis on giving up the false idea that we are in control of our destinies. We first see this in the way Daigo rather accidentally stumbles into his job. He is drawn to the cryptic newspaper ad, answering it without knowing what it entails. The boss takes his résumé and tosses it aside without reading it. Without an interview he is told abruptly he is hired, with the explanation that the boss uses his intuition on such matters. Later the boss says encoffining is Daigo's fate. Daigo does not know why he is drawn to it. He is physically repulsed by the job and vomits. Yet, when people ask him to quit, he refuses, even though it means social rejection and separation from his wife. The boss speaks as if he knows what will happen in advance, asking if his wife has returned *yet*. There is a mystical element in the character of the boss. It appears that he has developed an ability to understand the direction of fate, which is, after all, ultimately toward death. In the book Mr. Aoki explains that death and life are not separate, as modern people typically think. Instead, he speaks of a continuum he calls LifeDeath. Many years ago, the boss too was strangely drawn to the job and suffered socially in the same ways. However, the years have given him a special insight into the nature of reality. We see his abilities when Daigo is struggling with his misgivings. Planning to walk away from the job, he wanders in a rocky field by a river. Unexpectedly, the boss drives on the road next to him and calls out. Daigo cannot believe the boss has found him by chance and asks if it is another coincidence that he is passing by. The boss responds it is fate. In the book the two male characters are not a boss and his employee. Instead, Mr. Aoki speaks from the perspective of having done the job for decades, describing also his early experiences and social rejections. This corresponds to the feeling in the film that the older boss reflects the fate of the younger Daigo. This may be one way the boss knows so much about Daigo's fate. It can be seen also as a reference to **karmic affinity**, connections we have with certain other individuals due to connections in past lives. For Shin Buddhists, letting go of attachment to the ego by giving oneself up to fate is key. They believe our actions in life are largely guided by past karma that determines the direction of our lives to a large degree. Early in the film Daigo remembers his wedding vows and his plans to travel the world with his music career. He begins to realize dreams do not turn out as planned, that life is beyond our control. This is the outlook of Shin. At the end of our earthly lives, however, Shin says we will be taken to paradise by Amida Buddha, to whom we should now express gratitude for doing so.

Scholars have debated the origin and meaning of the belief in Amida and the Pure Land, tracing it from India, through China, into Korea and Japan. The first major figure to promote this type of devotional Buddhism in Japan was **Hōnen** (1133–1212 CE), founder of the Pure Land Tradition in that country. The decline of aristocratic culture saw a corresponding loss of interest in Buddhist doctrine, unwieldy rituals, and corrupt priests. This was replaced by a growing emphasis on direct experience and simple faith. From an early age, Hōnen studied **Tendai** Buddhism, a meditative and ritualistic tradition popular in earlier times. But eventually Hōnen decided that he was not seeking awakening but salvation by Amida in the Pure Land. He taught that this could be achieved by a mystical process initiated by invoking the name of Amida. The believer should wholeheartedly repeat the phrase "*Namu Amida Butsu*" ("Praise be Amida Buddha"), known as the *nembutsu*. The primary scriptural source for information on Amida is the *Larger Sūtra of Immeasurable Life*. According to this sūtra, Amida lived in the distant past as a Bodhisattva named Dharmakāra. As a Bodhisattva, he took 48 vows, including one to save all sentient beings from suffering. Because of his merit, he was able to manifest the Pure Land to which he would transport individuals during the age of *mappō,* when people could not awaken by their own power. It may be that Amida's paradise was first conceived not as a final Pure Land, but as a land of purification where one could temporarily live away from the degenerate world in order to work toward nirvāṇa. That is, after death, one would first go to the Pure Land and later reach nirvāṇa. As time went on, this view perhaps did not seem inclusive enough for *nembutsu* practitioners and the Pure Land came to be thought of as a place of immediate salvation for all people. This paradise is thought of as existing in the western quadrant of the heavens, which is also considered the direction souls go after death in Chinese **Daoism** and other folk traditions, possibly because it is where the sun sets, marking its symbolic death at the end of each day.

In Hōnen's time, repeating the *nembutsu* gained popularity among ordinary people outside of temples. This annoyed the priests of the established temples in Kyoto, who pressured the government to ban the practice and banish Hōnen from the capital. Although Hōnen did not attempt to build temples or organize follow-ers, his ideas continued to gain popularity. After his death, Pure Land Buddhists continued to be persecuted but this only seems to have strengthened their faith. People gave money to build statues of Amida and sub-groups developed. Today, many visitors to Japan visit the large statue of a Buddha in Kamakura. Although tourists may not realize it, the large Buddha does not represent the historical Buddha Siddhārtha Gautama, but the more popular Amida.

Hōnen's most influential follower was **Shinran** (1173–1263), the founder of Jōdo Shinshū, "the True Pure Land Tradition," also called Shin or Shin Buddhism. Whereas Hōnen taught that a person should repeat the *nembutsu* endlessly as a way to call on the savior Buddha, Shinran believed it should be repeated as thanks to Amida, who inevitably saves all people due to his vow to do so. Taking the belief to its logical extreme, Shinran taught that an individual's deeds and past misdeeds have nothing to do with going to the Pure Land since Amida vowed to save all sentient beings. Hōnen had said "even a bad man will be saved, how much more a good man!" But since Amida vowed to save those who most need it, Shinran turned Hōnen's words around saying, "even a good man will be saved, how much more a bad man!" Hōnen and Shinran agreed that people are naturally inclined to do evil and, given the opportunity, even a person considered good will do so.

Shinran married and had children. Although the Buddha left home and monks in other countries remained celibate, priests maintaining families became normal in later Japanese tradition. After all, this is considered to be the age of *mappō,* when people cannot understand the Dharma or practice it. Many priests in Japan do not shave their heads nor do they follow vegetarian diets as is the practice in other countries. Also in Japan, Buddhist priests became responsible for performing funerals because the other major religion of the country, **Shintō**, considers death impure and life pure. This is a strong folk tradition that remains a taboo today. The ancient Shintō record, the *Kojiki*, depicts this situation in the death of the female creator *kami*, spirit-being. In disbelief that she could have died, the male creator *kami* journeys to the land of the dead, which is underground, to bring his partner back to the earth's surface. Discovering her in a putrefied condition he is horrified. He runs out of the opening in the earth and seals it off. He proceeds to wash himself of death and in his act of cleansing he creates the Sun *kami*, Amaterasu, progenitor of the imperial family of Japan. In *Okuribito*, Daigo also attempts to wash off the stench of death, vigorously scrubbing his skin and rinsing his nostrils. Schoolgirls, representatives of the youth culture unconcerned with death, are seated on a bus across the aisle from him after he has touched a decaying corpse. Even at that distance they smell the unfamiliar odor of decay. A famous saying in Japan holds that Japanese people are born Shintō and die Buddhist. This is because Shintō priests perform birth rites while Buddhists handle funerals. We should wonder too if the name "Mika" is used to imply *miko*, a Shintō shamaness. The ordinary Japanese name "Mika" means "beautiful smell," which also contrasts with decay.

One influence of Buddhism, possibly mixing with Shintō is that most homes in Japan have an ancestral shrine called a **butsudan**, Buddha Altar, where people can pray, burn incense, and place fruits for the benefit of the spirits of deceased family members. At funerals in the film we sometimes see the corpse in front of a *butsudan* containing a Buddha image and a picture of the deceased. Incense is sometimes burned so the spirit can follow the smoke up towards the Pure Land. Chopsticks are stuck straight up in a bowl of rice for the departing, not to be eaten by the living. In Japan today, it is taboo to leave chopsticks sticking in a bowl when eating, for example, while drinking water or eating another dish. Another influence of Buddhism in regard to the dead in Japan is the popular **Obon** festival, held once a year when spirits are said to return to the villages of their previous homes. This is an ancient Buddhist observance from India that has developed in Japan as an occasion for family reunions. Over time, many aspects of Buddhism and Shintō blended together in Japan and some people identify Shintō *kami* as emanations of buddhas or Bodhisattvas.

The name "Daigo" is used in Buddhism to mean "ghee," the most pure part of clarified butter. In Buddhism this is a metaphor for the most sublime form of the Buddhist teachings. For example, according to the Japanese Zen Buddhist Dōgen (1200–1252 CE) in the chapter titled "*Daigo*" in his famous book *Treasury of the True Dharma Eye* (**Shōbōgenzō**), when practitioners of Zen meditation attain *daigo* ("great realization" or "awakening") they have risen above the discrimination between delusion and enlightenment. *Daigo* can also mean "nirvaṇa," Buddha Nature, Buddhist truth, or flawless personal character. In the film, Daigo is coming to realize his nature, which in its original essence is flawless. It is this nature from which we come and after the dramas of life, to which we return in death.

To see this is to go beyond the discriminating judgment that people are good or bad—for example, Daigo's father. As Daigo's coworker indicates, people become caught up in situations and feel helpless to change the course of events in their lives. However, this does not alter the core truth of Buddha Nature underlying all sentient beings. It is Buddha Nature that glows within all living things and shines as the light of Amida Buddha. In the book, Mr. Aoki describes events during which he became aware of this light. The film scene in which Daigo smells the badly decayed corpse draws from the actual experience of the author. In addition, Mr. Aoki witnessed maggots on the corpse and all around on the floor. Just as he was becoming ill at the sight, he noticed a glow coming from one of the maggots. This became a profound religious experience for him. Mr. Aoki began research-ing across cultures and times, finding reports from individuals who had reported seeing a light at the time of death. He quotes dying poets who speak of this. He also points out that people who have been revived after dying in a hospital often report having heard or somehow intuited the words "walk towards the light." A similar description is given in the *Tibetan Book of the Dead* of Tibetan Buddhism, although not referenced by Mr. Aoki. According to that book, after death, human consciousness travels through three in-between or *bardo* states. In the first, we see a light. If we walk toward the light, we will not suffer rebirth in the world. If we do not walk toward the light we go on to the next *bardo* state, where we find other tests. Because of the frequency of reports of the light, this has entered American pop culture and is found in novels, television shows, and films. For example, the television series and later film *Dead Like Me* (2009) is about a girl (Ellen Muth) who is killed and afterward is in an in-between state working as a grim reaper. Her job is to offer people the light. If the recently deceased accept the light they go beyond it. Neither she nor the viewing audience knows what is beyond the light. In Shin Buddhism the light is the Buddha Amida and is shared by all living beings. Accordingly, going toward the light at death is going to the Pure Land.

The opening sequence of *Departures* sets the stage for the interrelatedness of presumed opposites, a motif leading the viewer to the conclusion that death is intimately connected with life. We see the interrelationship of presumed opposites in the ongoing interplay of seriousness-humor and male-female dynamics, begin-ning with the deceased woman with male genitals. In another seemingly serious moment, when Daigo is talking about how much money he owes on his cello, the octopus comes alive. Through such scenes, the film proves not to be a traditional comedy. Instead it uses comedy as a contrast to seriousness so that viewers come to understand that many things that are considered opposites in life are really on a natural continuum. The octopus is both grotesque and strangely funny in its struggle to live. The ordinary thing to do might have been to kill it and eat it. There is much talk in the film about how we must kill and eat living things to survive. According to Shin belief, this makes us naturally defiled and only a super-natural Bodhisattva would be able to live without killing. This is more indication that we cannot rely on our own power for salvation. Instead of taking the natural path, Daigo and Mika throw the octopus into a river in hopes it will continue to live. But there is nothing they can do to sustain it, for as the Buddha taught, all things are subject to decay and death. The octopus floats lifelessly before them, vaguely resembling a human body. The camera shoots from below, as if from death, moving toward Daigo's disappointed face. He comments, "I think I'll quit," which signifies his larger decision to give up the struggle against fate and instead allow himself to be taken away in the current like the octopus. This is in keeping with the attitude of Shin.

We see this motif repeated in the metaphor of the cello. Playing with the orchestra and losing his job, Daigo comments that he should have acknowledged there is just so far a person of limited talents can go. This speaks directly to the idea that in the age of *mappō* we cannot rely on our own abilities. But even outside the theory of *mappō*, Buddhists such as the famous Indian philosopher Nāgārjuna (*c.* 150–250 CE) have explained that belief in the power of the ego-self to save an individual is the very ignorance the Buddha warned against. According to Shin, salvation is manifested to those who are most alienated and aware of their own profound shortcomings. This describes Daigo when he realizes the limits of his talents. He says he is think-ing of giving up. For Shin Buddhism, this is exactly what we *should* do. According to Shinran, we should stop making efforts and start living spontaneously and naturally.

Daigo's shortcomings as a cellist contrast with his extraordinary talent for pre-paring corpses. About the expensive cello he says it was too heavy for him in many ways. As long as we continue to struggle with the burdens of life, we will suffer. This was expressed by the Buddha in his Four Noble Truths. In Shin Buddhism this is also true in reference to continuing to believe that salvation can come through the actions of the ego-self. Daigo sells his cello and says he immediately feels a great burden has been taken off him. When he returns to his hometown he plays the smaller and symbolically lighter cello he had as a boy. It fits into grooves on the floor in his house, just as he fits better in his hometown. Later he watches salmon in their life struggle, attempting to return to where they were born, only to die trying. Daigo asks an old man why they would do such a thing. The man replies it is that important to them. Daigo is about to learn the importance of coming to terms with death, even when it means struggling against the stream of social taboos. Likewise, he has returned to his hometown to learn about death before his father dies and to understand his own mortality. Daigo holding the cello is analogous to him holding a dead body, which is shaped similarly. His art, playing the cello, is like the art he performs on bodies. Similarly, when Daigo's hands are shown moving the hands of the dead, there is in intertwining of life and death.

In the book, Mr. Aoki explains that he is a failed poet. This becomes a failed cellist for the protagonist in the film, perhaps because a musical score is a better or at least a more conventional motif for a film. This is also true in the classic film *Dr. Zhivago* (1965), wherein mystical moments experienced by the poet are expressed through music. The poets Mr. Aoki quotes have a special ability to see the light even before death, likely due to the same sensibility that has drawn them to poetry. Mr. Aoki shares this ability, even as a professed failed poet. In the film, Daigo's music is woven through the soundtrack into scenes of light, snow, and death. But not only does his small cello connect him with death and corpses, it is also analogous to his unborn child as well as himself as a child. These associations, interrelating seeming opposites, all go to express the idea of the continuum of LifeDeath.

After Daigo tells about his father leaving him, abandonment and devotion become major themes in the film. We see this, for example, when he sticks to his job in the face of derision, when his wife leaves him and returns, and when he resolves to see his dead father. The displays of indecision and resolve are analogous to the path leading to devotion in Shin. As the story unfolds, there are indications that Daigo's father continued to care about him and that he did not live with another woman chosen above his mother as assumed. This points to the idea that we cannot really know the heart of another person, which can be expressed only vaguely like the shape of rocks. In fact, Daigo's father seems to have been a lot like him. The house his mother had left him was also a snack bar called "Concerto" and was filled with vinyl records of classical music Daigo loves.

In the training video, Daigo and the boss sit in front of a Buddhist altar, containing a painting of Amida Buddha and his retinue of Bodhisattvas that will lead one to the Pure Land. Participating in the video serves as training to Daigo in several ways. He is experiencing how the body is washed before he has to do it to an actual corpse. He is also experiencing the position of the dead and sympathizing in a strange, new way. In the training video, the boss explains the Buddhist significance of how he treats the corpse: "Cleaning symbolizes the ridding of the world's fatigue, pain, and lust and also symbolizes the first bath for a new birth." The dead person then symbolically becomes clergy in preparation for entry into the Pure Land. The encoffiner simulates the tonsure by shaving the forehead and face of the corpse. The body is dressed in robes, and a Buddhist rosary (called a *nenju* in Japan and a *mala* in India) is placed in the hands. The arms are moved as if in prayer with the rosary.

In contrast to the shot from below when Daigo says, "I think I'll quit," as he watches the dead octopus taken by the current, later there is a shot from above looking down on him when he thinks he'll quit his new job. The classical film shot from above typically indicates the smallness of humanity from the point of view of God, as seen in such films as *High Noon* when the sheriff (Gary Cooper) appears to be doomed. In this case it shows the futility in Daigo's attempt to go back on his original resolve to quit, the opposite of the shot from below when he first decided to do so. We look down on him as from the God-like view of nature but also as from the upstairs view of the boss. The boss first appears at the time in Daigo's life when he needs a Bodhisattva's guidance, the time when he realizes his shortcomings and is in most need of salvation. The boss is a transformed person who can help Daigo and others in their transformations. In Shin, transforming one's life by living spontaneously as the boss has done by becoming a mortician, leads to living as a helper to others. In this way, other-power is manifested in the individual. It flows in two directions: inwardly from the other into the individual, and outwardly from the individual to others who need help. By becoming a mortician, Daigo also receives other-power in his life and sends out other-power by helping families and individuals. The fictional character of Daigo and the film-makers also help the viewing audience overcome the denial of death. That we must recognize the fact of our mortality is an important message of the Buddha. It is believed to lead to awakening. Many Buddhists have included contemplation of dead bodies as a part of their meditative practice. Even in disregard for social customs, the film and personal revelation it affords also may help us acknowledge the dignity others deserve in life and death.

Visitors to Kyoto are likely to see the two large temples of modern True Pure Land Tradition (Jōdo Shinshū) near Kyoto Station. These are the Western Temple of the Original Vow (Nishi Honganji) and the Eastern Temple of the Original Vow (Higashi Honganji). These temples played important roles in Japanese history. They survived attacks by warrior monks of the rival Tendai sect three times, by the warlord Oda Nobunaga (1534–1582 CE) and by the Shogun Tokugawa Ieyasu (1543–1616 CE), who split the original temple into the present-day two temples. The branch associated with the Eastern Temple is the largest within Jōdo Shinshū today. In America, a statue of Shinran that survived the atomic bomb dropped on Hiroshima can be seen on the Upper West Side of Manhattan. It is on Riverside Drive between 105th and 106th Streets, in front of the New York Buddhist Church, the largest of the overseas branches of Jōdo Shinshū.

As for *Departures*, although the film-maker was concerned about how his taboo topic mixed with humor would be accepted in Japan, it won numerous awards there. It also received the 2009 Academy Award for Best Foreign Language Film. The book *Coffinman: The Journal of a Buddhist Mortician* sold out after the success of the film, went into reprint, and is available in English translation.

Further Reading

Aoki Shinmon. *Coffinman: The Journal of a Buddhist Mortician*. Anaheim, CA: Buddhist Education Center, 2002.

Buddhaghosa, Bhadantācriya. *Visuddhimagga, the Path of Purification*. Seattle: BPS Pariyatti Editions, 1999.

Numata Center for Buddhist Translation. *The Three Pure Land Sutras: The Larger Sutra on Amitayus* [Taisho 360]; *The Sutra on Contemplation of Amitayus* [Taisho 365]; *The Smaller Sutra on Amitayus* [Taisho 366]. Berkeley: Numata Center for Buddhist Translation and Research, 2003.

Andreasen, Esben. *Popular Buddhism in Japan: Shin Buddhist Religion and Culture*. Honolulu: University of Hawaii Press, 1997.

Further Viewing

Shinran-sama: Negai*, *Soshite Hikari (*His Wish and Light*) (Group Tac, Japan, 2008). An animated film about the life of Shinran, founder of the Jōdo Shinshū tradition of Japanese Buddhism. Japanese with English subtitles.

The Taste of Tea (Japanese title: *Cha no aji*) (Katsuhito Ishii, Japan, 2004). A surrealistic comedy with Buddhist overtones. Japanese with English subtitles.

After Life (Japanese title: *Wandāfuru raifu*) (Hirokazu Koreeda, Japan, 1998). A drama/fantasy film about people choosing one memory from their lives to relive after death for eternity. Japanese with English subtitles.

Note

1 Inadvertently or not, the "*dachi*" had been left out of *tabidachi* 旅立ち.

9

THE BUDDHIST ORDER OF NUNS

Windhorse

1. Basic Plot

Windhorse (Paul Wagner, USA, 1998) focuses on three members of a Tibetan family whose lives are changed in different ways by the Chinese occupation of their country. They are a man named Dorjee (Jampa Kelsang), his sister Dolkar (Dadon), and their cousin Pema (not credited in the film). The film opens with the three as children happily jumping rope and singing a children's folksong of innocence, as Tibet is portrayed before Chinese invasion. But this lifestyle will soon be changed as we see Chinese soldiers approaching and entering their house. There is the sound of a gun firing, and we later learn Dorjee and Dolkar's grandfather has been killed for hanging up a poster advocating a free Tibet. The next scene takes place years later. In this scene, the head nun at a nunnery is forced by Chinese soldiers to read a statement to the women there. The statement condemns the Dalai Lama, then living in exile in India, for allegedly being a counter-revolutionary. The statement further instructs the nuns to remove all photographs and other images of the Dalai Lama, and to never mention or even think of him again. As the head nun reads this proclamation, her students wipe tears streaming down their faces. Later we realize that Pema, now grown up, has become a nun and is among those crying.

We also see Dorjee grown up. Having become dejected by seeing his family and country suffer under Chinese control, he spends his time playing pool and getting drunk. A friend approaches him to ask if he will join a secret organization that seeks peaceful ways to oppose the Chinese. Dorjee yells that if they have bombs, he will join. Later, he sees his grandmother defying the government prohibition by displaying a picture of the Dalai Lama on her home altar. This may cause him to think about acts of peaceful resistance of the government.

In the middle of the night at the nunnery, Pema and her roommate, Dolma, wake up to the sound of army trucks arriving. Quickly, they rise from bed and hide their pictures of the Dalai Lama. It is unclear how the soldiers became aware the Dalai Lama was still being revered, but they harshly interrogate the nuns as a group. Having found a picture, they demand to know whose it is. A nun named Tsering steps forward. The soldiers tell Tsering to renounce her religious and political affinity with the Dalai Lama. She refuses and instead chants a prayer. A soldier strikes Tsering and she is taken away in the back of one of the trucks.

Later, Pema goes to Lhasa and listlessly wanders through the city's marketplace thinking of her friend. Suddenly she begins shouting "Tibet belongs to Tibetans!" and "Long live the Dalai Lama!" Soldiers quickly come and struggle to detain her. The commotion is captured on film by an American woman, Amy (played by the poet Taije Silverman), visiting as a tourist.

Meanwhile, Dorjee's sister Dolkar has been making a living by singing at a nightclub, mostly for the occupying Chinese. She has learned the Chinese language well and has a Chinese boyfriend, Duan-ping (Richard Chang), who helps her career by introducing her to a Chinese official, Mr. Du (Lu Yu). The official tells Dolkar to learn a number of patriotic Chinese songs that depict Tibetans as happy under their rule. One night, as she is singing these songs, her brother Dorjee happens to be at the club. Dorjee angrily shouts at her and storms out.

At this point in the film we have seen in one family three reactions to Chinese occupation. Pema joined the Buddhist order and openly defied government prohibitions, Dorjee remained aloft and sunk into despair, and Dolkar accepted the occupation and found a way to make a living within it.

Dorjee and Amy meet and begin a friendship. At her request, Dorjee accompanies Amy to Lhasa and shows her various aspects of the city. They see a large painting of Padmasambhava (eighth century CE), who is said to have introduced esoteric Buddhism to Tibet. They turn big prayer wheels and visit the ruins of Shide monastery. There, Dorjee explains that the powerful spirits of old Tibet had been damaged by the Chinese. It is likely that this is also affecting Dorjee's idea about how he should respond to the occupation. Amy tells Dorjee that she filmed a scuffle between soldiers and a nun. Dorjee becomes interested. We also see that he and Amy are being filmed by security cameras as they walk through the streets of Lhasa.

By arrangement of Dolkar's Chinese boyfriend and his connection, Mr. Du, she is scheduled to appear on national television to sing a pro-occupation song. Thinking she has succeeded as a folk singer, her family becomes excited and borrows a television for the event. As this is happening, the family receives a message from the police, instructing them to pick up Pema from Drapchi Prison. Going there, Dorjee finds her badly beaten and unconscious. A doctor is called to their home and the family learns she will likely die soon from head trauma. In her delirium, Pema calls out to the Dalai Lama for his mercy. The Dalai Lama is considered the Bodhisattva of compassion. Later, when she comes around a little more,

Pema sings the childhood song she and Dolkar had sung while jumping rope. The song recalls the innocence of Tibet before the invasion. In tears, Dolkar joins in the song, which stands in stark contrast to the contrived political message of the Chinese songs she had sung.

Moments before time for Dolkar to sing live on television, we can see her struggling with what she should do. As she is being cued to go on, she stares blankly and walks out of the studio. In the streets she cries, prays, and runs around a large spinning prayer wheel frantically. Meanwhile, Dorjee has also made a conversion. Deciding to try to smuggle information about Chinese torture and repression to India, he asks Amy to record Pema and her testimony about the treatment of nuns in prison. On film, Pema tells a story of brutal treatment at the hands of Chinese and Tibetan officials. Although the nuns had been beaten until they could not move, Pema says she sang a song of encouragement about the Dalai Lama because she was afraid her friend and former roommate Dolma was about to die. Hearing this, the Tibetan prison warden had her dragged to his office and hit her more. When Pema asked him to not speak badly about the Dalai Lama and to not let the Chinese cause conflict among Tibetans, he beat her until she was close to death. After recording this, Amy attempts to smuggle the tape out of the country but is detained at the airport. She had been identified as potentially subversive through the security cameras in Lhasa. Thus, in the movie, the camera can be used to expose repression or to perpetuate it. While Amy is permitted to leave, her tape is confiscated by the authorities.

2.   Buddhist Themes

A **Wind Horse** is a mythical creature that entered the art and imagination of Tibetan Buddhism from folklore. Legend says it carries on its back prayers to the ancient spirits of the earth and sky. A drawing of the Wind Horse sometimes appears on prayer flags. As the prayer flag blows in the wind it is said to be constantly reciting the prayers written on them. The film's narrator, Dorjee, explains that sheets of paper with prayers written on them may also be tossed in the wind to relay prayers to the spirits. By extension, a Wind Horse can be any vehicle that delivers messages of praise to the old gods of the world in this modern age of suffering and materialism, even the people portrayed in this film. In this way, the three main characters, as well as Amy and others, may be seen as Wind Horses, as the title implies. The film also serves as a kind of Wind Horse.

Windhorse won several awards, including the Best US Independent Film award at the 1998 Santa Barbara International Film Festival. Apparently, because of Chinese pressure on the US, the film was removed from consideration at the Hawaii International Film Festival.[1] The story came to director Paul Wagner through his niece Julia Elliot, who was detained by Chinese officials after filming a demonstration in Lhasa.[2] Ms. Elliot was a co-writer of the screenplay. Interestingly, in making *Windhorse*, Mr. Wagner repeated this twice by smuggling footage out of Tibet that he had shot. Most of the drama, however, was recreated outside of the country. Along with numerous others in the film, the actress who played Pema was not credited in the film, for her protection. While she is not actually a nun, she is a Tibetan refugee living in exile. Among others in the film who have experienced Chinese repression in Tibet is the notable singer and actress Dadon Dawadolma, who plays Dolkar. In her six albums recorded in Tibet, which combine popular and traditional folk music, she criticized the situation in her country. In 1992, she fled and received political asylum in the United States.[3]

In the film we find women as key movers in resistance to China, often through Buddhism. In many ways this mirrors the activities of women as nuns in the Buddhist *sangha* from the earliest times. The film has been criticized as a propaganda film, too simplistic for modern audiences.[4] It has also been called formulaic and "more of a human-rights treatise than a truly satisfying movie".[5] However, it can also be quite illuminating concerning women in Buddhism. For instance, Pema is depicted as beaten in Drapchi Prison located in Lhasa. A number of Tibetan refugees in exile have reported of the brutality experienced by nuns in Drapchi.[6] In 1994, 13 nuns were sent there for protesting in Lhasa. In 1996, the inmates, including 100 women, went on a hunger strike to protest violence in the prison. Just as with Pema, because of fear they would die in prison, they were released.

Tibetan nuns have been at the forefront of demonstrations for human rights, dignity, and freedom as they see it for over 50 years. Many of them have been arrested, tortured and publicly executed as a result of these efforts. Meanwhile, other women in Tibet have been forced to have abortions and have been sterilized by the Chinese. Many Tibetans believe the Chinese want Tibet without the Tibetan people. Tibetan sources estimate that since the Chinese invasion of 1950 more than a million people have been tortured, executed, or starved to death for demonstrating.

Since the invasion, China has been incorporating Tibet as a part of their country and modernizing it accordingly. This modernization has meant the destruction of some traditional ways considered of the utmost importance to Tibetan identity and life, including those preserved through Buddhism. Those who have objected have faced death or harsh punishments. From the Chinese perspective, the process has involved building hospitals and providing medicines to replace archaic shamanistic practices. In this way, they claim to have diminished rampant diseases that were spreading throughout the country when they first occupied it. They also say they brought running water, sewage facilities and electrical stations, schools that replaced solely monastic education, reduced taxes, reduced unemployment, and alleviated some of the extreme poverty.[7] To facilitate the annexation of Tibet, China at first allowed the Dalai Lama to remain spiritual leader and figurative political leader until 1959. At that time, realizing that remaining in Tibet would likely cost him his life and end the institution of Dalai Lamas, he fled to Dharmasala, India at his advisors' insistence. Since that time, he has called for Tibetans to not only realize the inevitability of the situation but to follow Buddhist principles by looking on the Chinese occupiers with compassion, even those who torture them. Today, some 20,000 Tibetans who have escaped Chinese persecution live in exile in Dharamasala, the home of the Tibetan government-in-exile. While monastic Tibetans, American political leaders, and many others have revered the Dalai Lama for the wisdom of his non-violent stance toward the Chinese, other Buddhists and individuals outside his tradition have severely criticized him for not leading an armed uprising.

The 1959 Tibetan uprising was a combination of non-violent protests and armed insurgence partly fueled by covert CIA operations. Three times during March 1959, large groups of women demonstrated just below the Potala Palace in Lhasa. The city was shelled and many of these women were arrested, tortured, and sentenced to long prison terms.[8] This included the leader of the 1959 women's demonstrations, Pamo Kusang, who in 1970 encouraged other inmates to demonstrate by shouting anti-Chinese slogans, just as Pema did in the film. For this she was seized, interrogated, and tortured. Though Pamo Kusang declared she alone was responsible, like Tsering in the film, her companions were brutally interrogated in front of other demonstrators. Because they refused to relent, they were executed in front of the public. Those seeing the women reported they hardly recognized them because of abuse.[9] Pamo Kusang herself was crippled and had lost her hearing in one ear, as well as her hair, which had probably been pulled out by the roots. Also like Pema in the film, another protester, Dhemo Chime, died after being released from prison.

Among the many cases of sexual assault in prison is that of Tsultrim Dolma. Pema and Dolma in the film may have been modeled after her, although there are many similar stories. Arrested in 1988 for demonstrating with other nuns and monks, she was beaten with electric prods and iron rods. On one such occasion she said to the torturer, "Many monks, nuns, and lay people have been arrested, but we know that Tibet belongs to the Tibetans. You say there is freedom of religion, but there is no genuine freedom!" Angered by this, the guard knocked her to the ground with an electric cattle prod. She describes the horrible events that followed:

> They shouted at me to stand, but I couldn't and so one pulled up my robe and the other man inserted the instrument into my vagina. The shock and the pain was horrible. He repeated this action several times and also struck other parts of my body. Later the others made me stand and hit me with sticks and kicked me. Several times I fell on the floor. They would again force the prod inside of me and pull me up to repeat the beatings.[10]

While *Windhorse* shows us harsh conditions imposed on nuns from outside of Buddhism, nuns have also struggled within Buddhist institutions from the earliest times. According to early accounts, the Buddha established the **Bhikkhuni Sangha** (the order of nuns) that exists to this day. Since that time, women in many parts of the world have taken Buddhist vows to become nuns, engaged in practice, attained realizations, and worked for peace and the wellbeing of the smaller and larger communities to which they belong. In many Buddhist texts and in actual circumstances throughout the history of Buddhist communities around the world, women have often been afforded a lower status compared to men. It is possible that this attitude did not come from early Buddhist doctrine but from Indian society. Nevertheless, in numerous later Buddhist *sūtras* and commentaries, women are described as inferior, temptresses, and the personifications of evil. The **Larger Pure Land Sūtras** and many other scriptures explain that in order to attain enlightenment, women must first "despise their female nature" and be reborn as men.[11] According to the most famous biography of the Buddha's life and enlightenment, the **Buddha-Karita** attributed to the Sanskrit poet Aśvaghoṣa (first century CE), the tempter Mara sends his three daughters to try and distract the Buddha-to-be from meditation.[12] These daughters are portrayed as the manifestation of Lust, Delight, and Thirst. They embody female seduction. The Buddha's rejection of these temptresses represents the monastic transcendence of the bonds of women.[13] Likewise, earlier in the text, when Siddhartha is preparing to leave his father's palace in order to seek enlightenment, he becomes surrounded by "a herd of females," some of whom "pressed him with their full firm bosoms in gentle collisions."[14] Such descriptions are common in Buddhist literatures and sermons from at least the first century CE onward. Rare exceptions can be found in scriptures composed later, such as the *Śrimaladevi Sūtra*, wherein a women attains Buddhahood without the necessity of first being reborn as a man.[15] Also, an early scripture in the *Dīghanikāya* has the disciple **Ānanda** asking the Buddha how he should behave towards a woman. The Buddha replies, "You should keep out of her sight." When Ānanda asks how he should behave if he is seen by a woman, the Buddha replies, "Do not speak to her."[16] From this we might guess there could never be interaction between Buddhist men and women, much less a *Bhikkhuni Sangha*, but this is not the case.

The *Bhikkhuni Sangha* is said to have been founded by the Buddha himself. The story of its beginning can be found in an early Buddhist writing in Pāli language, the *Cullavagga* of the **Vinaya Piṭaka**.[17] With few alterations, the story appears in all known *vinaya* collections of the world. In summary, the story is as follows. After Buddha's father King Suddhodana died, his stepmother, who was also his aunt named Mahāpajāpatī, went with 500 palace women before the Buddha in Kapilavatthu requesting permission to join the *sangha*. The Buddha replied, "Do not ask this." However, Mahāpajāpatī repeated her request three times. Each time the Buddha's response was the same: "Do not ask this." Probably because early Buddhism generally took a very liberal and anti-caste stance in relation to the Buddhist *sangha*, as attested to by numerous scriptures, those who heard his words in this case did not understand why the Buddha refused to admit the women to the *sangha*.

Later, the Buddha traveled to Vesali, which took many days to reach by walking. Meanwhile, Mahāpajāpatī and the 500 palace women shaved their heads and also walked to Vesali, showing their determination to be accepted in the *sangha* and to follow the Buddha. In Vesali, Mahāpajāpatī and the others sat crying with swollen and bleeding feet from walking so far. Ānanda, who was the Buddha's cousin, personal attendant, and disciple with a gift for perfect recollection, saw the women and asked them why they were crying. After hearing their story and seeing their determination, Ānanda went to the Buddha on their behalf, telling him Mahāpajāpatī and the others had come in hopes of being granted permission to join the *sangha*. Again, the Buddha said, "Do not ask this." But Ānanda felt compassion for the women and appealed in another way. He said Mahāpajāpatī was both the aunt and stepmother who had fed the Buddha as a baby with her own milk. The Buddha still did not comply. Surprised, and after having failed three times, Ānanda asked if the reason was that women do not have the same capacity as men to become enlightened. Here, however, the Buddha says this is not the reason. Afterward, Ānanda implored the Buddha to accept women into the sangha on the grounds that they could attain enlightenment and would be able to do so through monastic discipline, and since Mahāpajāpatī has been so kind to the Buddha.

At this point the Buddha gives in to Ānanda's request and says he will allow women to join the *sangha*,[18] but only if Mahāpajāpatī agrees to accept eight important rules. Mahāpajāpatī accepts the rules and thus the *Bhikkhuni Sangha* is born about seven or eight years after the *Bhikkhu Sangha* (order of monks) had been formed. Afterward, the Buddha is reported to have made another famous and much-quoted statement about the negative consequences of forming the *Bhikkhuni Sangha*. Had he not allowed women to join the *sangha*, the statement goes, the Buddhist Dharma would have lasted 1,000 years. However, since he did allow the foundation of the *Bhikkhuni Sangha* it would last only 500 years.

In this story we see many possible points of ambivalence in the Buddha's attitude towards women. Scholars and practitioners have analyzed these in various ways, sometimes emphasizing either the negative or positive aspects of this view of women in Buddhism in support of their own positions. For example, the story has been used in Thailand where no *Bhikkhuni Sangha* has ever been allowed to officially exist. Women who want to join the *sangha* are refused on the bases that the Buddha did not really want them to do so. In response, a separate group of female Buddhist devotees has emerged in and around temples. These women, who shave their heads and wear white robes in contrast with the yellow robes of the official monks, are known as *Mae Jis*.[19]

At the other end of the spectrum, the Japanese Buddhologist Kajiyama Yuichi argues that the Buddha's prediction that the life of the Dharma would be shortened due to the formation of the *Bhikkhuni Sangha* was a later addition to the original story, perhaps reflecting the attitudes of the monks who recorded the Buddhist regulatory texts (*vinaya*) in Sri Lanka some 400 years after the Buddha.

If so, by implication, the story works contrary to the Buddha's intent. According to Kajiyama, the story was added at a period of time when the newer ideas of Mahāyāna Buddhism were threatening to supplant those of early Indian Buddhism, some 500 years after the Buddha's life.[20]

There are also indications that the eight rules Mahāpajāpatī accepted in order to become a nun may have been added later. In fact, a number of the eight important rules seem to make no sense other than deferring to male members of the sangha. The first rule states a nun must always rise and bow when she comes into the presence of a monk. This applies even to a senior nun who encounters a monk who has only been in the *sangha* for one day. The second rule says nuns must spend the rainy season in a location where they can be supervised by monks. The third rule says monks will determine the dates for nuns to confess twice a month. The fourth rule stipulates that monks will be a part of the interrogation of nuns accused of digressions against the *vinaya*. However, the opposite case does not apply. Fifth, monks were to participate in deciding the punishment of a digressing nun, but the opposite again does not apply. According to the sixth rule, women should train themselves for two years before receiving ordination. At that time, monks must participate in the ordination of nuns, while there was no necessity for nuns to participate in male ordination. However, when the Buddha accepted Mahāpajāpatī as a *bhikkhuni*, there does not appear to be a probationary period of two years, during which time she had to prove herself worthy of ordination. Seventh, a nun could never criticize a monk but a monk may criticize a nun. Eighth, a nun could never officially admonish a monk, but a monk could officially admonish a nun.[21]

Later writings such as the thirteenth century *Pūjāvaliya* of Sri Lanka (Ceylon) record that the Buddha's reluctance to accept women into the *sangha* and his prediction about the shortened life of the Dharma resulted from his feeling that women are fickle by nature.[22] In an even stronger statement, the academically influential late nineteenth century European Buddhologist Monier-Williams states in relation to this story, "Clearly the Buddha was originally a misogynist as well as a misogamist, and wished his followers to be misogynists also."[23] In contradistinction, a number of self-identified feminist Buddhist scholars have offered alternative explanations as speculation about why the Buddha may have hesitated to form a *Bhikkhuni Sangha*, if he in fact was hesitant.[24] It is first pointed out that the hesitancy was never related to a women's potential for enlightenment. Instead, the Buddha may have worried about the harsh conditions his aunt and other women would encounter as nuns. After all, in the story they were found crying with swollen feet. In addition, begging for food in the villages, they would sometimes receive very little for sustenance. It may have been painful to imagine the elderly queen Mahāpajāpatī and 500 palace women begging for alms in the streets. Likewise, since there were no monasteries at the time, living in the forests and caves would be difficult, perhaps especially so for those used to palace pampering.

Confucians in East Asia would later severely criticize Buddhism for destroying
the family. Early Buddhists heard similar criticisms directed toward the Buddha's
abandonment of his wife and children. The Buddha's decision to accept 500 women
into the *sangha* can be interpreted as destroying 500 families or potential families.
It is possible that the Buddha considered such issues. Interestingly, in this respect,
there is no mention that women had to sever ties with their families during the
two years of prescribed probation in preparation for ordination, nor does the consideration of broken families seem to be applied to men.

After the two-year probationary period, at the time of examination to receive
full ordination as a *bhikkhuni*, the aspirant is asked a series of questions specified in
the *vinaya*. These include:

> Are you a human being? Are you a woman? Are you a free woman? Are
> you without debt? Are you free from royal service? Have you received the
> consent of your parents and husband? Have you completed twenty years of
> age? Do you have a bowl and robes? What is your name? What is the name
> for your woman-proposer [that is, the *bhikkhuni* who recommends you]?[25]

Some feel there was no ordination of *sangha* members during the lifetime of the
Buddha. Joining the *sangha* was simply called "Going forth," that is, giving up
family life and living as a mendicant while following the Buddha's teachings. At
that time, when the Buddha's followers lived in the forests and caves, there may
also have been no real division in terms of a *Bhikkhu Sangha* and a *Bhikkhuni
Sangha*. Accordingly, this division developed as the Buddhist community began to
dwell in permanent structures. At some point while the Buddha was still alive, the
Buddhist community grew large and new aspirants were asked to recite the "refuge formula" three times in order to become full members of the *sangha*: "I take
refuge in the Buddha; I take refuge in the Dharma; I take refuge in the *sangha*." It
was around the time of the **First Council** that the community rules known as
the **pratimoksha** (Sanskrit: *prātimokśa*) were recorded, expanding the qualifications
for becoming a fully ordained member of the Buddhist *sangha*.[26]

According to legend and early records, the First Council met sometime
between a few days to three months after the Buddha's *parinirvana*. At that time,
500 *bhikkhus* gathered to recite the Buddha's teachings. It seems logical that
female followers would have also attended, but if so, this has been omitted from
the records. Before the recitation began, some of the *bhikkhus* reprimanded
Ānanda for what they said were eight mistakes he had made during the lifetime
of the Buddha, and they demanded that he confess to these and repent. Among
the offenses was that he had introduced women into the *sangha*. There is no indication that while the Buddha was alive some monks objected to his allowing
women in the *sangha*. Apparently, however, the Indian conservative backlash followed immediately afterward. Ānanda is reported to have responded that he did
not see it as a mistake, nor had he violated a precept in so doing. However, seeing

that the community was on the verge of sectarian splits and trying to keep the followers united, he agreed to confess. Soon afterward, the *pratimoksha* was written, recording the rules for the *sangha*. While there are 227 such rules recorded there for *bhikkhus*, those for *Bhikkhunis* are more stringent and number 331.

Regardless of the biases against them, there are numerous stories from many countries about *Bhikkhunis* who attained arhatship. A collection of such stories has been preserved from early Indian Buddhism in a writing known as the *Therīgāthā*. The text, attributed to women authors, relates struggles faced by *Bhikkhunis* in their quests for and attainment of enlightenment. However, the *Therīgāthā* maintains the view that the female body is particularly impure. It should be meditated upon as a putrefying corpse discarded in a cemetery.[27]

As we see exemplified in *Windhorse*, today nuns and other Buddhist women are determined to find ways to help improve society and lighten the burden of oppressed people. Attuned to the Buddhist path in right livelihood, some have worked in secular positions such as that of psychologists, helping women and children who have been hurt or marginalized.[28] Others have voiced the idea that nuns can improve the world by setting living examples of unpretentiousness and being in accord with the principle of *ahimsa*, non-hurting. Likewise, it has been suggested that nuns can and have helped with problems regarding abortion, prostitution, menopause, and other issues that women prefer to discuss with other women. They have also helped unwed mothers. Buddhist women in Thailand recently opened a home for women with unwanted pregnancies.[29]

In regards to academics and scriptural studies, today a number of Buddhist women and other Buddhologists are reexamining classical interpretations of Buddhist texts. They are publishing findings they consider examples of misogyny and those honoring the Buddhist practices of women. Some have suggested the need for a new, feminist reading of history and a "reconstruction of Buddhism" accordingly.[30] According to some, this undertaking repairs the Buddhist tradition, which has been damaged internally by its patriarchal forms. Some Buddhist women see it as their task to restore the fundamental values of Buddhism as well as restructure it in terms of feminism.[31]

In many places in the world, the *Bhikkhuni Sangha* is being restored or appearing for the first time in history. There is today a feeling the *Bhikkhuni Sangha* has great potential for producing an atmosphere conducive to bring women Buddhist attainment and that a ripple effect is attracting women to Buddhism throughout the world.[32]

Further Reading

Blackstone, Kathryn R. *Women in the Footsteps of the Buddha*. Great Britain: Curzon, 1998.

Dresser, Marianne (ed.). *Buddhist Women on the Edge*. Berkeley: North Atlantic Books, 1996.

Gross, Rita M. *Buddhism After Patriarchy, A Feminist History, Analysis, and Reconstruction of Buddhism*. New York: SUNY Press, 1993.

Kajiyama, Yuichi. "Women in Buddhism," *The Eastern Buddhist,* 15:2, 53–70, Autumn 1982.
Kabilsingh, Chatsumarn. *Thai Women in Buddhism.* Berkeley: Parallax Press, 1991.
Thubten Chodron (ed.). *Blossoms of the Dharma: Living as a Buddhist Nun.* Berkeley: North Atlantic Books, 2000.

Further Viewing

Come, Come, Come, Upward **directed by Kwon-taek Im, Korea, 1989** Korean title: *Aje aje bara aje.* This film depicts a woman struggling to become a nun while being condemned by the *Bhikkhuni Sangha* itself, sometimes rightly and sometimes wrongly. She is told by her teacher, the head nun of the nunnery, that in order to experience the truth of the world she must give up her own ambitions and completely sacrifice herself for other beings. To her astonishment and that of all involved, the opportunity comes when after saving an alcoholic man from suicide, he insists on her becoming his wife under the threat of killing himself. After repeated visits by the man to the nunnery to plead with her, she is punished by the head nun with the penitence of performing 10,000 prostrations before a Buddha image.[33] Some of the nuns are suspicious of her motives in saving the man. Others wrongly believe she has been physically involved with him. When the man continues to stalk her, she is expelled from the order and chastised by her formerly fellow nuns.

Satya: A Prayer for the Enemy **(USA),** A 28-minute documentary directed by Ellen Bruno about the torture and abuse of Tibetan nuns, 1995.[34]

Bhikkhuni: Revival of the Women's Order. A documentary about discrimination and the quest for gender equality in Buddhism, directed by Wiriya Sati and still in progress.[35]

The Women's Meditation Tradition in Tibet, A 62-minute lecture by the Venerable Wangdrak Rinpoche, June 11, 2010, sponsored by Google Tech Talks.[36]

BLESSINGS: The Tsoknyi Nangchen Nuns of Tibet **(USA)** is a 90-minute documentary directed by Victress Hitchcock and narrated by Richard Gere about 3,000 women who practice an ancient yogic tradition in nunneries and hermitages. Chariot Videos, 2009.

Notes

1 http://www.indiewire.com/article/windhorse_yanked_from_hawaii_fest_by_director, accessed 8/19/12.
2 http://weeklywire.com/ww/04-26-99/alibi_film1.html, accessed 8/19/12.
3 In 2001, Dadon composed the soundtrack for the film *Samsara*, directed by Pan Nalin. In 2006, she narrated *Vajra Sky Over Tibet*, a documentary by John Bush.
4 See "The Tibetan Propaganda Film 'Windhorse' is Half Tourist Brochure, Half Political Pamphlet," by Richard von Busack, http://www.metroactive.com/papers/metro/03.11.99/windhorse-9910.html, accessed 8/19/12.
5 http://buddhisttorrents.blogspot.com/2008/04/windhorse-1998.html, accessed 8/19/12.
6 See "Testimony Given by Passang Lhamo, Tibetan Nun and Former Political Prisoner, to the US Congressional Human Rights Caucus," May 1, 2002 in Washington, DC at http://web.archive.org/web/20070819034526/http://www.tibet.com/NewsRoom/drapchipassang.htm, accessed 8/19/12.
7 Felix Greene, *A Curtain of Ignorance.* The Dalai Lama has said Felix Greene, who reported this, changed his attitude in the 1970s after visiting him in India. See http://www.dalailama.com/news/post/535-his-holiness-the-dalai-lama-in-new-york-ny—may-22-2010, accessed 8/19/12.

8 See an account of the history of nuns and other Tibetan women in struggles against Chinese occupation at http://www.tibetjustice.org/reports/women/women.html, accessed 8/19/12.

9 *Ibid.*

10 Interviews conducted by Tibetan Centre for Human Rights and Democracy (TCHRD) reveal many such incidences of extreme sexual violence against nuns. This one is documented at http://web.archive.org/web/20120602214553/http://www.tchrd.org/report/topicalreport/Fearless%20Voices_1998.pdf, accessed 8/19/12.

11 Max Müller (trans.), "The Larger Sukhāvatī-vyūha," in E.B. Cowell (ed.), *Buddhist Mahāyāna Texts*, p. 19.

12 Aśvaghoṣa. "The Buddha-Karita of Asvaghosha," in E.B. Cowell (ed.), *Buddhist Mahāyāna Texts*, p. 136.

13 Diana Y., Paul *Women in Buddhism*, p. 7.

14 Aśvaghoṣa, "The Buddha-Karita of Asvaghosha," p. 40.

15 See *The Lion's Roar of Queen Śrimala*, Alex Wayman and Hideko Wayman (trans.).

16 Lamotte, Étienne, *History of Indian Buddhism, from the Origins to the Śaka Era*, p. 61.

17 I.B. Horner (trans.), *The Book of the Discipline*, pp. 352–7.

18 This may be the only time in scriptures where the Buddha is defeated in an argument or changes his mind, if we are to interpret the story this way.

19 For a description and discussion of *Mae Jis*, see Chatsumarn Kabilsingh, *Thai Women in Buddhism*, pp. 36–44.

20 Also see Rita M. Gross, *Buddhism After Patriarchy: A Feminist History, Analysis, and Reconstruction of Buddhism*, p. 33, and Kabilsingh, pp. 26–7.

21 Gross, pp. 36.

22 G.P. Malalasekera (ed.), *Encyclopaedia of Buddhism* III, p. 44.

23 M. Monier-Williams, *Buddhism*, p. 86.

24 Gross, pp. 34–5.

25 Quoted from the *vinaya* in Malalasekera (ed.), III, p. 45.

26 Robert E. Buswell Jr. (ed.), *Encyclopedia of Buddhism*, p. 741.

27 The *Visuddhimagga* also prescribes meditation on the female body as a decomposing corpse discarded in a cemetery. Although the whole Pāli canon is typically dated to the first century BCE, the earliest the *Therīgāthā* can currently be traced is through a mention of it by Dhammapāla in the fifth century CE. The *Visuddhimagga* was also composed in the fifth century CE by Dhammapāla's contemporary, Buddhaghosa.

28 See Anita Borrows' article, "The Light of Outrage: Women, Anger, and Buddhist Practice."

29 See "The History of the Bhikkhuni Sangha" by Chatsumarn Kabilsingh, in Thubten Chodron's *Blossoms of the Dharma: Living as a Buddhist Nun*. Also available online at: http://www.thubtenchodron.org/BuddhistNunsMonasticLife/LifeAsAWesternBuddhistNun/the_history_of_the_bhikkhuni_sangha.html, accessed 8/19/12.

30 See Gross.

31 *Ibid.*

32 Kabilsingh, "The History of the Bhikkhuni Sangha."

33 This difficult practice is a tradition in Tibetan Buddhism and a part of "preliminary practices" (*ngondro*) of initiation.

34 http://www.brunofilms.com/films/satya-a-prayer-for-the-enemy/, accessed 8/19/12.

35 See http://www.bhikkhunidocumentary.com/, accessed 8/19/12.

36 http://www.youtube.com/watch?v=nG-RiTO3vjY, accessed 8/19/12.

10

THAI BUDDHISM IN HORROR FILMS

Nang Nak and *Uncle Boonmee Who Can Recall His Past Lives*

Thai Buddhism preserves and propagates many vital features of Theravāda Buddhism. These include traditions of forest monks, mindfulness meditation practices, and in-depth phenomenological analysis of the Buddhist Abhidhamma. Generally, Thai horror films have focused instead on the sensational aspects of popular Buddhism associated with superstitions in the country. *Nang Nak* (Nonzee Nimibutr, Thailand, 1999) and *Uncle Boonmee Who Can Recall His Past Lives* (Apichatpong Weerasethakul, Thailand, 2010) represent two treatments of these aspects.

1. Basic Plot Summary of *Nang Nak*

Nang Nak is set in the mid-nineteenth century around a simple area of Bangkok with river huts and longboats. It starts with the unlucky coming of a solar eclipse at the beginning of the ninth lunar month, according to the opening intertitle. People are uneasy at this, pointing to the sky and jumping out of boats. A baby cries and even birds fly away. Buddhist monks chant a scripture. Temple bells ring and someone fires a shot into the sky as if to chase away an evil spirit with the clamor. In the next scene, a man named Mak (Winai Kraibutr) is called to war, leaving his wife, Nak (Intira Jaroenpura), crying for him. Time passes and a narrator tells us that, in Thai legend, Nang Nak (also called Mae Nak) was so deeply in love with her husband Mak that even death could not pull her from him. We see Nak touch her stomach as their baby grows inside.

At the end of a battle, Mak walks by fallen soldiers looking for his friend named Prig. Mak has also been wounded and, clutching his chest, he falls unconscious. We begin to see parallels and even telepathic transference in the lives of the separated couple, as, at the same time, back in their village Nak touches her chest and suddenly becomes ill. The scene changes back to Mak, who rises and finds his dead friend. Changing again, the scene is back to Nak. Seeing a spider beating the wall with its body and falling to the floor, she calls out for Mak. Mak is taken to an old business district of Bangkok and nearly dies there from his wounds. In a last effort to save him, he is taken to the Buddhist High Dignitary Toh at a nearby temple. Meanwhile, Nak visits her local temple elder to ask if he has heard news about her husband. She is told that Mak's fate is a result of his karma, that she should make offerings so that the elders' merit might offset some of Mak's karma. The priest also gives her a charm to protect her and the unborn baby.

We see Mak feverish and calling for Nak. Nak falls in a rainy field holding her stomach and calling for help. Mak is taken to a temple where in delirium he first thinks he sees Nak, then fires of hell covering both his dead friend and Nak. As he yells in anguish at this sight, Nak also screams as she struggles to give birth. At the temple, the High Dignitary administers medicines to Mak, while back in their home village the midwife tries to save Nak and the baby. Nak again calls out for Mak.

Time passes and by the end of the rainy season Mak recovers. Toh tells him life is uncertain, that some people who appear healthy die while others who are extremely ill live. He suggests that Mak become a monk to atone for his karma, but Mak says he must return to his wife and child. A young novice monk looks surprised at this, but Toh remains steadfast, telling Mak that whatever happens he should remain calmly aware that everything is related to karma and that attachment brings suffering.

Mak travels home by longboat, looking up at the tree branches in forests that seem somehow eerie to him. Finally reaching his hut, Nak comes out to happily greet him, holding their baby. Later Mak dreams fieldworkers yell at him for being with Nak. As he chases them away in his dream he suddenly sees his dead friend Prig, who becomes a decaying corpse in his arms. He wakes up terrified. The next day, Mak sees another friend Um in a boat. When Mak calls to him, his friend rows away quickly. That night, as Nak and Mak make love, scenes alternate between this and Nak's problems in childbirth. The viewer now sees that Nak did not give birth but died trying and that her midwife stole a ring from Nak's finger.

The next day Um goes to the local temple and tells the head monk that he has seen Mak living with Nak. The monk says it's tragic and asks if Mak knew yet. Mak visits a neighbor only to find her dead body being eaten by crocodiles. Later Nak tells him a number of people had died of cholera while he was away at war and the surviving neighbors had moved to avoid the illness. That night a storm rages and we see the midwife throwing the ring away, saying, "Take it, it's yours." A reptile-like figure, similar to the crocodile Mak had seen, appears in her house and she dies of fright. The storm passes and Nak sings. As she does, frightened villagers run to pray before altars for protection. The villagers sob, "She is coming." Later Mak wakes up to find Nak is outside pounding rice. When he asks her why she is doing this at night, she says she wants to serve him and might not have much time left. Crying, she says she will never leave him. He replies, "Till death do us part."

The next day Mak's friend Um finds him in the forest and tells him his wife and baby are dead. Mak becomes angry, hits Um, and tells him not to come back. Nak makes an excuse about why Um said this, saying people gossiped and hated her. That night another storm comes and Um is killed. After this, the villagers go to the temple and ask the head monk to bring in a ghost banisher (misprinted in the subtitles as banister). The priest tells the people that Mak will be inside the hut so they should not act rashly. Instead of following this advice, some of the group decide to burn down Mak and Nak's hut. Before this can happen, the priest goes to the house with two monks to try to reason with Mak. From the priest's perspective the house looks very dusty. Mak believes he offers the priest plates of food, but the plates are empty. Likewise, there is no baby in the cradle Mak rocks. Mak is again angered when the priest tells him Nak and the baby are dead, that he lives with ghosts. The priest leaves, giving Mak the parting advice that if he wants to see the truth, he should concentrate, keep the Buddha in mind, and look between his legs. Mak tells the priest to stay and he sees Nak. Startled, the priest hurries off.

The ghost banisher arrives. He looks like a Brahmin ascetic with long hair and a beard. Meanwhile, High Dignitary Toh tells his followers to pack an amulet, because he is leaving for the Phra Khanong district (also written Prakanong). At that time, the villagers also leave to burn down Mak's hut. Inside, as the ghost of Nak prepares food with a mortar and pestle, Mak remembers the priest's words and looks between his legs. When he does, Nak disappears. He then sees her ghost reach through the floorboards to pick up a lime. Terrified, he runs away from the hut and into the forest as Nak cries and murmurs his name. The villagers arrive and call for Mak to come out. Although he has left, they do not know this and set the house ablaze regardless. Nak comes outside, holding the baby as flames rise behind her. Now with a stern, echoing voice she chastises the villagers for their behavior. When they accuse her of killing people she denies it, saying their own karma killed them after they tried to harm her family. Now that these villagers have done the same, the burning house falls on them.

Mak arrives at the village temple and a circle of seated monks surround him. A storm is raging outside. Mak is wrapped in sacred thread while monks and laypersons chant for protection. At the same time the ghost banisher (Tul) is led to Nang Nak's grave, where the body is exhumed. In a particularly eerie scene, Nak appears in the temple, floating upside down above the circle of monks. She calls for Mak as she holds their baby. In pity, Mak starts to go to her, but the priest stops him. The ghost of Nak disappears and the priest says his sermon must have worked. But we are not sure if it is that or the banisher desecrating her dead body that made the ghost disappear. Mak rushes out in the storm and tells the banisher to leave the body alone. He is knocked down by the villagers as the banisher continues, striking Nak's corpse. Suddenly, the banisher is struck repeatedly by an unseen force as we hear Nak laughing. The storm stops abruptly as High Dignitary Toh arrives with the novice monk holding an umbrella over his head. Toh sits in front of the grave chanting. Nak rises in the grave holding the baby and crying. Toh instructs Mak to say his last goodbyes to Nak. Nak tells Mak the baby is sleeping and she must serve the High Dignitary until her karma is paid. Mak says their fates had been tied together. He hopes they can be reborn as husband and wife.

High Priest Toh chants and writes on Nak's forehead. Her body falls into the grave and the novice hammers out a piece of her skull. After this Toh explains that he has Nak's spirit in the piece of bone, that she will not haunt them further. Nak's body is cremated and Mak becomes a monk. A voiceover narrates that the High Dignitary Buddhacharn, Somdej Toh, placed the bone in his waistband and wore it for the rest of his life. It was then passed to Prince Chumborn and sometime later was lost. The narrator says, however, the story of the immortal love of a wife lives on in people's hearts.

2. Buddhist Themes

We can see through this film how popular Thai Buddhism combines local folklore, superstitions, and customs with Buddhist teachings. It is common for Buddhist traditions around the world to incorporate local customs. The film opens with a solar eclipse during the ninth month of the lunar calendar. Lunar months traditionally start on the day of the new moon and the full moon occurs in the middle of the month. Also, the official year in Thailand is not designated according to the so-called Common Era (CE). Instead, Thailand considers this the Buddha Era (BE), which began when the Buddha was born, 545 BCE, according to tradition. So, for example, 2013 CE is 2557 BE.

In Thailand there are various Buddhist celebrations related to specific months, especially at new moons and full moons. In Thailand and other countries where Theravāda Buddhism is strong, special days called **Uposatha** are times for Buddhist reflection. These are weekly celebrations occurring on the days of the full moon, new moon, waxing moon, and waning moon. Monthly celebrations are often observances of events in the life of the Buddha that are said to have occurred during the corresponding month. It is likely, however, that some elements of monthly observances predate Buddhism in Thailand. Of significance for the film, ghosts of the departed are said to roam freely during the ninth lunar month. Accordingly, in the ninth month there is a Buddhist celebration called *Boon Khao Pradub Din*, meaning "placing a gift of food on the ground" in honor of these spirits. Throughout *Nang Nak*, director Nonzee Nimibutr skillfully arranges many such cultural references to ghosts and Buddhism. During this celebration, people prepare food and wrap it in banana leaves. These are placed on the ground or hung in trees as offerings to deceased relatives. Many Thai people believe there are spirits everywhere including in water, land, and trees. While these can be malevolent, they may be kept peaceful with acts of respect such as offerings of food and drink. Through Buddhism, this is connected to merit making, which cancels out the bad karma that got the ghosts in a position of suffering in the first place. Since the ninth month occurs in the summer, it is a time of abundant crops. In part, placing food on the ground and in trees is a way of thanking the spirits of the earth for providing for the people. This may have been an older custom that was incorporated into Buddhism.[1] These days, the offerings made during the ninth month are sometimes thought of as given to monks who share with the ancestors.

The Buddhist basis for this festival when food is offered to the spirits of ancestors comes from a story taken from the life of the Buddha, recorded in the *Petavatthu*. The *Petavatthu*, literally "*Peta* Stories," is a collection of 51 tales explaining just how individuals' karma from unwholesome deeds resulted in rebirth as **peta**, **hungry ghosts**. This idea is central to the viewers' sympathy in *Nang Nak* because, not only is Nak subject to this law of retribution, but so are those who seek to harm her and her family. The *Petavatthu* is a part of the *Collection of Shorter Texts* (*Khuddaka Nikāya*) of the **Pāli Canon**, which are among the most important writings for Theravāda Buddhism.[2] The food-offering story in the *Petavatthu* is as follows.

Once the Buddha traveled to Rajagaha where he lectured to King Bimbisara (558–491 BCE) and a large gathering of people. At that time, the Buddha narrated the *Mahanarada Kassapa Jataka*, a story about a king who overcame his attachments to material pleasures. After hearing this, King Bimbisara and the others became **Stream Enterers**, embarking on the path of the Buddha. The next day Bimbisara offered donations of food to the Buddha and his followers. As he was doing this, there was a great earthquake and later that night the sounds of ghosts were heard in the palace. Frightened, the king asked the Buddha why this was happening. The Buddha explained that in a previous life, King Bimbisara and his relatives gave food-alms to a previous Buddha and Sangha, followers of the Buddha.[3] Those who did this dutifully were reborn in a higher realm. Those who refused and even stole from the sangha were reborn as *peta*. In their realm of suffering, these *peta* observed that some others among their fellow hungry ghosts were saved from the realm of suffering by the merit of their own living relatives who offered food-alms to the sangha on their behalf. However, the *peta* relatives of Bimbisara had no one to offer alms on their behalf and appealed to the previous Buddha for help. He answered that, in the future, King Bimbisara would be reborn and come to supervise the sharing of merit on behalf of them, his former relatives. Now, however, since Bimbisara offered food-alms without mentioning the *petas*, they moaned all night in sorrow. The Buddha then instructed Bimbisara to share his merit with the *petas* anytime he made an offering or carried out a noble deed. Afterward the king offered food, robes, bedding, and other necessary items to monks and shared the merit he earned in so doing with the *petas*. In this way, his ancestors were freed from their suffering and reborn in a higher realm.

This story is the basis for the present-day practice of offering food to the spirits of the deceased during the ninth month, when they are said to roam. There are a number of interesting points to it related to Thai horror movies. In Buddhism there is a widespread belief that this life is but one of **31 realms of existence**. This scheme, referred to in many Buddhist scriptures, includes immaterial and material realms, realms of happiness and those of suffering. Beings' existence in any of these is entirely dependent on karma. Among the unhappy realms are places of hungry ghosts. These places are sometimes called Buddhist hells. Hungry ghosts are depicted in drawings as beings with large stomachs that can never be filled because their mouths are the size of a pinhead. Owing to their insatiable cravings in life, they are reborn in such a condition. Indeed, they were metaphorically in this condition all along, which is one way to interpret the entire scheme of 31 realms, as psychological conditions in life. However, the literal interpretation of these heavens and hells is far more common and the basis of many films. It is also important to note that none of these realms are permanent states as we might think of concerning heaven or hell in other contexts. Instead, each is a temporary abode for working out the karmic consequences of actions, just as life is seen to be.

The eclipse that occurs at the beginning of the *Nang Nak* is also considered an inauspicious event. In some Asian countries, at times of eclipses people are advised to stay indoors. Since the life-giving sun is blocked, it is considered a time when germs, illness, and death gain strength. From Hindu mythology of India that entered Thailand, Rahu is responsible. Rahu is a snake or dragon Asura. Asuras are cosmic beings struggling with Deva, such as the sun, for divine control. Rahu occasionally swallows the sun and moon temporarily, causing eclipses. Because the Asura has momentary power over the Deva, people are cautioned to remain inside. As this story has been incorporated into Buddhism, monks should perform prayers and rituals at times of eclipse to subdue the dragon Rahu. In the film, we see and hear monks doing this during the solar eclipse. It is considered especially important for pregnant women to stay out of the solar eclipse, as it is believed this could kill them and their unborn babies or cause deformities. This is why it occurs in *Nang Nak*. In Thailand, amulets are bought to protect against such evils during an eclipse. Amulets of all kinds are popular in the country and important in the film. They can be obtained at Buddhist temples.

The story of Nang Nak is set in the Phra Khanong district of Bangkok. Mak goes to a local temple there called Wat Mahabut to escape Nak's ghost. *Wat* means "temple" or "monastery". Wat Mahabut was built around 1762 and is popular today because it has a shrine to Nak.[4] Most people call it *Wat Mae Nak Phra Khanong*, that is, "Phra Khanong Temple of Mae Nak." There is a statue of her cradling her baby. People come and offer gifts including baby toys. Some people go there to ask for babies. There is a pond outside where some come to release fish for merit. The temple looks like a ghost house. Most Thai families keep a small, dollhouse-like item in their homes as shrines to house the *peta* spirits of their ancestors. These ghost houses are painted buildings with many pointed roof spires, just like Wat Mahabut.

There are many versions of the Nang Nak story and it would be difficult to find a Thai person who has not heard of her. When children are misbehaving, parents sometimes tell them to calm down or Nak might get them. For over 50 years, as many as 20 movies have been made about the story. There have also been cartoons, a television series, and an opera.[5] In all versions, Mak is separated from Nak by war. Although the specifics of this war are not given in *Nang Nak*, other versions say it is a dispute between Thailand and Shan (Burma/Myanmar) which resulted in battles occurring on and off between 1849 and 1855. Some say that Nak hates war in general.

Among the cultural references director Nonzee makes to beliefs in supernatural forces is the spider Nak sees beating against the wall. There is a Thai superstition that a spider can cast an evil spell by beating its legs against its chest. Owls appear in the film as ominous symbols of what is to come. Throughout South and Southeast Asia, owls are seen as signs of bad luck and even messengers of the dead, probably because they are nocturnal. Also, as Nak is struggling to have the baby, the midwife yells at a man to not stand blocking the doorway, saying it is a bad omen. The superstition is that if you block a doorway or window the birth passage may be blocked. The midwife in the film calls out for someone to open a window. She also calls for water. Rinsing the mouth is thought to help dispel karmic obstructions. Later the local priest gives Mak advice that is again a mixture of Buddhism and local tradition. He says if he wants to see the truth he should concentrate, keep the Buddha in mind, and look between your legs. According to a Thai superstition, you should not bend down and look between your legs or you will see a ghost.[6]

Nonzee uses a montage technique to suggest that Nak and Mak are tied together closely by a karmic bond. Montage is an editing technique that splices scenes together in a way that can suggest to the viewer ideas such as time has passed or distance has been crossed. In this case, time and space are transcended by karmic affinity. The director illustrates this by juxtaposing scenes, such as Mak clutching his wounded chest as Nak touches the same spot on her body. Karmic affinity is considered extremely important in most traditions of Buddhism. An individual hears about the Dharma due to karmic affinity, connections from a previous life. This is thought of as seeds we carry that can grow in the right circumstances. The Buddha also is said to have attained Buddhahood due to his karmic affinity. He gained merit by performing good deeds in many past lives as narrated in Jataka tales. He also formed past-life relationships with others and this helped him eventually reach awakening. According to this theory, all Buddhas met previous Buddhas in past lives. A Jataka story says long ago in a previous life, the Bodhisattva, who would become the Buddha Śakyamuni (who we call the historical Buddha), met the previous Buddha Kassapa (Sanskrit: Kāśyapa). At that time the Bodhisattva was a boy who hurried to see the Buddha Kassapa as he passed through his village. Noticing Kassapa would have to walk through a mud puddle, the Bodhisattva put his long hair over the puddle so he could walk over it. The seeds from this karmic affinity and other acts eventually ripened into Buddhahood. Buddhist masters and disciples are also said to have this kind of karmic bond. We notice in the film when High Priest Toh arrives, the others listen carefully to him and obey even what his young disciple says.

Before Toh arrives to save Mak and calm the spirit of Nak, Mak goes for protection to the local temple, Wat Mahabut. There, the head monk and his followers form a circle with a Thai sacred thread known as *sai sin*. *Sai sin* is white thread used by monks to create a sacred space that cannot be penetrated by evil forces. In the movie, Mak is wrapped with the thread and placed inside a circle created by it. Thai Buddhists use *sai sin* in ceremonies to bless a new home or place of business. A ball of the thread is taken around the building and passed through the windows. *Sai sin* is also used in the ceremony to ordain a monk, symbolically binding him from evil. In this way, *sai sin* is similar to the sacred thread (*upanayanam*) conferred to Hindus and Indian Buddhists at initiation. In Thai services, the head priest holds the ball of thread during the ceremony. While chanting he unrolls it, passes the threads through his fingers, and passes the ball to a monk beside him. Each subsequent monk does the same until the ball comes back to the head priest. In some regions of Thailand, *sai sin* is used to bestow good luck for journeys and for good health. Like the Tibetan *khata* (white scarf), *sai sin* is also used to welcome guests. *Sai sin* bracelets blessed by monks may be available at Thai *wats*.

The name "High Dignitary" in the English subtitles of the film translates the designation *ajahn*, the Thai equivalent to the Pāli word *acariya* (Sanskrit: *ācārya*), which refers to an instructor or exemplar in religious matters. The High Dignitary in *Nang Nak* is the historical figure Somdej Phra Puttajan Toh (1788–1872 CE, 2331–2415 BE), also called, Somdej Toh or just Toh. The word *Somdej* is a title for a temple master.[7] Somdej Phra means reverend temple master. He is probably the most famous and highly respected Thai Buddhist in history. He is, of course, always greeted in the film with bows and hands together in the reverence gesture know as *wai* (the Añjali Mudrā). Similar to *namasté*, the Indian greeting that traditionally indicated recognition of the sacred in others, whenever possible Thai people greet one another with this hand sign of respect.[8]

Legend says King Rama I (1782–1809) announced that Somdej Toh was a *naga* (dragon) and asked him to oversee Wat Rakang Kositharam near the Phra Khanong district of Bangkok, near where Nak and Mak allegedly lived. The film's subtitles call this Rakang Temple when Mak is taken there to recover from his war wound. This is where Somdej Toh taught disciples, chanted scriptures, and crafted amulets for protection from a variety of potential misfortunes. These amulets may be seen as simple reminders not to fall into the bad habits of worldly life or to remember the teachings of the Buddha. More often they are interpreted as literally talismans with spiritual powers to ward off ghosts. Amulets are very popular in Thailand. Different types are seen as having different powers, from attracting a love interest to repelling evil influences. Some of them are made of ivory or bones seen, in part, as carrying some of the power of the being from which they came. Somdej Toh takes a piece of Nak's skull bone to lock in her spirit so he can help her overcome her karma through his merit. This part of the old story is related to Toh's amulet-making skills. The actual amulets made by Somdej Toh are today considered quite valuable, selling for around ten million Thai baht, the equivalent of about US $200,000. In *Nang Nak* we see Toh writing on Nak's skull bone while chanting. This writing on amulets is known as *yan* or *yant*, from the Sanskrit word **yantra**. Like a mantra, a *yantra* can be used like a spell. The root of the word, *yan*, means "to subdue." While mantra is chanted, *yantra* is drawn. It can be words or other symbols such as geometrical shapes. In the movie, Somdej Toh would have been writing in Khom, an ancient form of Khmer script used to write *yantra* and other Pāli language words from Buddhist scriptures. It is popular in Thailand for men to get *yantra* tattoos for protection. They are thought to be particularly efficacious if given by a monk according to certain rules. It is common to see *yantra* on taxis and busses for safe passage, as well as painted on the doors of houses to keep away unwanted visitors.

When Somdej Toh takes the bone in his hand he chants, "*Ma, a, ua*," a version of the most well-known mantra, "*Oṃ*," also written *Auṃ*. *Oṃ* is said to be the seed syllable to all words because it contains the sounds *A*, *U*, and *M*, made with different parts of the throat. That is, it contains all sounds, words, and concepts. Because mantra is believed to be so important and powerful, mispronunciation could be disastrous. For this reason, some Vedic Hindus learn mantras backwards and forwards. Likewise, there may be special values obtained by chanting a mantra backwards. "*Ma, a, ua*" in the film is "*Oṃ*" chanted backwards.[9]

That Somdej Toh has special abilities is clear from his first appearance. We see him skillfully administering medicines to Mak through a montage of scene changes that contrast his talent with the poor treatment Nak receives at the hands of the midwife. While healing Mak, Toh chants the *The Victor's Cage Verses* (*Jinapañjara Gāthā*). This is a Pāli text used for protection. The text invokes the Buddha and his followers to form a protection ring around the practitioner so no evil forces can penetrate. This has the same function as the *sai sin* sacred thread. Three types of knowledge and skills are contrasted: that of the ghost banisher, that of folk tradition represented by the midwife and the villagers, and that of Somdej Toh, who represents the power of Buddhism. Whereas even the local head priest is afraid of Nang Nak, Toh is steadfast in the presence of the ghost. In the end, he tells Mak to say his last goodbyes to Nak. This mimics a properly performed Buddhist funeral service wherein survivors stand in front of the coffin with hands together in *wai* position. Survivors either remain silent or quietly say their last words. Weeping should not be done because it does not help the deceased. Cremation or burial are options chosen according to personal preference.

It is also clear in the film that Somdej Toh knew that Nak was dead even before allowing Mak to return home. He tells Mak to stay and become a monk in order to make up for karma. When Mak says he must return to his wife and child, Toh's young disciple looks shocked, indicating that he too knows Nak and the baby have died. Toh, however, does not flinch. He is not affected by the ways of the secular world. He is also wise enough to realize Mak has to work through his own karmic circumstances. In this way, not only do Nak and Mak have deep karmic affinity, but also they share in this with Toh who will help them. Toh works to save both Mak and Nak from karmic retribution. He carries the spirit of Nak with him to cancel her karma with his merit. He may have also saved her from possible harm at the hands of the ghost banisher. Although her vengeful spirit seems to have the banisher under control, she may have accrued more karma in so doing. From another perspective, the banisher's punishment was the result of his karma, as was that of the badly behaved villagers. Regardless, the ineffectualness of the Brahman is contrasted with the successful treatments by Toh as way of venerating Buddhism above other traditions in the film.

Mak becomes a monk, entering Wat Mahabut monastery and becoming a disciple of Somdej Toh. He does this on the 15th day of the 11th month of the lunar calendar, which is the day of the full moon. This day is known as *Ok Phansa*, a day of celebration at the end of the rainy season. In ancient times, the Buddha and his followers continuously roamed the countryside with no place of residency except during the rainy season, when they would stop for three months. In Thailand, during this time many young men enter a monastery for the three-month period. The end of this period is punctuated by a celebration of the successful completion of the term and a welcome home. The day marks the end of the rainy season and signals a time to make a fresh start. This is the feeling we have for Mak on that special day. The storms of the rainy season had been associated with the wrath of Mae Nak, which has now been calmed.

3. *Uncle Boonmee Who Can Recall His Past Lives,* a New Direction for Thai Horror Films

One does not have to see *Nang Nak* in order to appreciate *Uncle Boonmee Who Can Recall His Past Lives*, but the two make a nice pair. There is a very real sense that what *Uncle Boonmee* in the film can recall is the past lives of horror films in Thailand, including their representations of Buddhism. Through the plot, the cinematic techniques, and the images, the film is a direct response to classic Thai horror and what those films say about society. Director Apichatpong Weerasethakul based the script on a book, *The Man Who Can Remember His Past Lives*, about a dying man living at a monastery who claimed he could do just that. The book was written by a monk at the monastery who recorded his encounters with the dying man living there. Though the man died before Apichatpong could meet him, the director realized a broader application of the book's theme to Thai cinema. According to this movie, through older films we can see something of our past. It is not that these films overtly photograph an objective reality of the past. Instead, they tell us about the social circumstances such as shared stereotypes, political beliefs, and constraints under which they are made. At the same time, they also contribute to the creation of a manufactured past that we collectively accept as reality as we watch films. *Uncle Boonmee Who Can Recall His Past Lives* investigates

Thailand's rural and social landscapes through myth, fantasy, and memory according to cinematic history, all of which have a relationship with Thai Buddhism. In an interview in the *Bangkok Post*, Apichatpong said the film progresses through six cinematic styles, "old cinema with stiff acting and classical staging," "documentary style," "costume drama," and "my kind of film when you see long takes of animals and people driving." He also said, "When you make a film about recollection and death, you realize that cinema is also facing death. *Uncle Boonmee* is one of the last pictures shot on film—now everybody shoots digital. It's my own little lamentation."[10] These stylistic elements combine with the storyline to challenge viewers to examine the presentation of social values that shapes and is shaped by culture. Horror film rhetoric is reversed in places. Buddhists do not come to the rescue as traditionally expected but are ordinary people doing ordinary things.

So many Thai films depict Buddhists in prominent roles that people sometimes say there is a Thai monk genre. Typically these characters are wise, benevolent, and spiritually powerful. Apichatpong seems to want us to consider how such images contribute to the creation and maintenance of social and political status quos. Undignified portrayals of Buddhists in films have been somewhat policed by Thai censors, who, for example, cautioned Apichatpong against showing a monk playing a guitar in his 2006 film *Syndromes and a Century*. The director decided to remove the movie from consideration for awards at film festivals rather than compromise his art, which, after all, could set a bad precedence for government censorship. The same year, Thailand temporarily blocked YouTube, demanding that Google remove 20 videos officials felt insulted the country and its traditions.[11] *The King and I* is banned in Thailand, as is the 1999 remake of *Anna and the King*, due to alleged signs of disrespect to the royal family. The Thai government would not allow the latter to be made in Thailand nor permit it to be shown or distributed in the country.

Buddhism is the national religion of Thailand. Politicians routinely make public displays of their reverence toward monks, especially during election times. Most Thai men become monks for several months at some time during their lives. Buddhist services, festivals, prayers, and amulets are parts of everyday life. It is no wonder these elements find their way into Thai films as pervasive spiritual and political forces. A medium that preserves the status quo is by definition a conservative force. While this may be good for the continual transmission and preservation of certain values, both in art and society it can both stifle creativity and champion the interests of those in power over the underclass. Viewers of *Uncle Boonmee Who Can Recall His Past Lives* who are familiar with the history of Thai cinema it addresses come to see this point as well as examples of what can be done to challenge the negative stereotypes of earlier films. *Nang Nak* is sometimes seen as a turning point in the history of Thai horror films in several ways. *Uncle Boonmee Who Can Recall His Past Lives* can likewise be seen as an additional turning away from usual representations of social norms. *Nang Nak* breaks from reliance on comedy to support horror. It stars Winai Kraibutr and Intira Jaroenpura, who were popular box office attractions. For this film, Nonzee came to be considered the first of Thailand's "New Wave" film-makers that was later to include Apichatpong Weerasethakul. Nonzee is credited with having pulled Thai films up from its artistic slump in the late 1990s. Before that time Thai horror films generally had poor acting (some of which seems intentional) and cheap effects, weak plots, and lots of screaming chase scenes. Ghosts in Thai films are typically taken from well-known folklore. Traditional ghosts (*phi*) are overwhelmingly female. Their representations in films carry serious overtones in terms of perpetuating stereotypes and reinforcing repressive gender roles for women. Sometimes they are made into sexy ghosts in films. Among the ghost spirits repeated in numerous Thai films are *Phi Kraseu* that manifest as beautiful women. They float with no body, just entrails dangling below an attractive head.[12] Likewise, many comic horror films center around legends of the *Phi Pop*, an ogress condemned to live on human intestines. This story was remade and made into sequels 13 times between 1989 and 1994.[13] There are also films depicting *Phi Nang Tani*, a fallen female angel condemned to live in a banana tree.[14] Others focus on ghosts called *Tai Hong*, spirits of those who died a violent death and seek revenge, as in the 2010 film *Tai Hong*, with four sequences by four directors.[15] *Nang Nak* is related to this type and she is specifically a *Phi Tai Tang Glom*, one who died along with her child while giving birth. This situation doubles her malevolent powers. It is easy to see the misogyny in these films once we realize how often negative female stereotypes are repeated in them and how this is related to social conditions and Buddhism. Like ancient Japan, some have suggested that ancient Thailand was a matrilineal society.[16] In both cultures the switch to patriarchy is said to have been accompanied by the creation of mythology about female demonic spirits.[17] The spread of Buddhism to Thailand may have helped to facilitate and reinforce that transition.[18]

Thai horror often depicts women as vengeful ghosts breaking taboos concerning social norms. These representations of female maliciousness and their punishments may serve to curtail people from such behavior. This can be seen as part of the social message behind Nang Nak deceiving her husband. He believes she is a good wife. We should also question the implied definition of this and the proposition that Nak's kind of devotional love or the desire to serve her husband transcends the earthly realm after death. The other part of the message is women cannot be trusted. Both film and Buddhism in Thailand and elsewhere have served to maintain such structures of society in a variety of ways, including the reinforcing atmospheres at social gatherings.

Thai Buddhism is and always has been dominated by men. It is illegal for a woman to join the monastic community. Birth as a woman is considered lower than as a man. Women represent a distraction to religious men, which is implied metaphorically in Thai horror films. Thailand has traditionally had no *Bhikkhuni Sangha*. Although the Buddha agreed with his cousin Ānanda that women should be allowed to join the *sangha*, the tradition of Thai Buddhism upholds an opinion that developed in India, that Ānanda had wrongly pressured the Buddha into this. Women in Thailand who have been determined to follow the teachings of the Buddha in disregard for secular law and monastic bias have shaved their heads, worn white robes in contrast to the monastic ochre robes, and lived homelessly outside of temples. Recently, in defiance of the prohibitions against the *Bhikkhuni Sangha*, some women have been ordained as nuns outside of Thailand and returned to the country to propagate the order. A few monks have joined them in an effort to overturn Thai law.[19] But it is an uphill battle that Thai cinema has not made easier—until now.

Uncle Boonmee Who Can Recall His Past Lives challenges the haunting wife motif. When the ghost of Boonmee's wife appears to him he does not run, as audiences have come to expect in Thai horror films. Instead, the two calmly have a conversation. In fact, she changes his catheter for him. There is no need for a Buddhist exorcist because there is no problem. Indeed the Buddhist monk, who is Boonmee's nephew, comes home, changes out of his robes, and watches television. We would be hard pressed to think of a more ordinary activity to represent. Watching television also suggests a different way of transmitting social values, that is, film in contrast to temple scriptures and lectures. The implication of this image is no less radical than that of the monk playing a guitar, which censure opposed. However, censuring this film would have caused an international outcry. In May 2011, *Uncle Boonmee Who Can Recall His Past Lives* won the top prize, the Palme d'Or, at perhaps the world's most prestigious film competition, the Cannes Film Festival.

The film opens with an ox breaking free from a tree where it was tied. The scene evokes the Zen *Ox Herding* drawings as seen in *Why Has Bodhi-Dharma Left for the East?* In that case, however, it indicates a stage of awakening. Apichatpong takes a different direction. Like the film's critique of cinema, the ox breaks free of social constraints, only to be led back. The rural setting is also suggestive of Thailand's past. The scene changes to a ride inside a bus. Boonmee's sister-in-law and her son are coming to visit. This scene goes on longer than our expectation of how time is portrayed in films, making us uncomfortable, which seems to be Apichatpong's intent in this strategy throughout the film. From the windows of the bus we see the landscape that plays an important role in the film in our coming to understand relationships of culture and place. That night, when Boonmee and his guest sit outside at a table, they are visited by the ghost of his wife. They are not frightened and Boonmee smiles. Next Boonmee's son comes to the table. None of the family has seen him in many years and he has changed drastically. He appears to be part wild animal, having hair all over his face and the body of a gorilla. He explains that he had become a photographer because of Boonmee's interest in this art. One day he took a picture in the forest and saw a spirit-creature in it. He decided to go back into the forest and discover what was there. He says he became obsessed with this new creature and tried to chase it down. Eventually he mated with a monkey ghost and thereby became one. The monkey ghost (*ling phi*) seems to have been invented for the film and is male, again departing from the horror genre's reliance on traditional ghost stories. It is also interesting that Boonmee's son becomes obsessed with these ghosts and transformation through film. Because of this and other such references, it becomes clear that Apichatpong is making this film reflect his own biography as film-maker, as well as Thailand's as a country in change. Boonmee's wife is preserved, just as film preserves its subject. In contrast, he cannot recognize his son, who has become natural and something the country tried to forget.

Later we see a monkey ghost in still shots being led to execution by the Thai military. This is a reference to violent repression of the Communist Party in Thailand's north during the 1970s. Boonmee also explains that he had been one of the soldiers who had killed communists. He believes the illness that is killing him is a result of the karma he accrued from this. By implication, Thailand's repressive culture resulted from suppressing dissent. As more still shots are shown, Boonmee says he had a dream that present people traveled to the future. There they were shown pictures of the past projected on a screen. Once they were shown these, the people of the past were transformed. This narrative is key in understanding the leitmotif of the film. The "other" in the film is anything defined by society as foreign and off limits to us, whether it be communism, nature spirits, or the unacceptable behavior represented by women or female ghosts. Instead of embracing the artistic possibilities, we try to eliminate alterity from the world and stay within the lines drawn by the dominant culture. Film plays two roles in this process. It serves as a tool for conservatively defining who we are and how we should act. It also offers a potential for transformation by redefining who we are and what we are capable of. The seemingly impossible transformation of society and individuals can be achieved by embracing the other. There are several scenes in the film in which the audience can be made aware that the cinematic part of this transformation process is not only being represented in the film, but is happening to the viewer at that very moment when the film is watched. In one such scene, Boonmee's nephew hangs up his monk's robes and watches television. Then, as he's leaving for a café with his aunt, Boomee's sister-in-law, he sees himself and his aunt watching TV. At the café, his aunt leans back and stares at him blankly. The scene changes back to the room, where they stare with the same expression at the TV. This is also suggestive of the longer-than-expected shots. We are staring at them rather blankly, wondering if we can make sense of it.

At the end of the film, after Boonmee has died, his sister-in-law is asked by her daughter if she would like to write some things about uncle Boonmee's life in a book of remembrances. She says she didn't know him that well. The daughter suggests she make up something. This brings up two points. We are seeing the country's history on screen but it is an imagined Thailand. This made-up world becomes our reality. Also, this film is at least partially based on the book *The Man Who Can Remember His Past Lives*, which is in fact what was written in the book of remembrances. This implies that the source book was made up, just as film reconstructs the past in a way that transforms us.

In these ways, *Uncle Boonmee Who Can Recall His Past Lives* questions and critiques traditionalist society, cinematic reinforcements of social standards, and Buddhism as a conservative force. However, Apichatpong's critique is in line with basic Buddhist analysis of perception, as found in Theravāda scriptures, including those of the *Abhidhamma Piṭaka* preserved by Thai Buddhists. Generally, Buddhists feel that we constantly construct reality and form attachments to our illusions based on attractions and aversions. Seldom do we realize these are empty of real, individual existence. Just as Apichatpong indicates in a different way, Buddhists believe this constructed reality perpetuates suffering. In addition, the director's suggestion that we embrace the presumed "other" is close to the Buddhist idea of dependent origination that says there really is no "other." The movie suggests art and cinema might help overcome suffering. This is in line with Buddhist directors, such as Khyentse Norbu (*The Cup*), who propose films can be tools functioning even as amulets against our own phantom, ultimately pointing us to the Buddha's Dharma.

Further Reading

DeCaroli, Robert. *Haunting the Buddha, Indian Popular Religions and the Formation of Buddhism.* Oxford: Oxford University Press, 2004.

McDaniel Justin. "The Emotional Lives of Buddhist Monks in Modern Thai Film," in *Journal of Religion and Film* 14:2, October 2010. Available at https://www.unomaha.edu/jrf/vol14.no2/McDanielEmtionBuddhist.html, accessed 8/18/12.

Sukwong, Dome and Sawasdi Suwannapak. *A Century of Thai Cinema.* Thailand: River Books Guides, 2006.

Terwiel, B.J. *Monks and Magic: An Analysis of Religious Ceremonies in Central Thailand.* Scandinavian Institute of Asian Studies Monograph Series 24. London: Curzon Press Ltd., 1975; republished by NIAS Press (Nordic Institute of Asian Studies), 2011.

Further Viewing

Ghost of Mak Nak (Mark Duffield, Thailand, 2005). Retells the *Nang Nak* story in a modern urban setting.

The Coffin (Ekachai Uekrongtham, Thailand, South Korea, Singapore, 2008). A horror film about a Thai practice for getting rid of karma by spending the night inside a closed coffin.

Phobia 2 (various directors, Thailand, 2009). The first sequence in this film depicts a juvenile delinquent who is sent to a monastery for rehabilitation. After making light of Buddhism and ghosts, he has a chilling experience.

OK Baytong (Nonzee Nimibutr, Thailand, 2003). A latter film by the director of *Nang Nak*. A Buddhist must leave his monastic life to take care of his dead sister's child. In secular life he is confronted with sexuality, drunkenness, business, and the communities fear and hatred of Muslims. It is not a horror film.

Mysterious Object at Noon (*Dokfa nai meuman*, literally "Dokfa in the Devil's Hand," Apichatpong Weerasethaku, Thailand, 2000) is an experimental independent film that was unscripted. It was made using the "exquisite corpse" idea, that each person adds something to the film to go with what has previously been said or done.

Notes

1 Somchai Wanlu, Songkhoon Chantachon, and Boonlert Rachote, "An Application of Isan Local Indigenous Knowledge in Suppression of Social Disputes," *Social Sciences* 4:2, 2009, pp. 180–5. http://www.medwelljournals.com/fulltext/?doi=sscience.2009.180.185, accessed 8/18/12.

2 I.B. Horner (trans.), *Minor Anthologies*, vol. 4: *Vimanavatthu: Stories of the Mansions, and Petavatthu*.

3 According to some accounts the Buddha in our age is the twenty-fourth Buddha. Each lived tens of thousands of years earlier than the next. Other texts say there have been six Buddhas in our age (*kalpa*).

4 The shrine dedicated to Nang Nak is down a side road along On Nut, Sukhumvit Soi 77. Because of boundary changes in 1997, the temple and shrine are currently located in the Suan Luang. Local people have petitioned to have the boundaries moved back to include the temple once again in the Phra Khanong district.

5 Well-known versions include *Mae Nak Prakanong*, 1959; *Mae Nak Rampage*, 1989; *Mae Nak Prakanong* (Mae Nak's Contract of the Heart), 1992; *Nang Nak*, 1999; *Ghost of Mak Nak*, 2005.

6 There are numerous other cultural references unrelated to Buddhism in the film. For example, Nak shares with Mak beechnuts that turn their teeth black, an old custom in Thailand.

7 He is also known as Somdet Phra Phutthachan or Buddhachan.

8 Visitors should do this, as well. Even Ronald McDonald outside of restaurants in Thailand holds his hands in *wei*. See http://en.wikipedia.org/wiki/Thai_greeting, accessed 3/17/2011.

9 See "The Emotional Lives of Buddhist Monks in Modern Thai Film" by Justin McDaniel, *Journal of Religion and Film* 14:2, October 2010. Available at https://www.unomaha.edu/jrf/vol14.no2/McDanielEmtionBuddhist.html. Accessed 8/18/12.

10 "Of monkey ghosts and men," by Kong Rithdee, *Bangkok Post*, May 28, 2010. http://pages.citebite.com/o3d3t4pouuj, accessed 8/18/12.

11 See *Time* magazine, April 5, 2007, at http://www.time.com/time/world/article/0,8599,1607121,00.html.

12 This is seen in a number of films, including *Krasue Valentine*, 1996, directed by Yuthlert Sippapak and released in America as *Ghost of Valentine*.

13 "What Lurks Beneath Horror," by Kamjohn Louiyapong. *Bangkok Post*, August 24, 2005.

14 For a film about a tree spirit, see *Takien the Haunted Tree* (*Nang Takien*), directed by Saiyon Srisawat, 2010.

15 The directors are Chartchai Ketknust, Manus Worrasingha, Tanwarin Sukkhapisit, and Poj Arnon.

16 This point of view is explained by Kamjohn Louiyapong in "What Lurks Beneath the Horror."

17 In the case of Japan this can be seen in the *Kojiki* in the figure of Izunami, whose dead spirit in a putrefying body chases her still-living male companion from the underworld.

18 This is explained by Kamjohn Louiyapong in "What Lurks Beneath the Horror."

19 For information on this, see http://www.thaibhikkhunis.org/eng/, accessed 8/18/12.

GLOSSARY

108. A sacred number in Indian religions. Buddhist *mala* (prayer beads) typically have 108 beads and the number appears in many Buddhist and Hindu contexts. In Buddhism, 108 is sometimes thought of as the number of defilements we must overcome.

31 realms (or planes) of existence. The Buddhist idea that all of our actions result in karma that manifests in one of 31 ways. These ways may be seen during our lifetime or may occur as the specifics of rebirth. In the case of rebirth, we will be born in one of 31 realms, depending on our karma.

Abhidhamma Piṭaka. One of the three baskets (*Piṭaka*) of Buddhist teachings. It analyzes and enumerates the points made in sūtras.

Ahimsa. Non-hurting, an important concept in Hinduism, Buddhism, and Jainism. Mohandas K. Gandhi stressed the importance of *ahimsa*. It is a principal idea for socially engaged Buddhists.

Amida, *Amitābha*. A cosmic Buddha said to reign in the Western Paradise. He is the principal Buddha of Pure Land Buddhism.

Ānanda. The Buddha's cousin and disciple. He is known for having a perfect memory and for his loving kindness. He is often a speaker in sūtras.

Anātman (Pāli: *anatta*). The Buddha's refutation of the doctrine of *ātman*.

Arahant (Sanskrit: *arhat*), also **arhatship**. An awakened being according to Theravāda tradition. The term *"arahant"* means "worthy one" and is sometimes used as a name for the Buddha.

Ātman (Pāli: *atta*). Sometimes translated as "Self," it is the principle that Brahman (eternal and all pervasive holiness or transcendent Self) is within all people. The Buddha refuted the notion of a permanent self.

Avidyā. Ignorance, blindness.

Bardo. The "in-between" states, usually referring to those between bodily death and rebirth.

Bhikkhu. A Buddhist monk.

Bhikkhuni Sangha. The order of Buddhist nuns.

Bodhi Tree. The tree of awakening, under which the Buddha sat.

Bodhidharma. Fifth or sixth century Indian monk who came to China and propagated Chan (Zen, Seon). He is considered the first patriarch of Chinese Chan Buddhism.

Bodhisattva. An awakening being. One advancing towards Buddhahood.

Bodhisattva Vows. Vows to overcome blind desires, to penetrate the Dharma, to save all sentient beings, and to attain awakening.

Buddha-Karita. A famous telling of the life of the Buddha, written by the Sanskrit poet Aśvaghoṣa, (c. 80–c. 150 CE).

Buddha Nature. The principle that all beings have a seed or potential for awakening to Buddhahood.

Butsudan. A Buddhist altar.

Chakras. Wheels; circles. Centers of energy in the body.

Dalai Lama. The traditional political and religious leader of Tibet. The current Dalai Lama, Tenzin Gyatso, is the 14th Dalai Lama.

Daoism. A Chinese religion and philosophy of nature. A principal writing in Daoism is the *Daodejing*, attributed to Laozi.

Deer Park. Where the Buddha set the wheel of Dharma into motion, that is, gave his first talk on Buddhism to five ascetics.

Dependent origination (or **dependent co-arising**). The principle that what appears to be individual existences are compositions of interdependent physical and psychological elements that mutually condition one another.

Dhamma-eye (Pāli: *dhammacakkhu*, also called **Dharma-eye**). An eye that looks towards the Dharma or sees by the wisdom of Dharma rather than viewing objects with desires and aversions as we usually do.

The Dhammapada. Verses on the Dhamma (Dharma), teachings of the Buddha. One of the best-known and easily understood collections of the Buddha's sayings.

Dharma (Pāli: **Dhamma**). The teachings of the Buddha.

Dhyāna. Meditation.

Dōgen (1200–1253). Japanese Buddhist who studied in China and founded the Sōtō Zen tradition in his country.

Dream Yoga. Tibetan Buddhist practice of using dreams for awakening and other purposes.

Dukkha. Usually translated as "suffering," *dukkha* is perpetual dissatisfaction or unease (perceived as a dis-ease).

Eightfold Path. The Buddha's eight-step program for overcoming *dukkha*. The steps are Right Understanding, Right Resolve, Right Speech, Right Actions, Right Livelihood, Right Effort, Right Mindfulness, Right Concentration.

Fetters. Mental chains that bind us to rebirth. These are listed in varying numbers in scriptures. Generally they are: (1) belief in a self, (2) doubt or uncertainty, especially about the teachings, (3) attachment to rites and rituals, (4) sensual desire, (5) ill-will, (6) lust for material existence and rebirth, (7) lust for im-material existence and rebirth in a formless realm, (8) conceit, (9) disquietude, and (10) ignorance.

First Council. The meeting of Buddhists that came after the Buddha's *parinirvana*.

Five aggregates or "five heaps." Form, feelings, perceptions, mental fabrications, and consciousness. The Buddha said these five are all the constituents making a person.

Five Precepts (Pāli: *pañca-sīlāni*). Five basic vows of Buddhists. Not to kill, not to steal, not to lie, not to cause harm through sexuality, not to indulge in intoxicants to heedlessness.

Four Noble Truths. A basic teaching of the Buddha. (1) Life is filled with dissatisfaction. (2) Dissatisfaction is caused by desires. (3) To overcome dissatisfaction one must eliminate desires. (4) To eliminate desires one should follow the Eightfold Path.

Four Sights. When Siddhartha left home to attain Buddhahood he made four observations, illustrated in his life story as four sights. He saw that people have sickness, old age, death, and he saw asceticism.

Going forth. Embarking on the path of Buddhism.

Great Departure. The Buddha's leaving of palace life, his going forth.

Hōnen (1133–1212), the founder of the Pure Land Tradition in Japan.

Hungry ghosts. beings with large stomachs that can never be filled because their mouths are the size of a pinhead.

Insight Meditation. See **Vipassana**.

Jataka. Didactic stories, mostly of the previous lives of the Buddha.

Jiriki. A Japanese term referring to reliance on one's own abilities in order to reach awakening, rather than appealing to a savior for help.

Kami. A spirit or god, usually associated with Japanese Shintō.

Karmic affinity. The Buddhist idea that individuals have unseen connections due to previous actions, which might have occurred in past lives.

Karuna. Compassion. One of the principal qualities sought by Buddhists and informing their actions.

Kāśyapa. In Zen (Chan, Seon) Buddhism, Kāśyapa is said to be the disciple of the Buddha who received the mind-to-mind transmission of the Dharma, a transmission occurring outside the Buddha's lectures that are recorded in sūtras. Thereby, he became a patriarch of Zen. Kāśyapa is also the name of a Buddha who is said to have lived before the historical Buddha Śakyamuni.

Koan (Chinese: *gong'an*). Literally "public case." A story or saying given by some Zen (Chan, Seon) teachers to help a student awaken.

Loving Kindness. The principal outlook Buddhist practitioners should develop toward all beings, even those formerly considered enemies.

Mahāyāna. The "Greater Vehicle." The type of Buddhism predominant in East Asia.

Mandala. Circle. Buddhist and Hindu concentric diagrams with spiritual and ritual significance.

Mantra. A sound or group of syllables believed to have spiritually transformative properties.

Mappō. The last age of the Dharma. The degenerative age when people cannot understand the teachings of the Buddha or live according to the Dharma.

Mara. The personification of death or temptation in Buddhism.

Maya. The Buddha's mother, whose name means "illusion."

Middle Path or **Middle Way**. A name for Buddhism. Buddhism is the Middle Path between extremes such as harsh asceticism and hedonism, as well as between doctrines of existence and non-existence.

Mudra. Highly symbolic finger gesture.

Nāgārjuna (*c.* 150–250 CE). The most famous Mahāyāna Buddhist philosopher of the Middle Path after the Buddha.

Nembutsu. The chant and the practice of chanting "Namu Amida Butsu" in Pure Land Buddhism.

Nirvana. Extinction of desires and extinction of the process of creating new desires. Ending the cycle of rebirth.

Non-returning. The stage of Buddhist attainment when the practitioner overcomes the fetters (chains) of attachments and so will not be reborn.

No-self. Buddhist refutation of the Indian *ātman* doctrine.

Obon. Japanese Buddhist celebration in honor of the spirits of ancestors in order to relieve their suffering.

Once-returning. The stage of Buddhist attainment when the practitioner is free of the first three fetters and has weakened two more: sensuous desire and ill-will. This stage gets its name from the idea that upon reaching it the person is partially awakened and only has one more lifetime until full awakening.

Pāli Canon. The collection of scriptures most important to Theravāda Buddhism, written in Pāli language.

Parinirvana. Final nirvana attained at bodily death.

Peta. The spirit of a departed person; a hungry ghost.

Potala Palace. Located in Lhasa, Tibet, Potala Palace was the chief residence of the Dalai Lama until he left the country in 1959.

Prajñā. Insightful wisdom.

Prapancha. Unprofitable elaboration of perceptions.

Pratimoksha (Sanskrit: *prātimokśa*). The basic vows taken by Buddhist for liberation.

Pure Land Buddhism. A tradition of Mahāyāna Buddhism focused on receiving salvation from suffering by grace of Amitābha Buddha (Japanese: *Amida*). Accordingly, *Amitābha* Buddha will save sentient beings by bringing them to the Pure Land after death.

Pure Land Sūtras. The scriptures that explain the Pure Land.

Rinpoche. An honorific title give to a Tibetan monk, literally "precious one."

Samsara. The cycles of rebirth.

Sangha. The community of Buddhists.

Shin Buddhism (Japanese: *Jōdo Shinshū*). A tradition of Pure Land Buddhism founded by the monk Shinran.

Shinran (1173–1263). The founder of *Jōdo Shinshū*, "the True Pure Land Tradition," also called Shin or Shin Buddhism.

Shintō. A Japanese religious tradition that reveres spirits of nature.

Shōbōgenzō. The "Treasury of the True Dharma-Eye," a book written by Japanese Zen master Dōgen about awakening.

Shwedagon Pagoda. A famous stupa and temple complex located in Yangon, Myanmar. Eight hairs of the Buddha are said to be buried there.

Siddhartha Gautama. The historical Buddha of our time period.

Siddhi. The unusual skill or perfection achieved by a Buddhist master.

Skill-in-means or *upāya.* The skillful practices employed by a Bodhisattva to lure people to awakening.

Socially engaged Buddhism. The use of Buddhist ideas and practices to help change oppressive social conditions of society. Currently, this is a major trend in Buddhism worldwide.

Stream Enterers, Stream entry (Pāli: *sotāpanna*). A person who eradicated the first fetters that bind us to rebirth has attained stream entry. Metaphorically, to cross the stream is to reach *nibbāna* (nirvana).

Stupa is a mound of earth that enshrines a Buddhist relic. Most typically, the relic is the remains of the Buddha, such as a single finger joint.

Suchness. See **Thusness**.

Tantric Buddhism, also called **esoteric Buddhism** or **Vajrayana.** A tradition of Mahāyāna Buddhism that emphasizes the use of mudra, mantra, and mandala in practices leading to awakening.

Tariki. "Other power." Reliance on another being for salvation.

Tathāgata. A title for the Buddha that means "thus gone" or "thus come," the one who has gone to *Tathātā* (thusness).

Tendai (Chinese: *Tiantai*). A tradition of Japanese Buddhism that incorporates the *Lotus Sūtra*, meditation, and some esoteric practices.

Theravāda. A longstanding tradition of Buddhism that is most widely practiced in Southeast Asia today.

Three Jewels of Buddhism, also called the **Three Treasures**. The Buddha, the *Sangha* (community of Buddhists), and the Dharma. These are of utmost importance to Buddhists. In many traditions, a person becomes a Buddhist by publicly declaring that he or she takes refuge from suffering in the Three Jewels.

Thusness; Suchness; *Tathātā*. Experiencing reality as it is, without imposing judgments.

Torana (Japanese: *torii*). A gateway marking the entry to a sacred space, typically temple grounds.

Trikāya. The idea that there are three bodies of the Buddha. They are: *Nirmānakāya*, representing the physical, historical Buddha; *Sambhogakāya*, representing the Buddha as perceived through mediation; *Dharmakāya*, which is the universal body of the Buddha's teachings, or the universe itself.

Tripiṭaka, or three baskets of teachings. The three baskets are the sūtras, the *vinaya* or collections of vows, and the *Abhidhamma*.

Two truths (provisional truth and ultimate truth). This is an idea proposed by Nāgārjuna and others that some conceptual ideas can be said to be true provisionally but not ultimately.

Uposatha. Special Buddhist days of observance, usually determined by the lunar calendar.

Vairocana. A universal or cosmic Buddha, in contrast to the historical Buddha. Vairocana can represent the universal teachings of the historical Buddha, that is, the Dharmakāya (see *Trikāya*). Vairocana is revered by some Mahāyāna Buddhists, including Tantric Buddhists.

Vajra. A ritual instrument that symbolizes a diamond that cuts through delusion.

Vajrayana. The vehicle of the *vajra*, esoteric Buddhism.

Vinaya Piṭaka. One of the three divisions of the Buddhist scriptural canon. It is primarily concerned with monastic rules and vows.

Vipassana; **Insight Meditation**. A type of Buddhist meditation that stresses mindfulness, obtained through meditative contemplation on the breath, body, mind, and mental activities.

Wheel of Life. Pictorial depictions of the cycles of rebirth and/or states of consciousness.

Wind Horse. A mythical creature that entered the art and imagination of Tibetan Buddhism from folklore. Legend says it carries on its back prayers to the ancient spirits of the earth and sky.

Yantra. Geometric symbols drawn on paper, tattoos, and elsewhere for focusing spiritual energy.

Zeami Motokiyo (*c.* 1363–*c.* 1443 CE). Japanese playwright and Nō drama theorist.

SELECTED LIST OF FILMS WITH BUDDHIST CONTENT

1. Dramatic films with overt Buddhist themes arranged by release or completion date

Doomsday Book *(Pil-Sung Yim and Jee-woon Kim, Korea, 2012)*

A science fiction comedy suggesting three doomsday scenarios. In the middle sequence, a futuristic sentient robot created to serve visitors to a monastery in Korea seems to have attained Buddhahood. Considering this a malfunction and a threat to the Buddhist institution, the manufacturer comes to terminate it.

Flowers in Hell *(Korean title: Jiokhwa, literally "Fire in Hell," Lee Sang-woo, Korea, 2012)*

A monk is banished from a temple for having an affair with a parishioner. In the secular world his passions grow beyond control and he accidentally kills a woman from the Philippines. He goes to her family's home in that country to deliver her ashes but falls in love with her sister. The film explores karma.

Mindfulness and Murder *(Thai title: Sop-mai-ngeap, Tom Waller, Thailand, 2011)*

When a murder takes place in a monastery in Bangkok, a resident senior monk and former homicide is called upon to investigate. Based on a Thai book series about detective-monk Father Ananda by American writer Nick Wilgus.

Abraxas *(Naoki Katô, Japan, 2010)*

A Japanese Zen Buddhist persists in his secular attachment to punk rock music. His master suggests he perform a live concert.

Rolling Home with a Bull *(Korean title:* So-wa hamque Yeohang-ha-neun Beob, *Soonrye Yim, Korea, 2010)*

When sent by his father to purchase a bull, a reluctant son undertakes what turns into a pilgrimage of sorts, and comes to understand something important for his life.

9 Wat *(a.k.a.* Secret Sunday, *Saranyoo Jiralak, Thailand, 2010)*

Three people undertake a journey to nine temples, each for a different reason. Along the way they discover their karmic affinities.

Phobia 2 *(various directors, Thailand, 2009)*

Five horror film segments by different directors. One segment, "The Novice," is about a 14-year-old boy whose mother makes him become a monk after he is caught being a thief. Thinking this would free him from suspicion, he joins the monastic order and continues his lifestyle. He faces the karmic consequences of this.

Enter the Void *(Gaspar Noé, France, 2009)*

A film with sometimes shocking sequences depicting incest and conception, it follows the trek of the disembodied consciousness of a fallen drug dealer in the *bardo* state between death and rebirth, as described in *The Tibetan Book of the Dead*.

In the Shadow of the Naga *(Thai title:* Nak prok, *Nasorn Panungkasiri, Thailand, released 2010, completed 2008)*

Three criminals become Buddhist monks in order to recover stolen goods buried beneath a temple. Release of this film was delayed due to protests by Buddhists in Thailand.

Okuribito *(English title:* Departures, *Yôjirô Takita, Japan, 2008)*

Based on ideas from Jōdo Shinshū in Japan, as told in the book *Coffinman: The Journal of a Buddhist Mortician* by Shinmon Aoki, 2004. Encoffiners prepare corpses and families of the departed. It received the 2009 Academy Award for Best Foreign Language Film.

God Man Dog *(Singing Chen, Taiwan, 2008)*

Chance and karmic interactions of five individuals from different social-economic backgrounds are depicted in scenes of alcoholism, postpartum depression, religious desperation, compassion, and redemption.

Only the Way *(Dang Tak-Wing, Hong Kong, 2008)*

A washed-out songwriter's bad karma begins to catch up with him. His life goes downhill as his girlfriend leaves him, his career declines, and his mother passes away. All these setbacks make him live in even greater spite of the world, until he encounters a temple street vendor who introduces him to Buddhism.

The Coffin *(Ekachai Uekrongtham, USA, 2008)*

Following a Thai custom aimed at cheating death and ridding oneself of bad karma, a man who lies in a coffin for an evening has a series of terrifying experiences.

12 Lotus *(Royston Tan, Singapore, 2008)*

Also called *1028* (or *Ten 28*), *12 Lotus* is a musical. A girl steals an image of the Bodhisattva Guanyin and cares for it. The lead actor, Qi Yu Wu, was himself named Guan Yin in Royston Tan's previous film, *881*.

Un Buda *(Diego Rafecas, Argentina, 2005)*

In Argentina, two brothers are orphaned as children when their parents are killed. As adults, one becomes a skilled Buddhist practitioner, the other a university philosophy professor, influenced by their father and mother respectively.

Ghost of Mae Nak *(Mark Duffield, Thailand, 2005)*

From a Thai legend about a wife who dies in childbirth but refuses to leave her husband. Buddhist priests work to exorcize her relentless ghost. The story is also told in the Thai film *Nang Nak*, 1999 (see below).

A Chinese Tall Story *(Jeffrey Lau, Hong Kong, 2005)*

A science fiction comedy based on *Journey to the West* (sometimes called *Monkey* in English), which was also the model for the *Dragonball* animation series. The story takes place in the younger days of the famous Chinese monk Tripiṭaka (Xuangzang) and tells of the relationship between a monk and an alien.

Zen Noir *(Marc Rosenbush, USA, 2004)*

A detective investigates what seems to be a murder at a California Zen temple and ends up examining his own life.

I Heart Huckabees *(David O. Russell, USA, 2004)*

A man hires "existential detectives" to investigate his life. According to the director's commentary, ideas in the story are based on his college classes under noted Buddhologist Robert Thurman, who also serves as the model for Dustin Hoffman's detective character in the film.

The Simpsons *episode 332 (season 15), "Simple Simpson"* *(Jim Reardon, USA, 2004)*

Homer becomes a superhero, "The Pie Man," throwing pies in the faces of the deserving. Mr. Burns unmasks him and puts him to work for evil. As a part of this plan, The Pie Man is ordered to pie the Dalai Lama. Because Lisa has become a Buddhist, Homer is conscience-stricken. The Dalai Lama is depicted making jokes and flying.

Ok Baytong *(Nonzee Nimibutr, Thailand, 2003)*

A Thai Buddhist monk leaves the temple where he has lived since he was 5, after learning his sister has been killed by insurgents. He learns to live in the secular world and meets Muslims in south Thailand.

Travelers and Magicians *(Khyentse Norbu, Bhutan, 2003)*

A man seeking to immigrate to America is forced to travel with a monk. Their interactions take unexpected turns.

Spring, Summer, Fall, Winter and Spring *(Ki-duk Kim, Korea, 2003)*

The story takes place on an isolated lake, where an old monk lives in a small floating-island temple. The film follows the life of an apprentice monk who studies under the old master. Changes in the life of the younger monk are symbolized by the seasons and Buddhist imagery. The apprentice eventually leaves the temple, is involved in a murder, and decides to come back to take his own life. However, the old master has different ideas.

Hollywood Buddha *(Philippe Caland, 2003)*

A broke film-maker seeks advice from a Buddhist master in Los Angeles. The master convinces him to purchase an expensive statue of the Buddha. The release of this film was cancelled due to Buddhists protest about the poster and the content of the film.

The Anniversary *(Ham Tran, USA, 2003, 28 minutes)*

A Vietnamese monk is haunted by his memories of war and betrayal on the anniversary of his brother's death. Winner of 25 international awards, the USA Film Festival award for Best Short Film, and semi-finalist for a 2004 Academy Award.

Running on Karma *(Johnnie To and Ka-Fai Wai, Hong Kong, 2003)*

Big is an ex-martial-artist monk who has turned bodybuilder. He has the ability to see karmic connections. He befriends a female cop and helps her solve cases with his visions and fighting skills. But it is her destiny that really concerns him most.

Oseam *(Baek-yeob Seong, Korea, 2003)*

Animation about what an orphaned boy and girl learn after being taken in by a monastery.

A Little Monk *(Korean title:* Dong seung, *Kyung-jung Joo, Korea, 2002)*

Similar to *Why Has Bodhi-Dharma Left for the East?*, this film depicts a child monk, a middle-aged monk, and an old monk living together in a remote temple. The child is constantly longing for the mother he cannot remember.

Samsara *(Pan Nalin, An independent Italy/France/Indian/German film, 2001 Tibetan with English subtitles)*

A spiritual love story set in the majestic landscape of Ladakh in the Himalayas. *Samsara* is a quest; one man's struggle to find spiritual enlightenment by renouncing the world, and one woman's struggle to keep her enlightened love and life in the world. But their destiny turns, twists, and comes to a surprising end.

Echos of Enlightenment *(Daniel J. Coplan, US, 2001)*

Allegedly inspired by the "Skill-in-means" chapter of the *Lotus Sūtra*, which is referenced in the film.

Hi! Dharma! *(Korean title:* Dalmaya nolja, Cheol-kwan Park, Korea, 2001)

A comedy about a crime ring that comes to hide out in a monastery. The monks challenge the criminals to a series of competitions to determine if they can stay. A sequel was made called *Hi! Dharma 2: Showdown in Seoul* (Korean title: *Dalmaya, Seoul gaja*, Sang-Hyo Yook, 2004).

King of the Hill *episode 4.18, "Won't You Pimai Neighbor?"* (Boo Hwan Lim and Kyoung Hee Lim, USA, 2000)

In apparent parody of the *Kundun* story wherein the infant Lhamo Döndrub is identified as the 14th Dalai Lama, Bobby is examined as a potential Lama.

Enlightenment Guaranteed *(Doris Dörrie, Germany, 2000)*

Dörrie creates a comic work about two brothers who travel to Japan for a retreat in a Zen monastery in hopes of getting their lives back together.

The Cup *(Tibetan title:* Phörpa, Khyentse Norbu, Bhutan, 1999)

Young monks scheme to watch the World Cup in a Tibetan temple in exile in India.

Ghost Dog: The Way of the Samurai *(Jim Jarmusch, France, 1999)*

A hitman models himself after Buddhist-inspired Samurai philosophy.

Himalaya *or* Himalaya—l'enfance d'un chef *(Eric Valli, France/Switzerland/UK/Nepal, 1999)*

A beautifully shot film about the semi-nomadic people of the Dolpo, a remote region in the Himalayas. It was the first Nepalese film to be nominated in the Best Foreign Film category at the 72nd Academy Awards.

Nang Nak *(Nonzee Nimibutr, Thailand, 1999)*

Local monks struggle with the ghost of a woman who refuses to be parted from her husband in death. The story is also told in the Thai film *Ghost of Mae Nak*, 2005 (see above).

Hwaomgyong (also called Hwaomkyong. English title: Passage to Buddha, Sun-Woo Jang, Korea, 1993)

A boy travels seeking to understand life. Based on similar events in the *Avataṃsaka Sūtra*, some say this is the best Korean film on Buddhism to date.

Little Buddha (Bernardo Bertolucci, UK/France, 1993)

Tibetan monks find an American boy in Seattle who they identify as the reincarnation of their deceased master.

Come, Come, Come, Upward (Korean title: Aje aje bara aje, Kwon-taek Im, Korea, 1989)

Sun Nyog becomes a Buddhist nun and attempts to disentangle herself from a suicidal alcoholic she once saved.

Why Has Bodhi-Dharma Left for the East? (Young-Kyun Bae, South Korea, 1989)

A middle-aged man becomes a monk and practices at a remote mountain temple. There he struggles with his guilt about abandoning his ailing mother.

Fancy Dance (Masayuki Suo, Japan, 1987)

Yohei, a punk rocker, has to become a Buddhist monk in order to inherit a mountain temple. Yohei, though initially rebelling against the tough monastic discipline, learns to adjust. Then his girlfriend shows up, enticing him to return to his rock 'n' roll roots.

Mandala (Im Kwon-taek, South Korea, 1981)

A critically acclaimed firm by one of South Korea's most renowned film-makers. It follows the lives of two Seon Buddhists with contrasting lifestyles and practices.

Kung Fu (television series, 1972–1975) and The Way of the Tiger, the Sign of the Dragon, its feature-length pilot (Jerry Thorpe, USA, 1972)

David Carradine stars as Kwai Chang Caine, a Chinese-American Buddhist priest, trained in the Dharma and martial arts in China's famous Shaolin Temple. Caine travels around the American Wild West in the nineteenth century, philosophizing, righting wrongs, attempting to spread peace, and inevitably fighting bad guys.

Siddhartha *(Conrad Rooks, 1972)*

The story of a young Indian who embarks upon a journey to find the meaning of existence. Based on the novel by Hermann Hesse.

Mujō *(a.k.a* **This Transient Life,** *Akio Jissoji, Japan, 1970)*

First film in the Buddhist trilogy by Japanese "New Wave" auteur Akio Jissoji. All three films, including *Mandala* (Japanese: *Mandara*, 1971) and *Poem* (Japanese: *Uta*, 1972), explore Buddhism and eroticism in post-industrial capitalism.

The Burmese Harp *(Japanese title:* **Biruma no tategoto,** *Kon Ichikawa, Japan, 1956)*

At the end of World War II, a soldier of the Japanese army escapes capture by pretending to be a Burmese Buddhist with surprising consequences.

Lost Horizon *(Frank Capra, USA, 1937)*

After a plane crash in the Himalayas, a small group of civilians explore the fabled kingdom of Shangri-la, a seductive escape from the realities of World War II.

Broken Blossoms *(D.W. Griffith, USA, 1919)*

A Chinese Buddhist travels to London to teach the Dharma. There he discovers the harsh realities of everyday life and gives up his broad ambition. Applying his principles on an individual level, he meets a local girl who is abused by her father and tries to help her.

2.   Dramatic biographies of Buddhists

Zen *(Banmei Takahashi, Japan, 2009)*

A biopic on the life of Dōgen, founder of Japanese Soto Zen.

Shinran-same: His Wish and Light *(Japanese title:* **Shinran-sama: Negai, Soshite Hikari,** *Honganji-ha, Japan, 2008)*

Japanese animation about the life of the founder of the True Pure Land Tradition of Japanese Buddhism (Jōdo Shinshū) and released for the 750th anniversary of his passing.

Recalling a Buddha: Memories of HH Karmapa XVI
(Gregg Eller, USA, 2006)

The life story of Karmapa XVI is related by people who knew him in Tibet. Not only was *A Buddha* recalled, but so was the film. Likely because of complaints about production and content quality, the film-makers decided to rework it.

Milarepa *(Neten Chokling, Bhutan, 2006)*

A film about the early life of the Tibetan saint Milarepa.

Angry Monk: Reflections on Tibet *(Luc Schaedler, 2005)*

The story of the radical Tibetan monk Gendun Choephel.

Kundun *(Martin Scorsese, USA, 1997)*

Depiction of the life of the 14th Dalai Lama.

Seven Years in Tibet *(Jean-Jacques Annaud, 1997)*

True story of Heinrich Harrer, an Austrian mountain climber who became friends with the Dalai Lama at the time of China's takeover of Tibet.

Kūkai *(Setō Junya, Japan, 1984)*

Currently in Japanese with no foreign subtitles. But if you know the basics of his life story it's easy to follow.

Nichiren and the Great Mongol Invasion *(Japanese title: Nichiren to moko daishurai, Kunio Watanabe, Japan, 1958)*

Japanese with English subtitles.

3. Dramatic films with themes identified as Buddhist

3-Iron *(original Korean title means "Empty Houses," Kim Ki-duk, Korea, 2004)*

A man lives in empty houses while their owners are on vacation. He applies principles of a Buddhist mendicant and seems to develop extraordinary abilities.

Angulimala *(Sutape Tunnirut, Thailand, 2003)*

Based on a Jataka. Believing people seek release from suffering, Angulimala tries to kill 1,000 people for his own spiritual merit. After an hour and a half of murder and mayhem, Angulimala meets the Buddha and lives a converted life for the last ten minutes of the film.

Waking Life *(Richard Linklater, US, 2001)*

A young man seeking to awaken from a long vivid dream seeks the advice of philosophers.

After Life *(Japanese title:* Wandâfuru raifu, *Hirokazu Kore-eda, Japan, 1999)*

After people die, they spend a week with counselors, also dead, who help them pick one memory they can take to eternity. They describe the memory to the staff, who work with a crew to film it and screen it at week's end; eternity follows.

The Matrix *(Andy and Larry Wachowski, US, 1999)*

A group of people begin to see life is an illusion and work to help others realize this.

Fight Club *(David Fincher, USA, 1999)*

Analyzed by critics as a man's philosophical struggle with himself, the story progresses along the lines of the Buddha's Four Noble Truths and Eightfold Path.

Fearless *(Peter Weir, US, 1993)*

Following a plane crash, a survivor sees life from a new perspective.

Point Break *(Kathryn Bigelow, USA, 1991)*

A group of bank-robbing surfer/skydivers are led by a free spirit called Bodhi/Bodhisattva and are hunted by a federal agent who learns about life from them.

Dreams *(Akira Kurosawa, Japan, 1990), also called* Akira Kurosawa's Dreams

A classic film with eight segments showing human interaction with nature.

Jacob's Ladder *(Adrian Lyne, USA, 1990)*

A man wounded in Vietnam continues to live a nightmare in New York. His path of intrigue and horror seemingly leads to hell or heaven. Allegedly based in some part on the *Tibetan Book of the Dead* (*Bardo Thodol*).

4. Documentary films on aspects of Buddhism

I Am *(Tom Shadyac, USA, 2010)*

The Director Tam Shadyac tells about his brain injury and the resulting change of lifestyle that is close to Buddhism.

The Dhamma Brothers *(Andrew Kukura and Jenny Phillips, USA, 2008)*

A documentary about doing Mindfulness Meditation in an overcrowded maximum-security prison in Alabama.

How to Cook Your Life *(Doris Dörrie, Germany/USA, 2007)*

A Zen priest in San Francisco and cookbook author uses Zen Buddhism and cooking to relate to everyday life. By the director of *Enlightenment Guaranteed*, 2000 (see above).

Amongst White Clouds *(Edward A. Burger, USA, 2007)*

An exploration of Chinese Buddhist hermit monks.

10 Questions for The Dalai Lama *(Rick Ray, USA, 2006)*

Film-maker Rick Ray is allowed to ask the Dalai Lama ten questions of his choosing.

The Giant Buddhas *(Christian Frei, Germany, 2006)*

Investigation of the destruction by the Taliban of the huge Buddha cliff-carving in Afghanistan.

The Zen Mind *(Jon Braeley, USA, 2006)*

A documentary about Zen practice, the film features Soji Monastery, Kyoto Zen Center, Dōgen Sangha in Tokyo, Tenruji Temple, Nanzenji Temple, Ryoanji Temple, and Komazawa University.

On the Road with the Red God Macchendranath *(Kesang Tseten, Nepal, 2005)*

Documents the periodic trek of a large image of Macchendranath in Nepal.

Discovering Buddhism *(Christina Lundberg, USA, 2004)*

A film featuring Richard Gere, Keanu Reeves, the Dalai Lama, Lama Thubten Yeshe, Kirti Tsenshab Rinpoche, and Lama Zopa Rinpoche.

Words of My Perfect Teacher *(Lesley Ann Patten, Canada, 2003)*

Documentary film-maker Lesley Ann Patten turns the camera on her guru, Khyentse Norbu, one of the world's most admired Buddhist teachers, and accomplished filmmaker (*The Cup*, 1999, see above).

The Yogis of Tibet *(Jeffrey M. Pill, USA, 2002)*

A documentary showing Tibetan Buddhists discussing ideas and demonstrating practices.

To the Land of Bliss *(Wen-jie Qin, USA, 2002)*

Portrayal of the Chinese Pure Land Buddhist way of dying and living. Film-maker Wen-jie Qin is an anthropologist from Sichuan Province in southwest China.

Doing Time, Doing Vipassana *(Eilona Ariel and Ayelet Menahemi, USA, 1997, 52 minutes)*

A documentary about teaching Mindfulness Meditation in a prison in India.

The Marathon Monks of Mount Hiei *(Christopher J. Hayden, US, 1993)*

A documentary look at the extreme marathon training of monk Tanno Kakudo. The film depicts death-defying fasts, vegetarian training diets, handmade straw running shoes, and ritual feats of endurance.

The Reincarnation of Khensur Rinpoche *(Tenzing Sonam and Ritu Sarin, UK, 1991)*

A documentary on a life of devotion, and the continuity of Tibetan culture in exile. A disciple searches for the child who is the reincarnation of the late Khenshur Rinpoche.

BIBLIOGRAPHY

Addiss, Stephen, Stanley Lombardo, and Judith Roitman (eds.). *Zen Sourcebook: Traditional Documents from China, Korea, and Japan.* Indianapolis: Hackett Publishing, 2008.

Affron, Charles, *Lillian Gish, Her Legend, Her Life.* New York: Scribner, 2002.

Anuruddha, Caroline, Augusta Rhys Davids, and Shwe Hsang Aung. *Compendium of Philosophy.* London: published for the Pāli Text Society by Luzac, 1956.

Aoki Shinmon. *Coffinman: The Journal of a Buddhist Mortician.* Anaheim, CA: Buddhist Education Center, 2002.

Aśvaghoṣa. *Life of the Buddha* (Buddha-Karita), trans. Patrick Olivelle. New York: New York University Press, 2008.

———. "The Buddha-Karita of Asvaghosha," in E.B. Cowell (trans. and ed.), *Buddhist Mahāyāna Texts.* New York: Dover Publications, 1969.

Batchelor, Stephen (trans.). *Guide to the Bodhisattva's Way of Life.* Dharamsala: Library Tibetan Works Archives, 1987.

Blackstone, Kathryn R. *Women in the Footsteps of the Buddha.* Great Britain: Curzon, 1998.

Borrows, Anita. "The Light of Outrage: Women, Anger, and Buddhist Practice," in Marianne Dresser, *Buddhist Women on the Edge.* North Atlantic Books, Berkeley, 1996, pp. 51–6.

Buswell Jr., Robert E. (ed.). *Encyclopedia of Buddhism.* New York: Macmillan Reference USA, 2004.

Chanju Mun, *Ha Dongsan and Colonial Korean Buddhism: Balancing Sectarianism and Ecumenism.* Honolulu: Blue Pine Books, 2009.

Cho, Francisca. "Buddhism, Film, and Religious Knowing: Challenging the Literary Approach to Film," in Gregory J. Watkins (ed.), *Teaching Religion and Film.* Oxford: Oxford University Press, 2008.

Cleary, Thomas (trans.). *The Flower Ornament Scripture, A Translation of the Avatamsaka Sutra.* Boston: Shambhala, 1993.

———. *The Platform Sūtra of the Fifth Patriarch. The Sutra of Hui-Neng: Grand Master of Zen.* Boston: Shambhala, 1998.

Dhammacakkappavattana Sutta (*The Sūtra Setting the Wheel of Dharma in Motion*), in Bhikkhu Bodhi (trans.). *The Connected Discourses of the Buddha: A Translation of the Samyutta Nikaya*. Somerville, MA: Wisdom Publications, 2000.

The Dhammapada: Teachings of the Buddha. Fronsdal, Gil (trans.). Boston: Shambhala, 2008.

Digha Nikaya. The Long Discourses of the Buddha: A Translation of the Digha Nikaya. Walshe, Maurice (trans.). Somerville, MA: Wisdom Publications, 1995.

Discourse on the Four Foundations of Mindfulness, Satipaṭṭhāna Sutta, in Bhikkhu Bodhi (trans.) *The Connected Discourses of the Buddha: A Translation of the Samyutta Nikaya.* Somerville, MA: Wisdom Publications, 2000.

Dōgen, Numata Center for Buddhist Translation (trans.). *Shōbōgenzō: The True Dharma-Eye Treasury,* 3 vols. Berkeley: Numata Center for Buddhist Translation and Research, 2007.

Dumoulin, Heinrich. *Zen Buddhism: A History,* vol. 1. India, China and Bloomington, IN: World Wisdom, 2005.

Elison, William. "From the Himalayas to Hollywood: The Legacy of Lost Horizon," in *Tricycle Magazine,* December 1997.

Fields, Rick. *How the Swans Came to the Lake, A Narrative History of Buddhism in America.* Boston: Shambhala, 1992.

Fischer-Schreiber, Ingrid, Franz-Karl Ehrhard, Kurt Friedrichs, and Michael S. Diener. *The Encyclopedia of Eastern Philosophy and Religion,* Boston, Shambhala, 1994.

Garfield, Patricia. *Pathway to Ecstasy: The Way of the Dream Mandala, Your Child's Dream, Creative Dreaming.* New York: Fireside, Simon and Schuster, 1990.

Greene, Felix. *A Curtain of Ignorance.* London: Jonathan Cape, 1965.

Gross, Rita M. *Buddhism After Patriarchy, A Feminist History, Analysis, and Reconstruction of Buddhism.* New York: SUNY Press, 1993.

Horner, I.B. (trans.). *Minor Anthologies,* vol. 4: *Vimanavatthu: Stories of the Mansions, and Petavatthu.* Oxford: Pāli Text Society, 1974.

———. *The Book of the Discipline (Vinaya Piṭaka),* vol. 5: *Cullavagga.* London: Routledge & Kegan Paul, 1975.

Hubbard, Jamie. *Pruning the Bodhi Tree: The Storm Over Critical Buddhism.* Honolulu: University of Hawaii Press, 1997.

Jiheo, Ven. *Diary of a Korean Zen Monk.* Jon Kweon Yi and Frank Tedesco (trans.). Korea: Bulkwang Publishing, 2010.

Kabilsingh, Chatsumarn. *Thai Women in Buddhism.* Berkeley: Parallax Press, 1991.

Kalupahana, David J. *Causality: The Central Philosophy of Buddhism.* Honolulu: University of Hawaii Press, 1975.

Kamjohn Louiyapong in "What Lurks Beneath the Horror," *Bangkok Post,* August 24, 2005.

Kato, Bunno and Yoshiro Tamura (trans.). *The Threefold Lotus Sūtra.* Tokyo: Kōsei, 1989.

Khenpo Karthar Rinpoche. *Dharma Paths.* Ithaca, NY: Snow Lion Publications, 1993.

Kitagawa, Joseph M. *Religion in Japanese History.* NY: Columbia University Press, 1990.

Kong Rithdee "Of Monkey Ghosts and Men," in *Bangkok Post,* May 28, 2010.

Kovan, Martin, "The Burmese Alms-Boycott: Theory and Practice of the *Pattanikujjana* in Buddhist Non-Violent Resistance," originally presented at the International Association for Buddhist Studies Conference, Taiwan, June 20–25, 2011 and forthcoming in *Buddhism and Peace,* Chanju Mun and Ronald S. Green (ed.). Honolulu: Blue Pine Books, 2012.

Lamotte, Étienne *History of Indian Buddhism, From the Origins to the śaka Era*, trans. from French by Sara Webb-Boin. Paris: Peeters Press, 1976.

Loori, John Daido and Kazuaki Tanahashi (trans.). *The True Dharma Eye: Zen Master Dogen's Three Hundred Koans*. Boston: Shambhala, 2009.

Majjhima Nikaya. The Middle Length Discourses of the Buddha: A Translation of the Majjhima Nikaya. Bikkhu Nanamoli and Bhikkhu Bodhi (trans.). Somerville, MA: Wisdom Publications, 2000.

Malalasekera, G.P. (ed.). *Encyclopaedia of Buddhism*. Ceylon: Government of Ceylon, 1971.

Matsunaga, Daigan Matsunaga and Alicia Matsunaga. *Foundation of Japanese Buddhism*, vol. 2. Los Angeles and Tokyo: Buddhist Books International, 1987.

Metta Sutta, "Discourse on Loving Kindness (Karaniya Metta Sutta)," in *The Samyutta Nikaya, The Connected Discourses of the Buddha*. Bhikkhu Bodhi (trans.). Somerville, MA: Wisdom Publications, 2000.

Monier-Williams, M. *Buddhism*. India: Chowkhamba Sanskrit Series, 1964.

Mullin, Glenn H. (ed. and trans.). *The Practice of the Six Yogas of Naropa*, 2nd ed. Ithaca, NY: Snow Lion Publications, 2006.

Mueller, Max (ed.). *The Sacred Books of the East*, 50 vols. Oxford: Clarendon, 1879–1910.

Müller, Max (trans.). "The Larger Sukhāvatī-vyūha," in E.B. Cowell (ed.), *Buddhist Mahāyāna Texts*. New York: Dover Publications, 1969.

Nāgārjuna, A Translation of his Mūlamadhyamakakārikā. Inada, Kenneth K. (trans.). Delhi: Sri Satguru, 1993.

Olivelle, Patrick (trans.). *Upanishads*. Oxford: Oxford University Press, 1996.

Palahniuk, Chuck. *Fight Club, A Novel*. New York: W.W. Norton, 2005.

Paul, Diana Y. *Women in Buddhism*. Berkeley: Asian Humanities Press, 1979.

Prajñāpāramitā Sūtra, The Perfection of Wisdom in Eight Thousand Lines & Its Verse Summary. Edward Conze (trans.). San Francisco: Grey Fox Press, 2001.

Price, A.F. and Wong Mou-lam (trans.). *The Diamond Sutra and the Sutra of Hui-Neng*. Boston: Shambhala, 2005.

Reed, Charley. "Fight Club: An Exploration of Buddhism," in *Journal of Religion and Film* 11:2, October 2007.

Reps, Paul. *Zen Flesh, Zen Bones*. New York: Anchor Doubleday, 1961.

Samyutta Nikaya, The Connected Discourses of the Buddha. Bhikkhu Bodhi (trans.). Somerville, MA: Wisdom Publications, 2000.

Suzuki, Shunryu. *Zen Mind, Beginner's Mind*. New York and Tokyo: Weatherhill, 1988; Boston: Shambhala, 2006.

Takeyama Michio, *The Harp of Burma (Biruma no Tategoto)*. Rutland, VT and Tokyo: Charles E. Tuttle Co. Publishers, 1966.

Wanlu, Somchai, Songkhoon Chantachon, and Boonlert Rachote. "An Application of Isan Local Indigenous Knowledge in Suppression of Social Dispute," in *Social Sciences* 4:2, 2009, pp. 180–5.

Watson, Burton (trans.). *The Zen Teachings of Master Lin-Chi*. New York: Columbia University Press, 1993.

Wayman, Alex and Hideko Wayman (trans.). *The Lion's Roar of Queen Śrimala*. New York: Columbia University Press, 1974

Yamada, Koun (trans.). *The Gateless Gate (Mumonkan)*. Somerville, MA: Wisdom Publications, 2004.

Yamamoto, Kosho (trans.) and Tony Page (ed.). *The Mahayana Mahaparinirvana Sūtra*, 12 vols. London: Nirvana Publications, 1999–2000.

Yamazaki, Masakazu (ed.). *On the Art of the Nō Drama: The Major Treatises of Zeami*. J. Thomas Rimer (trans.). New Jersey: Princeton University Press, 1984.

Young, Serinity, "Dream Practices in Medieval Tibet." *Dreaming*, 9:1, 1999.

Yun, Hsing (trans.). *Sutra of the Medicine Buddha: With an Introduction, Comments and Prayers*. Hacienda Heights, CA: Buddha's Light Publishing, 2005.

INDEX

Abhidhamma 73, 118, 132, 135, 140
Amida 97, 98, 99, 101, 103, 136, 138
Ānanda 111, 112, 114, 129, 135
Anna and the King of Siam 128
A Passage to India 64
Apichatpong Weerasethakul xv, 118, 127, 128, 129, 132
Arnold, Edwin 6
Aśoka 76
ātman (Pāli, *atta*) 45, 47, 49, 50, 135

Bara, Theda 2, 3, 12
Bardo 35, 37, 39, 41, 42 101, 136, 142, 150
Barthelmess, Richard 4, 5
Blade Runner 15
Blavatsky, Helena 1, 6
Blue Cliff Record, The 21, 28
Bodhi Tree 18, 22, 35, 74, 80, 89, 136
Bodhidharma xvii, 21, 58, 59 68, 79, 130, 136
Bodhisattva xiii, xiv, 21, 32, 34, 38, 41, 73, 74, 85, 86, 87, 91, 92, 93, 99, 100, 101, 103, 107, 124, 136, 139, 143, 150, 153
Brahm, John 6
Brahmajala sutta 49
Bresson, Robert 64
Buddha Nature 61, 63, 65, 75, 100, 101, 136
Burma VJ 80
Butsudan 100, 136

Capra, Frank 6, 148
Chakras 17, 136

Clinton, William J. 10, 11
Colman, Ronald 7
Cy Twombly 53

Dalai Lama 1, 7, 9, 10, 11, 12, 36, 37, 42, 82, 85, 88, 106, 107, 108, 109, 110, 116, 136, 138, 144, 146, 149, 151, 152
Daoism 99, 136
David Lean 64
Dead Like Me 101
Deer Park 24, 89, 136
Dependent Origination (dependent co-arising) 19, 29, 35, 36, 38, 50, 51, 52, 53, 67, 132, 136
Dhammacakkappavattana Sutta (*The Sūtra Setting the Wheel of Dharma in Motion*) 47
Dhammapada 32, 33, 36, 39, 42, 55, 136
Dharamsala 10, 85
Dhamma Brothers 80, 152
Diamond Sūtra 63
Discourse on The Four Foundations of Mindfulness 24
Dōgen 21, 66, 100, 136, 139, 148, 152
Doing Time, Doing Vipassana 73, 151
Dona Sutta 31

Easy Rider 48
Edwards, J. Gordon 2
ego-self
Eightfold Path xv, xvi, 15, 20, 22, 24, 25, 32, 36, 89, 136, 137, 150
Emerson, Ralph Waldo 1

femme fatale 2, 13
film noir 5
Five Precepts 22, 23, 76, 137
Four Noble Truths xv, xvi, 15, 20, 24, 34,
    102, 137, 150
Four Sights 15, 16, 18, 74, 137

Garfield, Patricia 37
Gere, Richard 10, 116, 152
Ghost house 123
Glass, Phillip 10, 11
God 15, 29, 37, 38, 48, 62, 64, 103, 108,
    137, 143, 152
Griffith, D. W. 3, 4, 148
Groundhog Day 41

Haiku 24, 25, 41, 53, 66
Hesse, Hermann 60, 61, 64, 90, 148
High Plains Drifter 41
Hilton, James 6, 9
Hinduism 1, 17, 20, 47, 54, 135
Hirai Kinza 3
Hōnen 98, 99, 137
hungry ghosts 122, 123, 137, 138

It's a Wonderful Life 6

Jacob's Ladder 35, 42, 150
Jataka 62, 122, 124, 137, 150
Jiriki 97, 137
Jōdo Shinshū 97, 99, 104, 139, 142, 148
Jōdoshū 97

Kaccayana Gotta Sutta 46, 48
Kami 75, 100, 137
Karmic affinity 98, 124, 127, 137
Karuna 62, 74, 137
Kassapa (Kāśyapa, Mahākāśyapa) xiv, 58, 59,
    122, 124, 137
Kerouac, Jack xiii
Khata 87, 88, 125
Khyentse Norbu (Dzongsar Jamyang
    Khyentse Rinpoche) 13, 82, 84, 90, 92,
    132, 144, 146, 151
Koan 59, 60, 62, 63, 64, 65, 66, 137
Kundun 10, 11, 36, 85, 146, 149
Kung Fu 29, 59, 147

*Larger Sūtra of Immeasurable Life (Mahāyāna
    Amitāyus Sūtra)* 99
Life as Cinema xiii, xiv
Lord of the Flies 15
Lost Horizon 6, 7, 10, 11, 148, 154

Lotus 18, 38, 86, 87, 88, 89, 143
Lotus Sūtra 1, 21, 27, 29, 65, 66, 73, 139, 146

Mahākāśyapa *see* Kassapa
Mahāyāna xi, 27, 34, 61, 72, 73, 74, 76, 79,
    85, 113, 137, 138, 140
mandala xi, xiii, xiv, 37, 38, 86, 87, 138, 147
mantra 86, 87, 88, 126, 138
Mappō 97, 99, 102, 138
Mara 10, 18, 19, 20, 41, 74, 111, 138
Maya 16, 18, 138
Metta Sutta, Discourse on Loving Kindness
    11, 73, 74
Middle Path 9, 18, 23, 47, 51, 138
Mudra 86, 87, 88, 125, 138

Nāgārjuna 27, 47, 47, 52, 102, 138, 140
Nāropa 38
Nembutsu 99, 138
Net of Indra 53
Niddana 41
Nirvana 19, 25, 32, 35, 36, 37, 42, 58, 68,
    76, 90, 114, 138, 139
Non-violence 52
No-Self 44, 45, 46, 47, 50, 138

Obon 100, 138
Olcott, Henry Steel 1
Orientalism 2, 6, 9
Ox Herding Drawings 61, 62, 64, 68, 130

Palahniuk, Chuck 14, 15
Parinirvana 25, 37, 76, 114, 137, 138
Perverts Guide to the Cinema 26
Potala Palace 7, 8, 110, 138
prajñā, insightful wisdom 52, 62, 138
Principles and Practices of Zen 20
Psycho 26
Pulp Fiction 13
Pure Land xi, 22, 97, 98, 99, 100, 101, 103,
    104, 111, 135, 137, 135, 139, 148, 152

Sartre, Jean Paul 30
Scorsese, Martin 11, 149
Seven Years in Tibet 10, 11, 85, 93, 149
Shaman, shamanism 11, 38, 42, 64, 75,
    100, 109
Shambhala 6
Shaolin Temple 20, 59, 149
Shin Buddhism 97, 99, 101, 102, 139
Shinran 99, 102, 104, 139, 148
Shintō 75, 100, 137, 139
Shōbōgenzō 100, 139

Shōtoku 14
Shwedagon Pagoda 75, 79, 139
Siddhartha 60, 61, 64, 90, 148
Siddhi 38, 139
skill-in-means; *upāya* xiv, 139, 146
Slacker 31
Socially Engaged Buddhism 73
Sybil 26
Syndromes and a Century xv, 128

Tangaryō 20, 46
Tariki 97, 139
Tibetan Book of the Dead (Bardo Thodol) 35, 41, 42, 101, 142, 150
Tendai 98, 104, 139
thangka paintings 86, 88
The King and I 128
The Light of Asia by the British poet Sir Edwin Arnold 6
The Mask 45
The Newton Boys 31
The Outer Limits 6
The Shorter Instructions to Malunkya 48, 54
The Soul of Buddha 2, 3, 4
The True Dharma Eye 21, 28, 100, 139
Theosophical Society 1, 6
Theravāda xi, 22, 32, 33, 70, 72, 73, 74, 76, 79, 118, 121, 122, 132, 135, 138, 139

Thoreau, Henry David 1
Thurman, Robert 10, 13, 44, 46, 144
thusness; suchness; *tathātā* 16, 139
Toh (Somdej Phra Puttajan Toh) 119, 120 121, 125, 126, 127
Trikaya 27, 28, 139
tripiṭaka 73, 140, 143
Twilight Zone 6

Upanishads 20, 47

Valley of the Dolls 26
Vipassana 24, 72, 73, 140, 151
Vivekananda 73, 151

Way of the Tiger, Sign of the Dragon 20, 147
Wheel of Life 39, 40, 41, 140

Yantra 126, 140
Yeats, William Butler 1

Zahedi, Caveh 31, 41
Zen xi, xv, xxii, 20, 21, 22, 24, 25, 35, 41, 46, 48, 51, 53, 54, 57, 58, 59, 61, 62, 63, 64, 66, 67, 68, 74, 79, 92, 100, 130, 136, 137, 139, 142, 144, 146, 148, 151, 152
Zen Flesh, Zen Bones 61
Žižek, Slavoj 26, 28